KATARZYNA DODD

THE CHAMELEON'S GAME

When Love Becomes Manipulation:
Unmasking and Leaving a Covert Narcissist

Copyright © 2025 by Katarzyna Dodd

All rights reserved. No part of this publication may be reproduced, distributed, or transmitted in any form or by any means, including photocopying, recording, or other electronic or mechanical methods, without the prior written permission of the publisher, except in the case of brief quotations embodied in critical reviews and certain other noncommercial uses permitted by copyright law. For permission requests, write to the publisher, addressed "Attention: Permission Coordinator," at the address below.

Studio City, CA 91604

Book Design and Interior by Best Holistic Life Publishing
Stylistic and grammatical editing by Dr. Dixie Short
Illustrations by Paweł Furtak

This book is for informational purposes only. The ideas, procedures, and suggestions contained in this book are not intended to serve as a substitute for professional medical advice. The author and publisher specifically disclaim all liability arising directly or indirectly from the use of any information contained in this book. All matters regarding your health require medical supervision.

www.KatarzynaDodd.com
Printed in the USA

Library of Congress Control Number: 2025918482
Ordering Information: Special discounts are available on quantity purchases by corporations, associations, and others. For details, contact www.KatarzynaDodd.com.

Names: Dodd, Katarzyna, author.
Title: The chameleon's game : when love becomes manipulation: unmasking and leaving a covert narcissist / Katarzyna Dodd.
Description: Studio City, CA : Best Holistic Life Publishing, [2025] | Includes bibliographical references.
Identifiers: LCCN: 2025918482 | ISBN: 9798989215928 (hardcover) | 9798989215904 (paperback) | 9798989215935 (ebook) | 9798989215942 (audio)
Subjects: LCSH: Narcissists. | Manipulative behavior. | Psychology, Pathological. | Narcissistic injuries. | Psychic trauma. | Dysfunctional families. | Adult children of dysfunctional families. | Love--Psychological aspects. | Self-esteem. | Self-actualization (Psychology) | Self-realization. | Self-care, Health. | Interpersonal relations. | LCGFT: Self-help publications. | Autobiographies. | BISAC: FAMILY & RELATIONSHIPS / Dysfunctional Families. | PSYCHOLOGY / Interpersonal Relations. | PSYCHOLOGY / Psychopathology / Personality Disorders. | PSYCHOLOGY / Psychotherapy / Couples & Family. | SELF-HELP / Abuse. | SELF-HELP / Codependency.
Classification: LCC: BF575.N35 D63 2025 | DDC: 155.232--dc23

ISBN 979-8-9892159-2-8 (hardcover)
ISBN 979-8-9892159-0-4 (paperback)
ISBN 979-8-9892159-3-5 (ebook)
ISBN 979-8-9892159-4-2 (audio)

This book is inspired by real-life events and includes authentic examples. While it conveys the emotional and psychological truth of the experiences described, all names and identifying details—including locations—have been changed to preserve the privacy of those involved

TABLE OF CONTENTS

INTRODUCTION — ix
    The Enigma Relationship — xi
    Intro-Narcissist And Extro-Narcissist — xiii
    You Are The Alchemist — xiii

PART 1: THE ANATOMY OF SHADOW — 1

CHAPTER 1: COVERT NARCISSISM: A MIRROR WITH NO REFLECTION — 3
    Narcissist—A Diagnosis Or Just A Buzzword? — 3
    A Word That Lost Its Meaning — 4
    Not Every Difficult Person Is A Narcissist — 4
    The Ancients Already Knew — 6
    The Narcissistic Mirror—How It Works — 8
    The Disorder Of Being Human — 9
    How Does This Narcissist "Hide"? — 11
    Different Forms Of Narcissism — 13

CHAPTER 2: THE ABANDONED INNER CHILD AND THE MISSING INNER PARENT — 27
    The Structure Of The Self: The Inner Parent And Child — 27
    The Inner Child Is Perfect From Beginning To End — 31
    When The Inner Parent Fails — 32
    "I'll Never Be Like My Mother Or Father!" — 33
    The Inner Child Searching For The Parent — 37
    The Inner Parent Searching For The Child — 38
    The Narcissist's False Self — 39

CHAPTER 3: THE NEVER-ENDING STORY: THE NARCISSIST'S VICIOUS CYCLE — 49
    Act One: Love Bombing — 50
    Act Two: Devaluation — 50

Act Three: Discard	50
Act Four: Hoovering—The Narcissist's Return	51
Narcissistic Supply: The Oxygen A Narcissist Cannot Survive Without	52

CHAPTER 4: LOVE BOMBING: THE KIND OF LOVE THAT HOOKS YOUR SOUL — 55

Magic That Isn't Magic	55
Warning: Illusion Ahead!	56
Mirror, Mirror On The Wall…	57
Why You?	58
The Beginnings Of False Hope	59
Warning Map—7 Signs Of Love Bombing	65

CHAPTER 5: DEVALUATION–FROM PEDESTAL TO PAVEMENT — 67

The Subtle Onset Of Devaluation	67
The Effects Of Devaluation	68
Warning Map—7 Signs Of Devaluation	78

CHAPTER 6: DISCARD: TIME TO PUT ON THE INVISIBILITY CLOAK — 81

Closure? Never Heard Of Her	82
Warning Map—7 Signs Of Abandonment By A Covert Narcissist	95

CHAPTER 7: WHEN EGOCENTRISM STOPS BEING INNOCENT AND BECOMES A LACK OF RESPONSIBILITY — 97

Expectations And Entitlement	99
The Need For Constant Validation	103
Panic Fear Of Rejection	106
Guilt And Projection	108
Emotional Provocation	113
Lack Of Empathy	118
Testing Boundaries	122
Lack Of Responsibility And Awareness Of Consequences	126
Lack Of Sense Of Self And Changing Ideas Of Who They Are	129
Only Praise Allowed	133
Fantasy Life	136

Control	139
Name Games	146
Vacation That's Anything But	148
Sulking And Silence	153

CHAPTER 8: NO MAN'S LAND: BETWEEN 'I' AND 'WE'   **159**

The Birth Of Psychological Separateness	159
The Conflict: I Want To Be Close, I Want To Be Free	160
When Separation Hurts—A Stalled Development	161
An Adult Without Boundaries	162
Shame That Must Not Be Felt	162
Projection—Dumping Toxic Waste At Someone Else's Expense	164

CHAPTER 9: ARMAGEDDON–THE FINAL ACT IN THE THEATER OF ILLUSION   **169**

Still Together	169
Alone, But Still In Touch	199
"Never Enough"	204
"Time to Say Goodbye"	207
"The Diamond"	209
Completely On My Own	215

PART 2: THE ALCHEMY OF LIGHT

CHAPTER 10: A WIDER PERSPECTIVE™   **227**

Is A Healthy Childhood Everything?	228
A Kind Of Normalcy That Didn't Protect Me - But Actually Did…	229
The Answer Came In A Dream	230
The Unconscious Is Inherited Too	231
Dad Didn't Let It Break Him Either	232
The Last Link In The Line	233
Through The Looking Glass: The Meaning Of The Relationship	235

CHAPTER 11: HOW CONSCIOUSNESS COMES TO KNOW ITSELF   **237**

A Dance Between The Poles: Consciousness And Physicality	238
Why Do We Still Need Pain?	239

The Original Choice—The Source Of All Other Choices	240
Trauma Bond	241
The House That Lives In Shadow	243
The Trauma Bond As A Mechanism Of Consciousness	244

CHAPTER 12: THE LESSON OF DARKNESS — 247

Pure Darkness, Without Contamination	248
Darkness That Gently Envelopes With A Matte Softness	249
Unraveling Before Rebirth	250
When Light Acknowledges Darkness	251
Behind The Curtains Of Earth's Theater	254
The Power Of Learning Through Shadow	255
Becoming What You Carry	256
Three Layers Of Vision	257
The Dream That Closed The Circle	258

CHAPTER 13: COMPASSION AND DISTANCE–THE MOST IMPORTANT CHAPTER FOR YOU — 259

Between Empathy And Self-Erasure	259
Love Will Not Heal A Narcissist	260
Where The Mind And Heart Fall Short	261
When The Heart Understands That Love Means Boundaries	262
Not Every Intensity Is Love	263
From Passion Of Pain To The Passion Of Presence	264
Disconnected At The Root	265
The Absence That Awakened Presence Within	266

CLOSING WORDS — 269

The Truth About Women Who Live Alone Without A Man	269

ABOUT THE AUTHOR — 277

INTRODUCTION

When I think back on that relationship now, it feels like it happened in another world—another dimension, another timeline, another life—as if centuries ago. It was like a strange dream I woke up from, like time spent inside the Matrix—until I walked out of it.

Looking around at the collective consciousness, I get the sense that more and more people are starting to wake up from a kind of illusion of awareness. There's a growing hunger for authenticity—for living in alignment with who we truly are. People are saying it out loud now: they're tired of denying themselves to meet expectations and fit into someone else's mold.

And it's no coincidence that with this awakening, we're hearing more brave voices speak up—talking about the full range of human experience, not just the parts that check the boxes or please the crowd. Narcissism—this master of illusion, the king of fake and false—has finally been called out. There's so much information available now that it feels like everyone knows the term and is beginning to understand what it really means. And once we recognize it, we start to see how deeply it runs—not just in certain people or toxic relationships, but in the very patterns that shape humanity itself.

Personally, I'm glad to see more and more people feeling the need to experience a sense of inner wholeness. When we open our eyes in this way, we realize that no matter who someone is, where they live, or their status, we all belong to the same human village on planet Earth. Despite our different stories and paths, we share the same inner experiences. Within this human collective, we are all offered the same journey—a path of self-discovery and growing self-awareness.

That path winds through all kinds of experiences: challenges and struggles, triumphs and failures, resistance and flow, trial and error, fortunate turns and painful mistakes, gains and losses, connections and goodbyes, the familiar and the unknown. There isn't a single person on this planet who hasn't known the highs and lows of life, the ache of the soul, the soaring joys, the depths of love and despair. Even those we consider the greatest teachers and sages in human history often faced trials almost beyond endurance. Nothing shielded them from that. We look up to them not because they had perfect lives, but because they forged a meaningful relationship with life itself, with all its beauty and pain.

What truly connects us is what lies inside. That's where we meet, understand each other, and become one shared sense of awareness. However, there's a condition: *authenticity*—being true to ourselves. As long as we hide who we really are from the world, we sentence ourselves to inner isolation and loneliness. And from that place, a whole spectrum of defense mechanisms and dysfunctional behaviors grows.

It's a privilege to write this book—to share one of the many paths that wind across the Earth. This is my path: a journey of challenges, discoveries, life lessons, and deep exploration into the layers where the meaning of everything that happens can be found.

This kind of journey takes us from the inner naiveté of a child—who can only process what feels positive or within their control—to the inner wisdom of the Observer of all things, who sees in hardship a valuable signpost pointing toward the depths of the Self, a place they could never have reached otherwise.

The chapter of my path called "The Relationship with Maciek" has turned out, in hindsight, to be an incredible school of the Self. I've learned more about life, the human psyche, and myself than ever. I've learned that you can't predict what will happen on your path—and that's not the point. What matters is *what you do* with what happens along the way. Will you treat it as a teacher or as a tormentor? Will you surrender to helplessness or find even greater strength within it? Will you step into the role of the victim, or the explorer of life? And when it's time to leave this life behind, in that final moment, will you look back and pat yourself on the shoulder with a quiet "well done," or will you be met with despair and the feeling of a missed opportunity to know yourself truly?

The human mind is wired to think in images and stories. When we read about other people's experiences, we often find pieces of ourselves in them, and that gives us the comforting sense that we're all really on the same ship called humanity, and no one's an exception.

Even when the external stories seem worlds apart—like a king and a beggar—if the two of them sat down at the same table and spoke *honestly* about what they feel deep inside, through all their different struggles, they'd realize they're siblings from the same human family.

Let this story be a book of your own discoveries—about yourself and life on planet Earth.

The Enigma Relationship

I met Maciek long ago, before I began working as a therapist, though I had already completed my psychology training. One glance—and something magical happened. It felt like a cosmic space had opened and pulled me in like a vortex. The wave of emotions, physical sensations, and visions was incredible. It went on for several weeks, until he came to visit me. The depth of those experiences was so intense that I thought this must be what people mean by "love at first sight."

Looking back now, and through the lens of what I've come to understand about emotional-psychological processes—both from the field of psychology and from my own research—I can see that what we often call "love at first sight," those well-known "butterflies in the stomach," and that deep sense of "coming home" in another person, are signs of a *trauma bond*.

I'll explore this type of bond more in Chapter 10—unpacking not only its inner mechanics, but also the broader context of why these kinds of relationships exist, from both a collective-spiritual perspective and the viewpoint of human consciousness in its evolutionary process.

Maciek was my partner for over ten years. That relationship became a profound source of insight into the workings of self-awareness. It was one long emotional rollercoaster.

The first year felt almost idyllic—until the entire script flipped 180 degrees and his other side began to show. Emotional instability, sudden outbursts of anger with no apparent reason, fragmented thought patterns, mood swings from love to hatred, erratic behavior, conversations that turned into gaslighting, silent treatment and sulking, emotional provocations, constant projection, threats to leave, ongoing resentment that I was thriving in my own life instead of focusing solely on him—and more. All of it pushed me deeper and deeper into a search for answers and understanding.

At some point in the relationship, three questions began to haunt me constantly: What is going on here? Why is this happening? And what the hell am I doing in all of this?

Those questions stayed with me until the very end. I remained open the whole time, searching for answers, trying to see a bigger picture beyond my emotions. Running away or complaining were never options for me. And venting too early, before I truly understood what was going on, didn't feel like the answer either.

I know there's no such thing as bad luck, divine punishment, coincidence, curses, or bad genes. Those are just labels for things the mind doesn't yet understand—concepts it clings to to make sense of what feels overwhelming. Nothing is more terrifying to the mind than helplessness, so even powerlessness seems preferable—it lets us dodge the responsibility of facing ourselves.

That's why my only answer was presence: the mindfulness to see everything I possibly could, so I could make a conscious decision; the patience to give things time to reveal themselves so that I wouldn't act too quickly; and the openness to hear and feel even the uncomfortable truths so that I could be sure of my choices.

Given how intense and extraordinary that relationship began, something profound was clearly happening—I just didn't know what yet.

Years later, the pieces finally came together into a meaningful whole. That's the story I want to share with you here, as guidance for your own journey with covert narcissism. But back then, all I had were question marks.

Intro-Narcissist And Extro-Narcissist

As I deepened my understanding of narcissism, I realized that its expression largely depends on a person's temperament. A narcissist with an extroverted temperament manifests as the grandiose or overt type, while an introverted temperament gives rise to the covert type. In both cases, however, the core disturbance is the same — being the absolute center of attention, just expressed in different styles.

The extro-narcissist (grandiose/overt) seeks admiration and recognition, whereas the intro-narcissist (vulnerable/covert) craves ongoing empathy and understanding. The latter is much harder to detect, especially in Western culture.

At the core of this personality structure is a constant *posture of victimhood*. The covert narcissist sees themselves as someone the whole world is conspiring against. In Western society, where Christian cultural values have dominated for centuries, being a victim is often seen as something good, even noble.

Unfortunately, a lack of deeper understanding about the difference between self-sacrifice that stems from inner wholeness and sacrifice driven by a panicked fear of rejection has led to the glorification of a severe personality disorder.

What I offer here is a closer, more discerning look at these distinctions, so we can expand human self-awareness and move toward ending the unconscious perpetuation of this mistake.

You Are The Alchemist

This book is based on my personal story, and I've written it for women who are stuck in a relationship with a covert narcissist and want to break free, as well as for those who have physically left but still feel trapped in an emotional hell.

Throughout the book, I'll refer to the narcissist as "he" because my relationship was with a man. But let me be clear: covert narcissists are not exclusively male. This disorder is rooted in the structure of human self-awareness, not gender, and it shows up across all of humanity.

Each chapter includes different sections where I explore the traits of covert narcissism, the concept of the Inner Parent and Inner Child to help explain this personality dynamic, my personal experiences within such a relationship, and strategies for dealing with the aftermath.

By the end of this book, you should understand not only this disorder, but more importantly, yourself. Especially the parts of you that once believed in some kind of illusion and got pulled into the narcissist's destructive world of manipulation.

Understanding this dynamic—seeing how its mechanisms work, especially within the broader context of your family system and generational patterns—can help you step out of the victim role and reclaim responsibility for your Self.

Even in a relationship that brought harm, it's possible to use those experiences to uncover precious and beautiful parts of yourself—parts that, for various reasons, were buried so deep they could only be reached through painful moments.

What matters most isn't what happened, but what you choose to do with it now—and how you become your own inner alchemist, turning emotional mud into gold.

Don't let yourself get infected by the victim syndrome. Like following a thread back to its source, let this relationship be the path leading you to your inner treasures still waiting to be discovered.

PART 1

THE ANATOMY OF SHADOW

CHAPTER 1

COVERT NARCISSISM: A MIRROR WITH NO REFLECTION

Narcissist - A Diagnosis Or Just A Buzzword?

The words "narcissist" and "narcissism" have become so popular these days that they rank among the top search terms on Google. On one hand, that's a good thing—it means collective awareness is growing. People are realizing they're not alone in their struggles and that they're not crazy. That kind of recognition opens the door to making choices more aligned with who they really are, and taking responsibility for their lives and their inner world.

On the other hand, when a word gets repeated often enough, it starts to lose its original meaning. It gets watered down, applied to all sorts of things, and pretty soon, nobody really knows what it means anymore. That's precisely what happened with words like "imbecile," "idiot," and "moron."

You might even be smiling while reading this, because you've probably heard people throwing those words around in arguments or online fights. These days, they're mostly seen as just insults. For instance, the word "idiotic" doesn't even feel particularly offensive anymore—it's just part of everyday language. Haven't you ever casually said, "Oh wow, what an idiotic color combo!"?

A Word That Lost Its Meaning

Initially, those words were clinical terms used in psychiatry in the early 20th century to describe severe developmental disorders. "Idiot" referred to someone whose mental development exceeded that of a two-year-old child. "Imbecile" described someone functioning at about the level of a seven-year-old, and "moron" at around age twelve.

Today, someone might call another person an "idiot" just for making a small mistake. These words have entirely lost their original significance.

And now, something similar is starting to happen with the word "narcissist." In psychiatry, narcissism refers to a severe personality disorder that can cause deep emotional damage and devastation in relationships. It's so deeply rooted that very few people ever recover from it. Yet these days, someone only needs to act a little selfish or controlling, and they're immediately labeled a narcissist.

This is dangerous for two reasons. First, people who genuinely have this disorder can start hiding behind the word as if it's just a personality quirk, downplaying the seriousness of their condition.

Second, it harms those who aren't narcissistic at all but are labeled that way just because they have unresolved fears and, as a result, focus on themselves more than usual, or because they're highly sensitive and need extra care. Even more concerning, I've seen confident, strong-willed individuals called narcissists simply because they possess healthy self-assurance. These labels often come from people with low self-esteem, reacting with envy toward someone else's strength or presence.

Not Every Person Is A Narcissist

The word "narcissist" appears frequently in this book—after all, that's what the book is about. I describe many behaviors that are typical of narcissistic personality disorder, but that also show up in everyday people and situations. As a result, the term is often overused and has become a shortcut for expressing frustration.

> *Not every selfish, manipulative, or emotionally cold behavior is a sign of narcissism.*

There's a long road between making a selfish choice, having a difficult personality, or making a bad decision, and actually having a personality disorder.

After reading this book, I hope you can see the difference between isolated behaviors and a fixed personality pattern. These are key distinctions to keep in mind:

1. Everyone shows some degree of selfish behavior at times.
2. Selfish behavior is not the same as narcissistic personality disorder.
3. The average person's selfish behavior is occasional and doesn't cancel out their empathy. However, in someone with a personality disorder, selfishness is a consistent, foundational part of how they behave, and it comes without empathy.
4. A regular person and someone with narcissism might exhibit similar behavior on the surface, but underneath, the *intention* is very different. In the first case, it may come from a need to regulate the nervous system or a defense mechanism. In the narcissist, it's about getting *narcissistic supply*.

> *The hallmark of narcissism isn't one specific behavior—it's the overall pattern: the motive, the consistency, and the absence of self-reflection.*

Most of all, my hope is that by the end of this book, you will not only understand what's happening but also feel empowered, freer, and more connected to your true Self.

The Ancients Already Knew

I first encountered the myth of Narcissus in elementary school (in Poland), when we were learning about ancient culture. One of our required readings was Jan Parandowski's Mythology. At the time, I understood the story only in a simple, surface-level way—after all, I was still a child. Now, that understanding has deepened on many levels.

Narcissus, a figure from Greek mythology, was the son of the river god Cephissus and the nymph Liriope. From birth, he was known for his extraordinary beauty, which attracted the attention of both men and women. Still, Narcissus showed no interest in their admiration—he preferred to remain independent, which left many infatuated maidens heartbroken.

His aloofness enraged Nemesis, the goddess of revenge, who decided to punish him. She caused Narcissus to fall in love with his own reflection, which he saw in the perfectly still surface of a spring. He was mesmerized by his own image, yet could never touch it. Eventually, he died in despair—some versions of the myth say from hunger and thirst, others from a broken heart.

A beautiful flower grew in the place where he died—the one we now call the narcissus (*Metamorphoses*, Book III, Ovid).

When Narcissus first saw his reflection, he didn't realize he was looking at himself. He saw something beautiful, unreachable, drawing him in like a forbidden fruit. Every attempt to touch that perfect image ended in disappointment. The water he gazed into would ripple and distort the vision.

Covert narcissism works in much the same way. It builds an image of the Self that must remain a positive illusion—yet simultaneously, it's an image the narcissist can't truly connect with. Every crack in that illusion, every gesture that exposes the truth beneath the surface, feels like a threat.

The narcissist cannot recognize the Self, cannot truly see who they are. There is no internal mirror. Instead, they rely on the opinions and words of others to reflect a version of themselves. They choose empathic partners and friends who will never question their worth.

But what happens when the water starts to ripple?

When he's faced with a distorted reflection, the covert narcissist experiences terror, masked as anger and aggression. He can't allow others to see anything different than the image he wants them to see.

When a partner starts noticing his flaws, or when a friend no longer admires him the way they used to, his inner world begins to crumble. He no longer sees the possibility of real closeness—only a threat.

That's when he withdraws emotionally, resorts to manipulation, or disappears into passive aggression or silence—anything to avoid the shame of an imperfect reflection. He doesn't love people; he loves what he can extract from them, and only as long as it aligns with the image he wants to uphold.

In the myth, Narcissus didn't die because he loved himself—he died because he couldn't possess his own reflection. In other words, he couldn't truly recognize himself.

The same is true for the covert narcissist.

> *The covert narcissist doesn't suffer because they're losing the other person–they suffer because they're losing the idealized version of themselves reflected in the other person's eyes. It's not love. It's a powerful obsession with an identity that doesn't truly exist.*

That's why any relationship with a narcissist is doomed to fail—because he's only ever interested in himself, never in the other person. And even if, on the surface, it seems like he's trying to please someone, it's just a manipulation tactic, which I'll talk more about later.

The Narcissistic Mirror - How It Works

Every person on this Earth is, to some extent, disconnected from their true Self and seeks a reflection of that Self in others. If that weren't the case, we'd already be living at a different level of evolved self-awareness, and certain behavior patterns simply wouldn't exist anymore.

For now, though, our collective self-awareness is still in a developmental stage, like that of a child learning independence and inner responsibility. So, to varying degrees, we can observe behaviors rooted in internal immaturity in every one of us.

But in the case of narcissism, the internal disconnection is so extreme that the separated parts of the Self aren't even aware of each other's existence. The Self's structure is split at its very core, which leads to a profound sense of desperation and a constant internal state of survival, even when life, on the surface, is reasonable and safe.

In this narrowed, threat-based perception of reality, the narcissist sees virtually everything as either an enemy or a danger. As a result, their behavior oscillates between attack and defense.

Even if an angel were to descend from heaven, the narcissist would look for the devil in them, and eventually, they'd find one, even if he was never there.

Every relationship, sooner or later, is destined to be destroyed by the narcissist because they're striving for something that can never truly be reached.

It's a tragic place to be—when someone can't see themselves, and their entire emotional state depends on how others see them.

Praise and approval send them into euphoria, and they "love" the people who give it. Criticism or rejection shatters them, and they suddenly hate those same people. It's a constant surrendering of power, where other people essentially become the managers of the narcissist's inner world.

If their inner survival depends on others, then of course there's desperation—desperation to receive only positivity, only acceptance, only things they can control. Anything else feels like an attack on the Self's very existence.

And if you're an empath and feel compassion rising, don't be fooled. By the end of this book, you'll understand why.

The Disorder Of Being Human

Narcissistic Personality Disorder (NPD) is a serious and deep-rooted disruption in the structure of the Self. It has nothing to do with intelligence—many individuals with exceptionally high IQs can have NPD.

People with this disorder often function in society just like anyone else. They have families, run businesses, hold positions of power, and achieve success. They may be artists, inventors, or people going about their everyday lives.

But this disorder wreaks havoc in every relationship the narcissist is involved in. It could be a romantic partnership, a parent-child relationship, a friendship, or a workplace dynamic between a boss and their team.

The dysfunction plays out on the emotional level. The person may be knowledgeable, capable of behaving appropriately in society, pursuing goals, and presenting themselves in a completely normal—or even impressive—way. They may be well-liked or admired for certain qualities.

It's hard to spot this disorder because it doesn't look like something that would raise red flags or lead to consequences. It doesn't show up as criminal or visibly harmful behavior.

That's exactly why education on this topic is so important—because the narcissist's destructive behavior usually doesn't cross any legal lines. There's no official charge for emotional abuse caused by a covert narcissist, so no institution is going to protect you from it.

The only things that can truly help are your own awareness, knowledge, connection with your Self, and support. Only you can free yourself from this kind of relationship.

In this book, we'll take a close look at the specific behaviors of the covert narcissist—but not just those. We'll also look at specific behaviors that, on the surface, can seem totally normal and even identical to the behaviors of healthy individuals.

What makes them different is the *intention* behind them. That's the key to recognizing who you're really dealing with.

A perfect illustration is the saying, "Not everything that glitters is gold." You'll see, for example, how the same act of showing love can be empowering and nourishing in a healthy relationship, but when it comes from a narcissist, it turns into emotional blackmail and drains your energy completely.

Let's start by clarifying that narcissism falls under *personality disorders*, not mental disorders, because it is part of *identity*. That means it involves deeply rooted traits of character that develop from early childhood. These traits form the core and foundation of behavior and are almost entirely fixed.

They are not temporary episodes or states, like those seen in mental disorders—they are enduring patterns in how someone relates to the world and to other people. Unlike many mental dysfunctions, there is no pill for a personality disorder. Personality is the internal foundation on which a person's life unfolds, and it shapes every behavior.

It's also not the same as intellectual underdevelopment, where personality and cognitive functions are impaired.

> *Narcissists have no problem functioning intellectually. What's broken is their capacity for being human.*

By "capacity for being human," I mean the ability to feel empathy, rise above oneself, and act with integrity—that is, doing something for others when no one is watching. It's the ability to consider how others feel, welcome differences as an opportunity to expand one's perspective (rather than seeing them as a threat), delay instant gratification in favor of long-term well-being, and make choices that serve the whole rather than just the self. It means having a sense of honor and honesty, treating others as we would want to be treated. And a few more things that define true humanity.

What makes covert narcissism especially dangerous is that it can often hide behind the very traits I just described. That's what makes it so easy to be misled. The well-known saying "You'll know them by their fruits" is a good test in this case, because a covert narcissist's words rarely match reality. They're empty.

The core intention of a covert narcissist is to gain validation, attention, approval, praise, sympathy, recognition, and what they often interpret as "respect" (which really means: you must agree with them on everything). They manipulate in ways that allow them to dominate and control.

So if you notice that the real motivation behind all their "good deeds" is to be praised, admired, validated, or seen as special—and if you get punished for not giving them that (with words, silence, criticism, blame, or guilt-tripping)— know this: That is a massive red flag.

Another hallmark of the covert narcissist's "kindness" is that it's not consistent or steady—it's occasional. The prime opportunity for a narcissist to be "good" is when there's something in it for them—when there's a personal gain. That makes it insincere. Once there's no benefit left, the kindness disappears—and often turns into rejection or criticism of the person they treated as valuable.

There's no joy in doing good for the sake of doing good. The only satisfaction comes from being seen, acknowledged, or rewarded. A narcissist, in general, cannot maintain emotional or behavioral consistency. It's a constant rollercoaster. They're incapable of going beyond themselves and their own self-interest.

How Does This Narcissist "Hide"?

When we think of a narcissist, we usually picture a loud, arrogant person who has to dominate everyone and everything around them. They need to be the center of attention—the most special and important. No one measures up. They'll step on others without hesitation just to be on top. They look down on people as if they belong to a lesser species, use them for their own purposes, and don't care who they hurt as long as it keeps them above everyone else.

That's the overt narcissist—the one who doesn't hide their need for power and control.

The covert narcissist, on the other hand, has the same need for dominance and control, but hides it under the mask of being a wounded victim. They crave support, understanding, attention, forgiveness, special treatment, love, and help.

Their method of control isn't yelling or openly putting someone down. Instead, they manipulate you through your compassion, care, and instinct to help. And when you give it naturally, generously, they respond by telling you how wrong or inadequate it was.

In both cases, the narcissist's goal is the same: to diminish others, to prove that no matter what you do, it's not good enough.

The overt narcissist says it to your face.

The covert narcissist lures you in first—with their vulnerability, their pain, their need—and once you're emotionally invested, once you've given your time, energy, love, maybe even your money or started a family, that's when the emotional abuse begins.

It's more insidious because you don't see it coming. And by the time you do, some bonds make it much harder to walk away.

> Both types of narcissists treat you as someone of low value. The overt narcissist tells you that openly–he's better than you, and you're beneath him.
> The covert narcissist convinces you that you're a bad person because you're hurting him.

In the beginning, the covert narcissist often presents himself as a caring, attentive person—someone who seems to read your every need. That's because his sense of importance comes from feeling needed.

He may even lead you to believe—or create a situation in which it genuinely feels like—you can't function without him, that he's essential to your life.

And once that noose of dependence is around your neck, the devaluation of who you are begins.

For clarity, here's an overview of the different types of narcissism commonly discussed in psychological and popular-scientific literature.

Since this book is centered on my personal story with a covert narcissist, we'll focus specifically on the type of narcissism that shows up in close romantic relationships.

Different Forms Of Narcissism

1. **Overt Narcissism** – This is the classic image of a narcissist: arrogant, dominant, boastful, and convinced of their superiority. People with this type often showcase their achievements and expect admiration from others.
2. **Covert Narcissism**—A more subtle form, where the person may seem reserved on the outside, but hides a deep sense of specialness and a strong need for attention. They often play the victim and use emotional manipulation.
3. **Malignant Narcissism**—A severe and toxic version, often overlapping with psychopathy. These individuals are ruthless, manipulative, deceitful, and exploit others without remorse.
4. **Somatic Narcissism** – Focused on physical appearance, attractiveness, and sexual prowess. They seek attention through their body and lifestyle.
5. **Intellectual Narcissism** – These individuals base their worth on intelligence, knowledge, and mental ability. They see themselves as smarter than others and tend to belittle those with less education or intellectual ability.
6. **Spiritual Narcissism** – This involves using spirituality to reinforce a sense of superiority. These individuals see themselves as more enlightened and understanding than others.
7. **Social Narcissism** – Characterized by someone who appears extremely caring, empathetic, and socially active, but does it primarily for recognition and admiration.

8. **Parental Narcissism** – Found in parents who treat their children as extensions of themselves. They demand achievement and obedience to boost their own sense of worth.
9. **Organizational Narcissism** – Seen in leaders or companies that view themselves as exceptional and irreplaceable, while disregarding the needs and values of others.
10. **Media Narcissism** – A modern form, where individuals obsessively seek attention and validation through social media.

My working definition of narcissism is this:

> *A narcissist is a three-year-old child without a parent, trapped in the body of an adult.*

You could argue that every human being exhibits some form of narcissistic behavior at some point.

But it's essential to understand the difference between a *behavior* and a personality disorder—and that's what we'll be exploring here.

Narcissistic behavior happens to EVERYONE from time to time.

It's usually triggered by a significant life event—whether positive or negative—that involves strong emotions or when something feels extremely important. In those moments, all thoughts and attention turn inward, and the needs of others fade into the background.

But the key is: it's occasional.

In a personality disorder, however, these behaviors are not occasional—they're the baseline for how the person functions daily and how they relate to life and to others. External situations do not drive them—they come from within, from a distorted inner structure of self-awareness.

That's why public education on this topic is so important—so people don't mistake someone with occasional selfish behavior for a narcissist.

Narcissistic personality disorder is complex. It involves a whole cluster of traits and symptoms that must appear together. And even then, one must be careful not to confuse it with other complex internal conditions, like autism.

MEMORIES AND REFLECTIONS FROM THE CHAMELEON MATRIX

The Beginning Of The Covert Matrix

I want to begin my reflections on my relationship with a covert narcissist by pointing out the obvious: covert narcissism is hard to recognize. That's precisely why it's called covert.

The manipulation is subtle. He doesn't hit you. He doesn't do anything scandalous. He doesn't create the kind of extreme chaos that would instantly make you want to run.

In fact, through his twisted form of manipulation, he often creates the impression that he's sensitive—even hypersensitive—and that you need to be gentle with him, to be careful about how he feels.

Later, during the devaluation phase (which I'll describe shortly), he begins to allow more overt emotional abuse to come through. But by that point, you're already so entangled in his world that you can't quite believe what's happening. You think maybe he's having a bad day, and it'll blow over soon.

The covert narcissist eats away at the relationship from the root. He does it systematically and patiently. It shows up as passive-aggressive comments, constant opposition to everything, occasional criticism that knocks you to the ground, nonstop dissatisfaction and complaining, never-ending unhappiness, incessant demands for special treatment, deep pessimism, a lack of willingness to cooperate for the good of the relationship, resistance to any conversation that might lead to growth, control, emotional provocations and arguments, blaming you, saying hurtful things when you don't do what he wants—only to then turn around and tell you how amazing you are. Sabotaging anything that might create harmony in the relationship, giving you the silent treatment, and making you feel like no matter what you do, it's never enough, twisting reality to win your admiration. And countless other behaviors that prevent the relationship from growing, while reducing you to *narcissistic supply*—a caregiver, a rescuer, a mother figure, a savior from his own chaos. In this relationship, you don't exist as you—you exist as a source of his emotional needs.

A relationship with a covert narcissist can last for years. It's a deceptive tactic because, on the one hand, his behavior slowly erodes the relationship, but on the other hand, he plays the victim, triggering your empathy and making you want to help. And that very desire to help creates an even deeper bond with him. So the years pass, nothing changes, you feel increasingly drained, and the bond gets stronger until you wake up.

Straight From Real Life

As I describe the various behaviors and symptoms, I'll be sharing examples from my own relationship with a covert narcissist. I'm focusing specifically on the symptoms of the disorder, so I'll be filtering the story through that lens. That means it might sound like the relationship was 100% negative, because I'll mostly describe the negatives. If that were truly the case, I wouldn't have stayed in it for as long as I did. The emotional rollercoaster is characteristic in these relationships: there are positive periods, especially when his inner vacuum has been temporarily filled and he no longer feels the emptiness. But as soon as that emptiness returns, the entire script flips. He morphs like a chameleon into a toxic aggressor whose goal is to drag you down or destroy you. Then, once again, he's fine. It might look like bipolar depression, but it's not. The mechanisms underneath are different. Depression is not a personality disorder.

There are more negative periods and more moments of undermining the relationship. The positive moments give you hope—hope that maybe he really is capable of a healthy relationship. So you give it another chance. Until one day you realize: it's just the chameleon's strategy to keep feeding on your *narcissistic supply*.

The Book As Part Of The Process

When I finally ended that toxic relationship and immersed myself in the professional literature on narcissism, women suddenly began showing up in my therapy sessions—women trying to break free from relationships with narcissists, or women who had already left but still couldn't find their emotional balance. It was an incredible synchronicity. By the time my relationship with Maciek was nearing its end, I was already practicing as a therapist. That experience forced me to deeply explore the human foundations of functioning. My innate passion for understanding the inner universe, the painful relationship with Maciek that took me to the darkest corners of those depths, and the continuous work on my own inner world turned me into a specialist in this field.

When I talked with these women during sessions, explaining the mechanisms of narcissism and sometimes sharing examples from my own experience, it turned out to be so helpful that I heard more than once, "You should write something about this." At first, I thought I'd just write a few solid articles for my website—but the list of topics kept growing, and I thought, "This could be a book."

The Trait That Saved Me

There's one more thing that helped me deeply understand these mechanisms—the same ones I can now clearly explain to help you. It's an internal trait I've had for as long as I can remember—probably since birth. I call it "The Regenerating Sun." Thanks to this trait, I was able to maintain my inner integrity throughout the entire relationship. I didn't let myself get infected by the toxicity, and I treated each moment of mistreatment as a challenge to discover a new piece of myself, instead of falling into despair or collapse.

So, I want to share the insights I had and the deep understanding that came out of it with you now, so you can shorten your own time of emotional suffering, whether you're still in the relationship or already out of it. I want to treat this whole shared path with Maciek as a way of breaking a trail through the wilderness of this issue, so your journey can be easier. May the qualities I was born with, which have helped me navigate life, serve not just me, but you as well.

I'm writing this book first and foremost to empower you, to give you the right perspective so you can step out of the feeling of helplessness. After many sessions and conversations with women like you who've been stuck in relationships with narcissists, and after reading the professional literature, I've learned that people who've been through these relationships often end up emotionally shattered. They're devastated, stripped of all self-worth, disconnected from the world and people, and they've lost hope for a new tomorrow, not to mention the toll it takes on their physical health.

I asked myself why I didn't feel that way. The answer is this:

- "The Regenerating Sun"
- The EFT method (Emotional Freedom Techniques)
- Constant insight into what I'm feeling

If it's possible not to be destroyed by a narcissist, then that means **a relationship with one isn't a life sentence.** You just have to know what to do, how to approach it, and how to understand what's happening.

I know that if you turn inward—toward yourself—and rebuild your connection with your Self, you will reclaim your sense of who you are, your space, your freedom, your dignity, and your worth. Even if those things have been shaken or trampled, that doesn't mean it's the end. It just means it's time to love yourself. If you love yourself, even a narcissist can't break you. And loving yourself—that's entirely up to you. **No one can take that from you, and no one can forbid it**. It's time to stop sacrificing your relationship with yourself for someone who never truly wanted it in the first place. So… let's get to work.

The Regenerating Sun

If you're curious about the inner quality I've been referring to—the one that helped me survive this relationship without lasting damage and have the deep insights I'm now sharing with you—here's what it's about.

When I was younger, I never thought much about it. I just assumed everyone experienced life this way. It wasn't until later that I realized most people had no idea what I was talking about. And when I joined a group exploring states of consciousness in my late thirties, I discovered that what I was experiencing was considered one of the peak states of awareness.

In essence, I cannot remain in a negative emotional state for very long. When something challenging or painful happens, and I start to feel anxious, fearful, or unsettled, it never lasts. Suddenly, from a point just above my navel, a kind of sensation begins to radiate through my entire body. It feels like a wave of warm light moving outward. It's accompanied by a positive, uplifting energy—almost like a joy in simply being alive.

Emotionally, there's a deep sense of peace. Mentally, there's a quiet inner knowing that everything is exactly as it's meant to be. I experience a kind of inner concentration or energetic reorganization. It feels as if the whole universe pauses for a moment, focuses its attention on my inner world, and says, "I see you—and I know what you need."

What follows is a profound trust that everything I need is already "on its way." I can release all control and worry, and in truth, the synchronistic events that unfold afterward are often so astonishing, they're hard even to explain.

The original problem—the one that triggered the emotional low—becomes completely inaccessible in that state. It's as if my awareness has shifted into another dimension, where only flow exists. I simply can't "plug back in" to the negative emotion anymore.

Maybe you have this too, or at least you've had a similar experience. Perhaps it happened while you were out in nature, standing at the top of a mountain or drifting in the middle of the sea—somewhere you felt a perfect harmony with everything around you. A wave of gratitude and peace washed over you, and you felt a deep knowing that everything was all right.

What I experience is very much like that—only it doesn't depend on perfect external conditions. It rises on its own, from within. Especially when life gets shaken up and I need to restore harmony inside. It's like a reset to an optimal state.

This mechanism—and the synchronistic experiences that come with it—have been with me for as long as I can remember. At some point, when I realized that not everyone experiences life in the same way, I began observing it more consciously and trying to understand what it actually was. Out of curiosity, I tried to stop the warm wave of light with my will—but I never could. I tried to prolong the feeling of bad, but that didn't work either. During moments of injustice, I attempted to wallow in self-pity, using logic to convince myself I had the right to stay in that hurt, but soon it all started to feel abstract. I tried to intentionally bring myself into a negative state by exposing myself to heavy news, entering dark emotional spaces, and immersing my awareness in heavy energies, but those were always short-lived. Like being attached to a rubber band, I would be pulled right back to my center, where harmony and peace reside.

Today, I also understand that thanks to this quality of awareness, my general approach to life is to treat everything as an adventure—a puzzle to be solved—and anything that appears on my path isn't random or bad luck, but an opportunity to discover something new. That's why I don't know what it feels like to regret anything in my life. I can see and feel that every single experience—whether small or huge—was exactly what I needed at that particular moment to add another piece to the greater puzzle of understanding, even when it was a difficult experience.

People often chase happiness and peace by trying to control external circumstances, without realizing that true peace and happiness come from within, through self-discovery. Not intellectual understanding— but the kind that comes when *the mind settles into your deeper Self.* Everything you encounter on your path is there to help you make that discovery. There are no coincidences. What creates the illusion of randomness or "bad luck" is a lack of openness and trust, as well as the idea of divine punishment.

> *Peace and happiness are the result of knowing yourself, not intellectually, but through the state in which the mind comes to rest in your deeper Self.*

Thanks to this mechanism, my default internal state is peace. Of course, there are moments full of emotion, frustration when something doesn't go as planned, anxiety when something happens, but everything quickly returns, on its own, to a state of peace and warm light. And the solutions usually follow soon after. And if it doesn't resolve independently, I feel compelled to take action right away. I simply don't know how to sit in negative energy, complain, and do nothing.

A Gift Meant To Serve Others

All of this doesn't mean my path is lined with rose petals—everyone on this Earth has to go through their own hardships. But this state of awareness shapes the way I relate to the world, to challenges, difficulties, and even to painful experiences. It makes me more open to receiving them as activators of self-awareness. As a result, the connection with my inner Self continues to deepen, and with it, my sense of responsibility for myself.

I sincerely believe that every human being is fundamentally capable of experiencing life this way. Sometimes, though, we become disconnected from ourselves and need to help ourselves return to that inner space.

I'd also like to add—because I've encountered this in conversations about these states of awareness—that some people try to interpret it as emotional suppression, or as being "strong," putting on a brave face, or pretending. Let me say this: by its very nature, that would be impossible. You can't fool your inner system. Hiding behind that kind of mask might work for a little while, but eventually, the system would break down and fall apart emotionally, revealing what's really going on underneath.

Just watch a person—see whether what they say aligns with reality—and you'll know what's real and an illusion.

I once encountered another kind of reaction—and it really made me raise an eyebrow. A therapist with many years of experience (!) told me that it's better not to speak about these kinds of positive inner states or about the synchronistic moments that make life easier because people who don't experience them might feel worse. They might feel sad or discouraged. In other words, she suggested I hide who I am because it might "hurt" others.

But isn't that the whole point? To inspire those who feel broken or defeated? To help them see that if even one person can live this way, it's possible—that it's available to others, too? To shift their attention away from being stuck in pain and despair, and toward something that strengthens and uplifts them? I don't understand that kind of philosophy. Even the ancient texts said, "No one lights a lamp and then puts it under a basket."[1]

And if you don't have that inner state, don't worry. It's not required to heal from emotional hardship, and it's not the only way.

Maybe I have this state because I chose a path on this Earth that involves observing reality and working with its mechanics—and this state makes that easier.

If you're emotionally shattered right now, and you think you'll never come out of it because you don't have a state like this—or don't even know what that would feel like—just try one EFT exercise. It will guide you in the right direction within yourself and set you on the path back to who you are. Then continue, step by step. You'll already have come a long way in one month, two, or three.

The EFT Tapping

The second thing that saved me from the toxicity of that relationship was the Emotional Freedom Techniques (EFT). When I started that relationship, I was just beginning to explore EFT and wasn't yet working with clients. But I was already immersed in the practice and actively developing my skills.

If you're not familiar with EFT, I wholeheartedly recommend it. This method can help you through the worst hell on Earth. It's simple and unbelievably freeing.

I was so fascinated by the method that I practiced almost every day. As I slowly began working with clients, I would also conduct EFT sessions for them, using myself as a proxy. So I was also using those exercises on myself, actively working on my own system and emotions. You could say that my professional work saved me from emotional collapse—not because I had "something to do," but because I was systematically working on my emotional system, releasing everything I was aware of—and many things I wasn't. By doing exercises for others and with others, I probably cleared hundreds of negative emotions and beliefs I didn't even know I had.

---

[1] The Holy Bible, *New Living Translation*, Matthew 5:15. ©1996, 2004, 2015 by Tyndale House Foundation

Now I can see that whenever Maciek triggered some kind of emotional "excitement," it was processed and cleared almost immediately through EFT, and I came back to myself, to my center, to my integrity.

So, if you're currently caught in the chameleon matrix, I encourage you again to start doing EFT exercises today. You'll feel relief immediately and begin finding your way out of the emotional fog.

Constant Insight

I call it constant insight, but really, it's that my mind has been wired since birth to explore reality. I noticed it even when I was just a few years old. That's why I refer to it as reality engineering. I'm constantly curious about why things work the way they do and always observe what's happening around me. Instead of falling into despair, my mind switches into, "Hmm, what's going on here and why?" By default, I don't believe in bad luck or curses. That kind of thinking leads to a sense of powerlessness. If something unpleasant happens, it means the mechanism behind it has been thrown out of balance, and it's worth looking into. That's where the power of human potential begins.

This passion eventually led me to begin researching the structure of self-awareness in expanded states of awareness. I began exploring this work in depth during my relationship with Maciek. The depths of reality I explored would've made perfect scripts for a film.

My goal became to understand the mechanisms behind the Regenerating Sun. If this process happens naturally in me, then it means the system managing it is functioning properly. The key is to identify what disrupts it and how to restore it to harmonious operation. The foundations for this are already forming through a method I've co-developed called the Inherence Process˚.

Looking back now, I can see that everything Maciek brought into my life kept leading me to deeper and more difficult levels of awareness. So no matter which vulnerable part of me he hit, I would take it and go into the depths of that place that needed attention. And there, I would discover yet another unknown part of myself.

A Unique Position

The Regenerating Sun, the EFT Method, and deep insight gave me a unique position. On one hand, I was right at the heart of the chameleon matrix, but on the other, an Observer was present—one who calmly watched what was happening in the emotional storm—not only helping me stay centered and avoid being swallowed whole, but also learning how the entire dynamic actually worked.

That's why I hope this book reflects that experience: it takes you straight into the heart of this kind of relationship, where you'll recognize something that feels deeply familiar—and also see the perspective that frees you from feeling responsible for your partner's misery. And that will open the door to your freedom.

> *You are not his mother, his savior, his caregiver, or his rehabilitation center.*

If you find yourself smiling at certain points in this book, that's good. Some of it is so absurd that the only other option would be to cry. I've woven humor into the personal sections and title headings as a way to maintain a healthy distance. This book was written from a place of power, not despair, and I hope it helps awaken your own power too.

A Double-Edged Sword

All of this sounds great—but at the time, it turned out to be a double-edged sword. On one hand, the connection with my deep Self, the EFT Method, and constant insight saved my life and protected my inner integrity. On the other hand, I didn't feel bad enough on the inside to say, "Enough." It took a serious violation of boundaries for my detached common sense to finally step in and say, "That's it."

Beyond that, my optimistic belief that every person deep down wants to be healthy and happy kept me holding on to hope—that one day Maciek would wake up and join the people who truly enjoy life. After all, the first year was blissful—so clearly he could do it. What a mistake in thinking. That was my biggest wake-up call, a shock to my system. I saw with my own eyes that some people have such a deep attachment to destruction that they'll do anything not to let it go.

I also didn't realize that my peace and emotional stability wouldn't be something we could build the relationship on, but instead would be used as *narcissistic supply*.

So the obvious question arises: If I feel such deep harmony and peace within me, how in the world did I resonate with someone who destroys peace and happiness? What pulled me so strongly toward a person like that?

I searched for that answer for ten years. And it wasn't until I expanded my perspective that this strange connection finally made sense.

CHAPTER 2

THE ABANDONED INNER CHILD AND THE MISSING INNER PARENT

If you've read my previous book, *You Are the Dream of the Universe*, then you're already familiar with the concept of the Inner Parent and Inner Child as parts of the deeper Self. In this chapter, I'll give a brief overview of that idea to help illuminate the roots of narcissistic disorder. I invite you to read the above book for a more in-depth examination of the entire structure of the Self.

The Structure Of The Self: The Inner Parent And Child

In therapy, the concept of the Inner Child is well-known, and many therapists incorporate Inner Child work into their practice. Early in my own therapeutic work, I also often employed that approach. But over time, I started to feel that something was missing—like there was an unspoken piece no one was addressing. At the same time, through my continued exploration of levels of consciousness and my search to understand the mechanisms that govern the Self, a more complete picture began to emerge. I suddenly saw that our deep inner world doesn't consist only of the Inner Child—it also includes the Inner Parent. The Inner Child has no real problem at all. I couldn't understand why so much effort was being made to rescue or heal it. It became crystal clear to me: the real issue lies with the Inner Parent. That part needs healing, rebuilding, awakening, and maturing.

When we say the word *child*, we automatically assume the presence of a parent or caregiver. And when we say *parent*, we instinctively understand that this person has a child. You can't call someone a parent if they don't have—or aren't raising—a child. Likewise, we call someone a child when their life depends on the presence of a parent or caregiver. Without one, they can't survive.

We see that this is a functional whole composed of two poles: parent and child—one cannot exist without the other. Why, then, do we highlight only one half of this whole and focus exclusively on it in therapy? Perhaps it's because in order to see both sides of the system, you have to step back and take on the role of the Observer.

I suspect the idea of healing the Inner Child may have originated in the mind of a traumatized Inner Parent—one who, unconscious of their own pain, needed something onto which to project their wounds. The Inner Child was the closest and most convenient target.

In Western culture, the commandment "Honor your father and mother" has been repeated for centuries. Taken literally and without reflection, it distorts our perception of what it means to be a parent. According to this rule, parents are to be treated as flawless, almost sacred, forgetting that they are just ordinary people with the same struggles as anyone else. No wonder this also shows up in our inner world, where the only one seen as having a problem is the Child, while the Parent is overlooked—after all, they're "perfect." The reality is quite the opposite.

What Is This Pair?

The Inner Child and Inner Parent are two parts of the structure of our deeper Self. Each has its own qualities and functions, complementing and cooperating to create a functional whole. When both are operating properly, we experience outward signs of this inner balance in our moods and behavior: coherence, authenticity, confidence, a clear sense of Self, peace, trust in life, a harmonious relationship with reality, and the feeling of always being "at home," no matter where in the world you are. At the same time, when this system is working well, you're constantly learning from life and expanding your inner and outer horizons.

The Inner Child is the part of you that holds the energy of life, enthusiasm, joy, curiosity, openness to everything, playfulness, and trust. It's your power, warmth, fire, impulse, untamed force, emotional depth, and sensitivity. This is where your core potential lives—what you bring into the world. This part feels and experiences, but doesn't have the capacity for reasoning. It sits at the very center of the Self.

The Inner Parent is the part of you that is rational, intelligent, thoughtful, observant, and able to take a step back. It can pause, assess, and make conscious choices. It gives shape to the untamed energy of the Child and helps it express itself in life in a constructive way. It manages attention, time, and space, regulating everything to create harmony and a sense of flow. It sets the boundaries of the Self.

To put it metaphorically, we can compare the Inner Parent to a vase and the Inner Child to the water it contains. Water has no shape—if spilled on the floor or table, it must be cleaned up. A vase, when empty, can at best decorate a room and gather dust. However, when we pour water into the vase, the water takes on a shape. It becomes something specific and starts to play a role in reality. When filled with water, the vase begins to fulfill its function of organizing reality.

Together, water and vase—they gain meaning. Only then can they do something in the world: they can keep cut flowers alive. Water alone, spilled on the table, won't help the flowers. The vase alone, without water, won't help either—the flowers will dry up. Only together do they form a functional whole that makes sense in the world of cut flowers.

Our Self-structure works the same way. The Inner Child is untamed power—limitless energy that, without boundaries, becomes a "spilled substance." The Inner Parent sets those boundaries, giving the power a container so it can be held, shaped, and expressed in the world.

Translated into everyday life as an adult: when someone has that inner "water" without a container—an Inner Child without an Inner Parent—they behave uncontrolled. Their emotional reactions are disproportionate; they lack a sense of Self, can't access their potential, struggle in life and relationships, and have no inner or outer stability.

On the other hand, when the vase feels empty—when the Inner Parent doesn't hold the Child within—it results in a person who is rigid, perfectionistic, fanatical, stuck in routines, overly critical, constantly seeking control, anxious, and burdened by a deep sense of meaninglessness and emptiness.

Most often, it's a mix of both—some of this, some of that.

The Fully Formed Inner Child

When a child is born, the structure of the Self is still undeveloped. But here's the important part: the central element of that structure—the Inner Child—is already fully formed. What's missing is the Inner Parent.

That's why a small child behaves like a wild and enthusiastic force of nature. The Inner Child doesn't need to develop further—it's beautifully shaped from the beginning and stays that way forever.

What it needs is the emergence of the Inner Parent.

At first, that role is played by the actual parents. It's around them that the child feels safe and can begin to explore the world and discover themselves. They are the ones who hold and contain that untamed energy, so it doesn't "spill out" too far and end up causing harm to itself.

As the child grows, the Inner Parent begins to take shape. It learns from physical parents, caregivers, and the external world. It copies and absorbs information about life and how the world works.

The older the child gets, the more complex the Inner Parent becomes—until eventually, it's developed enough to take care of the Inner Child on its own, without needing outside guidance. At that point, the person becomes emotionally independent, and the Self-structure is complete, made up of both the Inner Child and the Inner Parent. It all sounds straightforward—but in practice, it's not.

As the Inner Parent develops, it soaks up behaviors and patterns from those with whom the child has emotional connections—whether those connections are positive or negative doesn't really matter. Most often, these influences come from parents and close family members. The developing Inner Parent takes these caregivers as the blueprint for what it learns from them.

For example, if your parents repeatedly told you that you were worthless, your Inner Parent absorbed that message, and now you tell your Inner Child that it's worthless, or at least you often feel that way. If they believed in you, your Inner Parent now believes in your power—in your Inner Child. If they were constantly worried about you, your Inner Parent now fears the Inner Child's enthusiasm. If they were overly controlling, your Inner Parent now suppresses the Inner Child. And so on.

The Inner Child Is Perfect From Beginning To End

Notice that nothing has actually happened to the Inner Child's structure. It's still that same vital force wanting to express itself in the world. What stands in the way is the Inner Parent. That's the part that has the problem. That's the part that didn't fully or healthily develop. That's the part that never gained the skills—or the connection—to become an extension of the Inner Child in the outside world.

Let's repeat this: a person is born with a fully formed Inner Child, and that structure stays the same throughout their life. As we grow, the Inner Parent structure develops—and that's the part we become as physically mature adults. We stop being pure, untamed energy and transition into rational beings. The Inner Child becomes the heart of the system, the core in the center. It's no longer that overflowing force spilling outward.

So, if we're unhappy or struggling in our adult lives, it's not because there's something wrong with the Inner Child that needs to be "healed." The Inner Child is perfect from beginning to end. The issue lies in the poorly formed Inner Parent structure because that's the part responsible for our behavior in adulthood.

When The Inner Parent Fails

A healthy Inner Parent should be fully connected to the Inner Child—able to see it, receive its power, recognize its potential, talents, and preferences, and always stay in touch with it, acknowledging its needs. At the same time, the Inner Parent observes the external world and serves as a mediator and regulator of the exchange between the heart of the system—the Inner Child—and the world.

However, when the Inner Parent is built on faulty models of how life and relationships work, it can't fulfill its role as the guardian and guide for the Inner Child. The Inner Child remains perfect and intact, but it can't function in the world by itself. It needs a caretaker who organizes its life. The Child itself has no problem, flaw, or wound.

The Difference Between A Child And The Inner Child

When people talk about "healing the Inner Child," they're usually referring to working with childhood trauma. This is where two different things get confused: the physical child and the structure of the Inner Child that exists within them.

This structure—the Inner Child—is already fully developed and mature in the child. What's not there yet, and what is still developing (and vulnerable to mistakes or developmental damage), is the Inner Parent structure. That's the part that gets poorly formed by unhealthy environmental patterns. That's the part that has problems, can't function properly, carries dysfunctional beliefs and behavioral scripts—and that's the part that needs healing.

The Immature Inner Parent – Limited Self-Awareness

Our self-awareness is also partially offline when the Inner Parent structure is dysfunctional. We act more out of automatic patterns than from conscious choice. That's why an Inner Parent with low self-awareness isn't able to see or recognize itself clearly enough to realize that it's the one with the problem—and so it projects that problem onto the Inner Child. In other words, it does precisely what caregivers often do when they project their own issues onto their children.

I encourage all Inner Parents to stop trying to rescue something that doesn't need saving. Instead, take a good look in the mirror and uncover the mask made of false beliefs and distorted images.

> What we call "Inner Child work" is actually work with the false **image** of the Inner Child that is recorded within the structure of the Inner Parent.

"I'll Never Be Like My Mother Or Father!"

Here's the paradox we often see in someone who had difficult or dysfunctional parents and swore they'd never be like their mother or father. On the outside, it might even look like they've succeeded.

Let's take an example. A child grows up with a narcissistic mother who never truly sees them. She focused only on herself and her own problems, blamed the child for anything that was hard for her, and burdened them with responsibilities that weren't theirs. She prioritized her own needs and used the child to fulfill them. She criticized the child constantly, but when she needed something, she suddenly became sweet and "loving."

The child tried to please her in every way they could. But as the child's Inner Parent structure developed, it learned that life meant not being seen, being abandoned, feeling unwanted, unimportant, and unloved. Since this is naturally unpleasant and deeply wrong, the child made a vow: "I will never treat others this way." Being selfish and dismissive of others' needs and well-being seemed unbearable.

And so, as an adult, this person becomes someone who "would give you the shirt off their back." They live by that inner vow—kind, generous, never acting superior, never using people. They consider others' needs and feelings so much that they neglect their own, because "I'll manage, I can handle myself."

Years pass. They're still good to others. But their life is stuck. And what do we find out? It turns out that yes, on the outside, they may be the complete opposite of their mother. However, the structure of their Inner Parent treats their Inner Child exactly the same way their mother treated this person. It doesn't see the Child—its needs, its talents, its potential—because everyone out there is more important.

So much for the vow, "I'll never be like my mother." Sure, they're different toward others—but toward themselves, this person is their mother.

Notice that even though the Inner Child is unseen, it isn't damaged in itself. What's malfunctioning is the Inner Parent. Without a real connection to the Child, the Parent doesn't allow that vital energy to manifest in the world. As a result, the whole Self-structure suffers—but the power at its core remains untouched.

So let's stop trying to heal the Inner Child. Let's start healing the Parent.

To sum it up: on this planet, the condition for functioning is having a structure that can move through the physical dimension and process its laws. That structure—the one that knows how to live here because it understands this dimension—is the Inner Parent. Raw power alone, meaning the Inner Child, cannot function in this world. Without the Inner Parent, it will always be lost.

In childhood, since the Inner Parent has yet to form, the Inner Child shines through the child's behavior. Over time, the Inner Child sinks deeper into the core of the Self-structure, eventually becoming its center. The person begins to function from the platform of a developing Inner Parent, starting to act more rationally than impulsively.

The Child sits in the center, ready for life and untouched. The Parent organizes things in a way that allows it to see, understand, and guide the Child through life. But most often, the Inner Parent doesn't operate from that inner connection to the Child—it acts from distorted and false recordings it absorbed during its development.

The Inner Child without the Parent is power without eyes–it moves blindly and without restraint. The Inner Parent without the Child is an empty shell–it feels no life and no meaning.

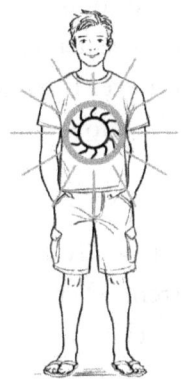

Inner Child without Parent   Inner Child and Inner Parent

○ Inner Child
◎ Inner Parent
∼ Radiant Power of the Inner Child
— Radiant Mind of the Inner Parent after Integrating the Child's Power

A Confused Child In An Empty Mirror

Let's place narcissistic disorder within the framework of the Inner Parent and Inner Child. As you already know, the Inner Child—your essence and potential with which you came into this world—is pure life itself. It's the living you. The Inner Parent is (in ideal circumstances) a wise guide through this world.

When you bring your awareness to the very center—into the Inner Child—the state you feel is: '*I am.*' When your Inner Parent is well-developed—that is, when you become self-aware—the state you feel is: *I know who I am.*

Our essence pulses with life, but it doesn't know itself. That's where the Inner Parent comes in—it's the mirror in which essence can see its own reflection. The Inner Child gets reflected back, and the Inner Parent gets to know it. In childhood, caregivers play the role of a mirror—they reflect to the child who they are. The child's developing Inner Parent learns about itself and its essence through this feedback.

The problem starts when caregivers' feedback doesn't match who the child's Inner Child really is. What gets recorded inside the child is a distorted message about themselves. Their Inner Parent—the internal mirror of the Self—can't accurately reflect what's really there. And so the Inner Parent never fully gets to know the Inner Child. The result is not the state of "I know who I am," but rather, *I know who they want me to be.*

In the average person, the connection between the Inner Child and the Inner Parent is partly intact, partly disconnected, and in some cases, entirely nonexistent. Picture it as a bicycle wheel with spokes: the rim represents the Inner Parent, the hub is the Inner Child, and the spokes are the Parent's attention. Some spokes are solid and connect the rim to the hub. Others are broken, and some are missing altogether. In other words, the person knows themselves and their essence to some extent and feels good about it. Still, other parts remain unseen, and those gaps are usually compensated for with various behaviors.

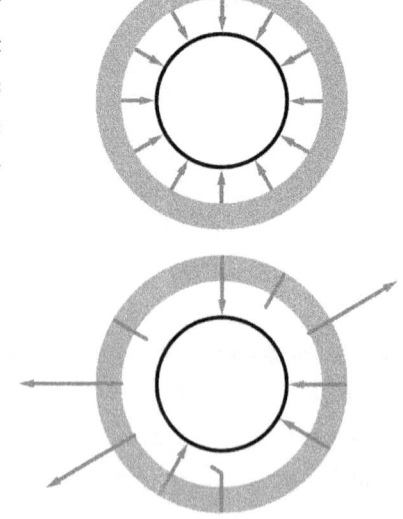

A healthy Inner Parent—its attention is fully focused on the Inner Child, reflecting it completely. As a result, it knows the Child—its needs, talents, and potential—and can express it authentically in the world. This creates a fully integrated Self.

Inner Parent – partially disconnected from the Inner Child, with some attention turned outward, searching for the Child in the external world (and never finding it). It only reflects the Child partially. This creates a Self "with holes."

In narcissism, there are no "spokes"—or rather, they technically exist, but they're all directed outward. The disconnection between the Inner Child and the Inner Parent is so extreme that one is unaware of the other's existence. In psychology, this is referred to as a split Self. That's why narcissists swing from one extreme to the other. One moment, they're acting out in a completely uncontrolled, emotionally driven way, with no discernment—then suddenly, awareness flips to the other extreme, and they become a cold tyrant who feels nothing.

Narcissist's Inner Parent – its attention is turned away from the Inner Child. It doesn't see it, doesn't know it. Its focus is directed outward, reflecting everything except the Inner Child. This creates a false Self based on external reflections, rather than a true Self rooted in one's own essence.

The Inner Child Searching For A Parent

As a result of such a severe internal split, both parts of the Self begin to function dysfunctionally. The development of the Self-system becomes frozen at the level of a three-year-old.

The Inner Child, having an Inner Parent who doesn't see it at all—as if it doesn't exist—begins to search for care and attention outside of itself. This is especially visible in covert narcissism. The person constantly steps into the role of the victim—the one who needs help, support, saving, rescuing, empathy, understanding, praise, appreciation… all the things a child needs for healthy emotional development.

But in adulthood, it is no longer possible for any external source of attention to truly help. That option is available only to children who have yet to develop an Inner Parent.

In adults, the Inner Parent already exists—and only *that* Parent, through deep inner work, can give the narcissist what they didn't receive in childhood.

The desperation to get this kind of attention is so intense that the narcissist resorts to manipulation, specifically by triggering guilt in others, especially those closest to them, in order to extract more attention and care. They can turn the smallest, most meaningless thing into a weapon and blame you for causing them harm. For example, let's say your face looks tense because your stomach hurts. A covert narcissist might accuse you of making that expression as yet another sign of how little you respect them, how you don't want them around, how you're using passive-aggressive tactics to show how much you dislike them. If you explain that your stomach is simply hurting, they'll say: "You always have an answer for everything." And there you are, looking at this bizarre exchange, while your brain twists itself in knots trying to figure out what just happened.

You'll get pulled into the game if you're an empath with weak boundaries (which means a weak Inner Parent). You'll feel guilty, offer reassurance, and try to soothe them. But if you're an empath with healthy boundaries, you might say something like, "I can see you're not in the best mood. Maybe we can talk later." And you'll walk away. The narcissist doesn't care about facts. They only care about emotional manipulation, provoking emotion in others. I'll explain why that is in the upcoming chapters.

The Inner Parent Searching For The Child

Just as the Inner Child in a narcissist seeks any kind of caregiver outside of itself, the Inner Parent likewise looks outward for its Child. The Inner Parent's greatest task is to see and reflect the Inner Child. The Parent is the mirror in which the image of the Child is meant to appear. When the Parent doesn't see the Child and is turned away from it, it falls into despair and desperately tries to reflect something—ANYTHING—to feel like it's fulfilling its function. However, the Parent looks outward, not inward, where the Child actually is, so it ends up reflecting and mistaking something external for its own Child.

In this way, the narcissist's Self becomes extremely unstable because the outside world is constantly shifting, and so the image in the Inner

Parent's mirror keeps changing. As a result, their sense of Self becomes someone different from one moment to the next. By reflecting external objects, the Inner Parent constructs a false Self, because by its very nature, nothing external can ever truly belong to the Self. A true Self can only be formed when the Parent sees its one and only Inner Child and creates the Self *with* it.

The Narcissist's False Self

The covert narcissist is like a chameleon—mirroring and adopting whatever is visible on the outside, treating it as if it were their own. As a result, they are constantly shifting, reinventing their false Self, changing their appearance, and changing their preferences. They are perpetually dissatisfied, unfulfilled, and always searching for something that will finally give them a sense of existence. When they encounter something new, they become filled with excitement—the Inner Parent is euphoric, believing it has finally found the Self. But because the true Self doesn't exist outside, the euphoria quickly fades, especially when the object turns out to be different from the imagined ideal. One minor flaw is enough to shift them from euphoria to hatred and the urge to destroy. The Inner Parent's disappointment—realizing once again it hasn't found its Self—turns into boredom with what was supposed to be "it," into anger and the impulse to destroy, and eventually, abandonment.

A narcissist will never find outside what they are truly searching for—their essence—because they are running from the only place it actually exists: their Inner Child, which they have rejected.

MEMORIES AND REFLECTIONS FROM THE CHAMELEON MATRIX
Love On Steroids–With Side Effects

If I had known back then what I know now about narcissistic personality disorder, my bags would've been packed just a few weeks after moving in with him. He revealed his true nature fairly quickly, but I didn't recognize those as warning signs. Besides, the rest of the first year was amazing.

The very beginning was absolutely extraordinary. We met online. I was living in Lakeland at the time, and he was in Pacifica. When I saw his photo, something shifted—like a vast starry space opened up and pulled me in, as if I were entering another dimension. This wasn't just an emotional reaction—my body was feeling something much deeper, something energetic, with sensations I had never experienced before in my life. It was intense. There were waves of energy so strong they were almost painful at times—tightness in the upper abdomen, sharp pains in the heart, a sudden connection to him, a feeling of being uplifted, and a deep knowing that I had known him for eons.

We messaged each other daily and occasionally had video calls. During that time, I also began having visions and dreams that felt like they came from other dimensions. Everything was so extraordinary that every cell in my body was convinced: *this is it.*

Dream - A Premonition Before The Premiere

I still remember one dream in particular, where I experienced something that was blurry in visuals but deeply stirring in message. I woke up with my heart racing, feeling like something strange was unfolding between masculine and feminine energy. A strong intuition came over me—that the feminine must not allow itself to be dominated by the masculine; that the most important thing in a relationship is to maintain one's integrity. Alongside this feeling came a vision of two substances—one radiating fullness and independence, and the other trying to absorb it, but failing.

At the time, I didn't understand the vision. Now I see that it was an early glimpse into the energetic dynamic of the relationship. But the interpretation only came later, once I learned to observe reality through expanded states of awareness.

Secondly, I had no idea where this vision came from. There was no abuse in my family; my parents respected each other, my father always supported my mother, and vice versa. They loved each other until the very end. I hadn't experienced any abuse or neglect from them either. I didn't know what it meant, so I dismissed it. Only years later, when I began exploring the topic of generational trauma, did it start to make sense. But more on that later.

Sensitive Boy Looking For A Mother - Urgent

During the few weeks we corresponded and talked before he came to Lakeland, we exchanged many deep thoughts. To this day, I still have that correspondence—and now, I look at it as a collection of red flags and material for deep reflection. Back then, I was over the moon.

Within just a few days, he was already telling me I was his "home," that he loved me, that he had visions of us holding hands in old age, that he'd never felt so good and safe with any other woman, and that he had finally found someone who truly understood him—because all his past partners had been worthless. He also said that since nothing had ever worked out for him before, he had basically given up… but now, it looked like he finally had a chance, because this time it felt different, unlike anything else.

Now I know that this behavior is called *love bombing* and is a classic narcissistic strategy. I'll talk more about it in the next chapter. But this kind of immediate, intense bonding, declarations of love, and imagining a lifelong future together before even meeting in person is a hallmark of a trauma bond.

During our correspondence, something arose that I now recognize as a red flag, but it seemed extraordinary at the time. Maciek started talking about masculine energy and how, when it's weakened, it can be beautifully strengthened by feminine energy. He said he hoped that my gentle, feminine energy could help him with that.

Sounds like honey to the ears, right? At first glance, you might think, what a sensitive man—someone who knows himself and is open to growing together. Don't be fooled. That's just another hook designed to reel you in.

First, if a man tells you right from the start that he needs nurturing from your feminine energy, it means he hasn't resolved his relationship with his mother—and he'll be looking for her in you. Not a partner, but a mother. And since he likely harbors resentment toward his mother, he'll end up projecting that resentment onto you—giant red flag. A relationship with a boy pretending to be a man will always lead to emotional chaos, because you're not his mother.

Second, unresolved mother issues brought into a romantic relationship inevitably lead to attempts at domination through immature masculine energy. And so much for that illusion of being open to mutual growth.

The Alarm Went Off, But The Music Was Too Loud

I remember during our correspondence, I once said something that set a boundary—and it was immediately labeled as "kicking him in the balls." ("You kicked my balls.") I apologized, saying I hadn't realized it could be taken that way, and I started watching my words more carefully. I didn't know then that this reaction would mark the beginning of a pattern.

Later, throughout our more than ten-year relationship, it turned out that this phrase was one of his favorites. All it took was the slightest thing that made him uncomfortable—even by a millimeter—and I was suddenly accused of "kicking him in the balls." It was his way of maintaining his completely fabricated role as the victim while casting me as the bad guy. Watching my words made no difference in the end.

Eventually, I couldn't take it anymore. After hearing it for the thousandth time, I snapped and said, "I'm surprised you even still have any balls. After everything that's supposedly kicked them, I'm not sure there's anything left down there."

The truth is, you won't find courage or accountability in a covert narcissist. Those symbolic "balls"—meaning mature masculinity—he left at his mother's house a long time ago and never went back to get them.

Red Flags? I Thought They Were Decorations.

Looking back after all these years, I write from the perspective of someone who has finally detached and gained a healthy, rational distance. It's easy now to talk about red flags and signs of narcissism. From this vantage point, common sense also asks, "Why did you get involved in the first place? Didn't you see all the warning signs?" The answer is: "No."

You don't see the whole picture when you're energetically and chemically pulled into a relationship like that. You see only a narrow slice of what's happening, filtered through what you feel inside. And those feelings are incredibly intense.

Our internal system tends to accept as truth whatever feels emotionally familiar, rather than what is truly healthy. That part of us doesn't distinguish whether we feel good or bad. For it, *familiarity* equals truth. And that's where the conflict begins—between what's healthy and real, and what's merely familiar. Trauma can feel familiar because our emotional system has adapted to it over time. Or even deeper, there may be inherited generational traumas that feel even more like "deeply mine." Only later does life correct this, and the conscious mind learns that what once felt "real" was harmful.

It's no coincidence that people say "love is blind." In that state, it's hard to hear your inner warnings—even when they're subtle and recurring.

Love—those intense feelings of something deep—can easily override common sense. Emotional bonds are among the most powerful forces between people. It's important to note, though, that emotional bonds *rooted in trauma* are even stronger because they tap into the survival instinct, and nothing in living organisms is more powerful than that.

Love Amphetamine: How To Lose Your Mind With A Smile

That's why these bonds are so seductive, gripping, and immediate. In that state, a person feels absolutely certain this is the real thing, so sure they're ready to sacrifice or give up their life for it. Of course they are, because on a felt level, everything aligns perfectly—like a key fitting into a lock. What they don't realize is that it's the key and lock of trauma.

When you're in that state of emotional "high," you don't see things clearly. When red flags show up, you rationalize them—because they don't fit what you're feeling in your intoxication. It's an emotional addiction, and as with any addiction, you need another "hit" to keep the euphoria going. The system simply doesn't want to see or hear the subtle whispers of intuition, because that would mean withdrawal pain and the loss of something that feels deeply precious.

I went through all of this myself. Today, I recognize those behaviors as red flags—but back then, they felt unimportant, like an annoying fly buzzing near my ear that I just needed to swat away. So the rationalizations would come: "He's just having a bad day," "Everyone loses it sometimes," "We'll talk it through later and it'll all make sense," "I won't make a mountain out of a molehill," "In a good relationship, you forgive little flaws," "I understand people and their weaknesses," and so on. The mind becomes a brilliant storyteller when it's trying to protect its own illusions—and it will lie to itself to keep the story alive.

For me, the biggest hook—which sank deep into my very marrow—was something he sent me to read during those first weeks of our correspondence.

Let's go back for a moment to the narcissist's early strategy when seducing someone: love bombing. One of the key tactics in this strategy is to listen carefully and read between the lines to figure out what matters most to you—what you value and hold dear. Once the narcissist has that information, he begins to manipulate his words and actions to give you exactly that. Of course, he isn't being sincere and has no intention of actually living out the things he promises or expresses. It's purely a tactic to make you see in him that part of yourself that feels most important to you. That's when you open up to him with your deepest Self, a bond forms, and just like that, you're hooked. And from that point on, you're hanging on the line.

The Perfect Con

I met Maciek through an online platform that connected people interested in spirituality. As I mentioned earlier, I wasn't a therapist yet, but I had already completed my psychology training, and I'd been fascinated by how people function since I was a child. When we started corresponding and talking, we shared many common interests. I was intrigued that he was into energy work and shamanism, and that he not only attended various workshops but also facilitated sessions meant to help others.

So when he picked up on the fact that I was into these things too—and when he heard me say that, in my experience, the most important thing in a relationship is communication, especially when something feels off—he responded by saying that relationships are meant to bring hidden things from the darkness into the light, so that both people can grow. And then he sent me this text. Looking back, I realize it hit me like a declaration of a spiritual relationship—that's why it resonated so deeply. Here's what it said, title included:

Sacred Union Of Man And Woman ~ Questions For The Heart ♂♀
Intent ~ Be Clear ~ About Intent
Imperative to be clear about one's own intent around the union.

1. Can I surrender to life on my own?
2. Can I surrender to life with another?
3. Time, nothing but time, will enable me to get to know someone more deeply—that is, if I have moved beyond my own personal criteria or the building of the box I would like my partner to fit into.
4. If they fit into the box initially but fall short of what I think they should be later in life, will I destroy the box?
5. I must be able to show up for myself fully, without condemnation, before showing up fully for my lover.
6. Am I clear enough about my intent in regards to what partnership represents to me?
7. What do I think my current desires are?
8. Am I prepared for my partner to change and evolve—and can I accept that change as it occurs, yet still be able to love?
9. Am I willing to surrender to another's desires on the physical, emotional, and spiritual level?
10. Will I ask the question, "What can I bring to the relationship for the highest good of us both?" — not "What can I get from it?"
11. How much of a person's past will I allow to influence my ability to show up for them in a loving, non-judging way?
12. Can I start fresh in the newness of every day's now-moment, with clear eyes, an open heart, and the willingness to face whatever challenges might arise for us in all the areas of our lives?

13. Is the outward expression of life with another harmonizing the time I spend on the inner realms?
14. Do I truly wish to be loved while living in love with another?
15. Have I been sold a bill of goods about "romantic love" and my cultural, religious, and societal inculcation of what partnership means?
16. Do I lose sight of the now-moment with my partner because I am unable to forgive the past hurts?
17. Can I be of deep integrity even if I feel abandoned?
18. Do I know what it is like to feel abandoned by myself and my Creator?
19. Is love for the sake of love enough for me?
20. Will I choose to remain faithful to my lover?
21. Can I feel blame, pain, despair, hatred, madness, and ego deflation at the sword tip of my lover?
22. Is there room for silence in the relationship, because I have made room for it in my own life?
23. Is there space in my perception for the transliminal and transcendental, which is beyond the threshold of awareness?
24. Am I willing to honor the harmonic relationship between the measurable intrinsic rhythms of life and the unmeasurable natural rhythms inside our bodies, minds, and spirits that are always connected to nature?
25. Can I be there for my lover no matter how uncomfortable or deeply triggered I may become?
26. Do I view the relationship as a gift?
27. Can I make the decision every day to show up fully, so that I might be able to participate in the manifestation of our highest good?
28. Will I honor the universe, fate, and grace for their role in the grand architecture of the mystery in the union of two souls?

When I read it, I nearly fainted from the impact. He had struck directly at the heart of what I considered the most valuable quality in a human being—growth and transcendence. The impression was intensified even further when he told me he had written it himself, that it had just "come to him" like a revelation. That completely swept me into the current, because being with someone who feels and understands so deeply felt almost like grabbing God by the ankle. I thought the piece was so beautiful that a few years later, when I created my first website, I posted those questions on my blog as a guide for anyone who seriously wanted to reflect on their relationship.

More than ten years later, when the relationship finally collapsed—and as the dust settled, many hidden truths came to light—I found out he hadn't written that text at all. He had copied it from another source and lied about it being his, just to impress me. Lies like that are completely normal for narcissists, especially in the early phase of a relationship, when they're luring you into their matrix and mimicking your deepest values like a chameleon. They want to be the perfect ideal in your eyes—someone you won't be able to resist.

The text itself is brilliant, but the fact that Maciek claimed it as his own and lied about it is just astounding. Throughout the entire relationship, NOT A SINGLE one of those points was fulfilled by him—or even considered, for that matter. It was just bait. Now, as I write this, it's hard to believe how effortlessly he took something so profound and treated it with the carefree attitude of a child, utterly oblivious to its weight or consequences. It reminds me of how actions speak far louder than ideals.

My mistake then was that I never suspected someone could lie so boldly and shamelessly. I don't do that myself, so I didn't expect it from others. This narcissistic tactic of adapting to you like a perfect puzzle piece hits such a central part of you—something that feels so aligned—that you don't even question it. You simply can't believe that something that feels so right could be a manipulation. After all, scams are supposed to feel wrong.

Now I know: when something seems too perfect, too aligned, and too intense right from the start, it's worth pausing and asking, "Is this real?"

CHAPTER 3

THE NEVER-ENDING STORY: THE NARCISSIST'S VICIOUS CYCLE

A narcissist doesn't love. A narcissist doesn't build. A narcissist follows a script—a loop that repeats endlessly. The mechanism is always the same no matter who stands across from them. They may switch up the scenery like a machine programmed to follow a single pattern, but the story never changes. And the goal remains the same: narcissistic supply.

The three main stages that form the cycle the narcissist gets trapped in are *love bombing, devaluation, and discard.*

At first, you're treated like "the chosen one." Then, you're treated like a nuisance. And finally, like someone who's no longer of use.

There's also a fourth phase, which often appears but not always: *hoovering*—the narcissist's return.

While the framework of these phases is consistent across all types of narcissism, how it plays out can vary depending on the narcissist's personality, intelligence, environment, and life experience.

Here's a brief look at each phase—we'll explore them in depth in the next chapters.

Act One: Love Bombing

The covert narcissist doesn't enter your life as just another person. They don't build a relationship slowly or leave space for doubts. They arrive like a storm, a tornado, a force of nature that turns your inner world upside down. It's not about their dramatic behavior—it can be subtle, even shy. What storms through is the emotional upheaval you feel from the very beginning. You sense that something extraordinary has entered your life from the first moment. This isn't just another acquaintance. This feels like something rare, something exceptional. They seem perfect.

"Perfect" doesn't mean flawless. This ideal isn't about external things. It's about the perfect resonance with you. It might even be someone with issues, but if you're an empath who naturally understands and compensates for others' struggles, he'll gladly step into the role of the wounded soul in need of saving. And to you, it'll feel like a divine revelation—"such a sensitive man…" That emotional resonance will create a bond that feels truly special. Until the day comes when it suddenly doesn't.

Act Two: Devaluation

This is the stage where it becomes clear that the earlier "love" was merely an investment, and now it's time to collect the returns. The narcissist gradually withdraws their affection and emotional engagement, and any attempt on your part to discuss what's going on is interpreted as an attack. The emotional games begin: manipulation, silent treatment, accusations, and passive-aggressive behavior. You become both the target of their frustration and the provider of emotional fuel they thrive on.

This is when the classic narcissistic tactics start to surface—gaslighting, stonewalling, projection, empty promises—all designed to keep you in a state of confusion and powerlessness.

Act Three: Discard

When the narcissist grows bored with you or you're no longer a sufficient source of supply, the discard phase begins. Don't expect them to leave you the way you deserve. They won't sit down and have an honest discussion about what's going on. Narcissists don't end relationships—they vanish. Sometimes it's abrupt, sometimes it's emotional withdrawal. Sometimes it's triggered by a sudden affair, other times it's a slow fade until one day… they're just gone.

Because they never gave you the chance to talk things through or make mutual decisions about the future, you're left in a state of shock, with one burning question: How do I fix this?

There are often practical entanglements—shared debts, a home, unfinished projects—but none of that matters to them. They leave you to deal with it alone.

Act Four: Hoovering - The Narcissist's Return

There's often a fourth stage in the narcissistic cycle, known as hoovering. The term comes from the vacuum cleaner brand Hoover—because, just like a vacuum, the narcissist tries to suck you back in.

This tactic can occur immediately after they leave, or it may manifest weeks or even months later. After disappearing, the narcissist suddenly reappears as if nothing ever happened. You might think they've had time to reflect, realized what they've lost, and are coming back to try again. Don't be fooled. This isn't love—it's a signal that they've run out of fuel and are checking whether you're still a source of supply.

If you're still deep in the trauma bond, it's easy to fall for it and say "yes." If you've regained clarity and seen through the game, you'll say "no."

> *A narcissist only comes back*
> *so they can disappear again.*

If you say "yes"—because they tell you again that you're the only person who's ever truly loved them—and you open the door, you'll kick off the same narcissistic cycle all over again. If you say "no," you'll strike at the narcissist's deepest wound—rejection—and they'll launch a smear campaign against you, since they cannot integrate difficult emotions and must project them onto someone else. You'll usually be the one in their crosshairs.

Narcissistic Supply: The Oxygen A Narcissist Cannot Survive Without

Depending on who a narcissist is, what they do, and their life status, they may require different kinds of narcissistic supply. Most often, it's attention and validation, money and material goods, sex and intimacy, status and connections, and even your identity and personality. Here, we'll focus on what a covert narcissist craves above all else—your attention and the emotional energy you provide.

> *A covert narcissist doesn't build a relationship or form a genuine bond with you. Instead, they hook in emotionally solely to feed on your energy.*

Most of what they do—their words, interactions with you, every bit of drama they stir up—isn't accidental. It's their way of getting what matters most to them: narcissistic supply. The more you give them, the higher their euphoria.

This isn't a metaphor. It's a very real psychological need, a mechanism without which their entire inner structure would collapse. As you may recall, his Inner Child has no Inner Parent, so it latches onto someone outside itself. Their Inner Parent has no Child, so they need to absorb someone from the outside. Their system becomes parasitic.

For the covert narcissist, supply comes from the emotional reactions they trigger in other people. It could be admiration, praise, but also fear, despair, or rage. All emotions are equally valuable to them, as long as they're directed their way.

A covert narcissist cannot be ignored. Ignoring them is like emotional death. They feed on two main types of emotional energy:

1. **Positive supply** – comes from admiration, love, and awe. Every compliment, message filled with longing, and glance that says "You're amazing" is the purest form of energy for them. When you don't give it to them or are in a bad mood, they'll go after the second kind of fuel.
2. **Negative supply** – comes from your struggle with them. Yelling, crying, despair, trying to explain yourself, searching for answers, and frustration. All of that negativity is just as valuable to them as your admiration. That's all that matters because they are at the center of both cases. Even if they provoke a conflict and then apologize, saying it was their fault, know that this is just manipulation meant to pacify you, to soothe you, so they don't lose you—meaning, their source of supply. The apologies are never real, because soon enough, they'll do the exact same thing again. This means, in truth, that it didn't affect them at all; otherwise, they wouldn't be able to repeat the pattern so easily.

A narcissist doesn't want peace. Peace not only bores them, it actually unsettles them. Because in peace—where there's no drama—contact with the true Self begins to surface. And that's exactly what the narcissist avoids like the plague. Because where their true Self should be, there's only the despair of disconnection—something they refuse to heal. The more you try to create peace, the more they will stir up emotion. Peace offers nothing to fill their emptiness. That's why there's no stability in a relationship with them—no balance.

Just like after the initial euphoria and love bombing—where the excitement of the chase is intoxicating—once things start to stabilize, the narcissist begins to feel internally starved and therefore dissatisfied. They start getting irritated over the smallest things, just to provoke some kind of emotional "action" to feed on.

A narcissist has no identity, no self-worth, and no stable sense of Self. They are a void that must constantly be filled with other people's emotions. That's why they react so intensely to rejection. That's why, when you stop feeding them, you suddenly become the target of their emotional attack.

CHAPTER 4

LOVE BOMBING:
THE KIND OF LOVE THAT HOOKS YOUR SOUL

When a narcissist enters your life, everything starts to look different. From one day to the next, the world seems to light up in colors you've never seen before. This doesn't feel like just another relationship. It feels bigger—something you've never felt before. Finally, someone sees you the way you feel inside. In their eyes, you're one of a kind. They tell you exactly what you want to hear. They give you exactly what you need. One look, one gesture, one conversation—and you start to believe this is destiny. This is the relationship you've been waiting for all your life. It's resonance on steroids.

Magic That Isn't Magic

That's how it begins. A fairytale, with a storyline carefully crafted just for you. But it's not a fairytale—it's bait.

A covert narcissist doesn't capture their target in an obvious way. They're not the king of the stage, demanding admiration. They don't ask for praise outright. Instead, they shape a reality where you naturally begin to admire them, because they adapt to you like a chameleon, creating the feeling of a perfect match. But only in the beginning. They construct a world where you seem to be the center of their attention, but it's only to distract you from the truth: they're the only true center of everything.

The love they give you is like a rope thrown around your soul. At first, it feels soft, velvet-like, barely noticeable—it wraps you in warmth and makes you feel like you've entered paradise. But before you know it, that rope turns into a hook, and you're already hanging from it.

Love bombing is never random. It's carefully performed. From day one, you're meant to believe you've found someone who understands you like no one else. Someone who sees something in you that others missed. Someone who has come to save you, especially if you're going through a difficult time. Conversation feels like they're reading your mind, like they've known you forever. That part of you that others never quite understood—they get it. The sensitivity that once felt like a burden—now it's seen as a gift. You feel, maybe for the first time, like you've finally found where you belong.

Warning: Illusion Ahead!

To recap, narcissistic disorder stems from an inability of the Inner Parent to reflect the Inner Child. The mirror in which the core Self should see itself—so it can grow in self-awareness—is broken. Instead of reflecting inward, it's turned outward, mirroring someone or something else and forming a false Self.

The illusion of an ideal beginning with a narcissist lies in the fact that they don't show you who they truly are. Instead, they hold up a mirror in which you see your own desires, not who they are. This is a calculated strategy to fast-track a deep emotional connection—not to truly know or respect you, but to capture you and drain your inner resources.

What you feel as unique, magical, special, or meant-to-be isn't actually the relationship itself—it's your resonance with your own values and desires. The narcissist simply mirrors back what matters most to you, creating the false impression that they are that person.

> The narcissist doesn't show you who they are—
> they hold up a mirror reflecting your desires,
> so you fall for your own reflection.

Mirror, Mirror On The Wall...

Mirroring is a core tactic narcissists use during the love bombing phase. It's a manipulative technique where they mimic your behaviors, beliefs, and emotions to create the illusion of a deep connection and similarity. They imitate you to give the impression that you share so much in common. You feel an immediate, intense bond—like you've known each other forever. Like you've finally found someone who loves you and understands you without needing words. It almost feels telepathic.

But in reality, they're building a connection based on a false sense of shared beliefs, experiences, thoughts, and feelings. It's not genuine—it's a carefully constructed illusion meant to win your trust and gain control over you.

In the beginning, they absorb everything about you—your thoughts, tastes, emotions, and even your way of speaking—because that allows them to craft the perfect lie. If you paint, they'll start painting to align with you. If you're into inner work, they'll say it's their top priority and send you deep, soulful texts. If you have children and they're important to you, they'll tell you kids are amazing and that they'll be their best friend, when in reality, they despise children. If you love dogs, they'll echo your joy when you talk about your pet, all the while secretly wishing all dogs would disappear. And so on.

They'll do and say whatever it takes to earn your admiration and acceptance. The more amazed you are by them, the deeper you fall. And once you're hooked, they no longer need to reflect you because they've already captured you.

That's when you notice they've changed their stance on things they "loved" before. They begin to dismiss what once seemed meaningful to both of you. What they once admired now becomes a source of criticism. And suddenly, they complain that you're "too different."

A covert narcissist was never the person they claimed to be. They were just an illusion tailored to your expectations. If you ever hear the words, "I'll be whoever you want me to be," run, no matter how intoxicating and alluring those words may feel. That's not love, devotion, or respect. That's a chameleon laying a trap.

Why You?

It's no accident that they chose you. Covert narcissists target people with a certain kind of sensitivity—those who crave deep connection, who love boldly and honestly, without pretense. Those who are loyal. Those who carry empathy and emotional insight. They create an atmosphere where it seems like all of that can flourish. At least, that's how the beginning is designed to look.

Then everything starts to shift, though not in a way that's immediately obvious. There's no dramatic end to the fairy tale. Just a subtle change in the air, one that leaves you feeling confused. Everything seems the same on the surface, but something's different. You begin to notice moments where you no longer feel truly seen, but you hesitate to bring it up. By now, you've learned to watch what you say, because the slightest "wrong" word might cause offense or accusations. You're told you're overreacting, ungrateful, that they've done so much for you. Maybe you're the problem. The roles of victim and villain begin to emerge, where they're always the victim, and you're the one to blame.

Love bombing was never about love. It was a tactic—a tool to get what they wanted. And what they want is emotional dependency. A covert narcissist doesn't love you—they possess you. They need you as a source of narcissistic supply. For them, that means your attention, your energy, your sensitivity, your empathy, your understanding, your support, your help, your time, your body—and sometimes, your material resources too.

As long as you keep providing that supply—filling the emotional vacuum they constantly crave—the narcissist is satisfied, maybe even "happy." But this isn't happiness the way you or I would define it. In a healthy emotional bond, happiness comes from mutual connection, where each partner feels like an expansion of the other, not a condition for existing.

> *For the narcissist, "happiness" is the rush they feel from being showered with attention and compliments— the temporary high of filling their internal void. The more they receive, the higher the euphoria.*

But that void is bottomless. The emptiness quickly drains, and you're expected to refill it again. Just like with any addiction, the original "dose" stops being enough—they need more and more. Eventually, the tolerance grows so high that you're no longer sufficient, and they have to replace you with another source of supply in order to avoid the agony of their inner emptiness.

The Beginnings Of False Hope

By the time the love bombing phase ends, the relationship is usually far enough that it's not so easy to pack your bags and leave. Plus, you're caught in a web of cognitive dissonance, because not everything is bad. There are good moments that spark new hope in you, making you believe something might have shifted for the better. So you hang on, from hope to hope, until your jar of hopes overflows and the saying "Hope is the mother of fools" becomes your lived reality.

A covert narcissist often works to cut you off from the world, so you come to rely on them more than anyone else. Sometimes this is just intense emotional dependence, but other times it involves shared living arrangements, joint loans, buying a home together, or starting a family. In some cases, they'll create financial dependence—at first, showering you with promises and support, saying you don't need to lift a finger—only to use that power later to devalue and control you.

You're left hanging on a hook—one that wore the mask of love.

 REALITY CHECK

When two people fall in love, they're often blinded by emotion and hormones. Everything feels heightened and otherworldly, making it hard to see the full picture. That doesn't automatically mean you're in a relationship with a narcissist. The difference is that in a normal, healthy relationship, when the initial magic gives way to everyday problems, challenges, or bad days, people still support each other, love each other, and treat one another with kindness and respect.

A covert narcissist, on the other hand, will start revealing their true nature the moment their illusion is no longer perfect, or even just slightly smudged. They begin to shift when there's a speck of dust on their projected fantasy. You'll start noticing discontent that's totally out of proportion, subtle accusations, passive-aggressive remarks, or nitpicking your flaws. At times, they'll be downright mean. Pay attention to this. Watch whether they can stay grounded and consistent regardless of circumstances, or if they shift like a weathervane—more like Dr. Jekyll and Mr. Hyde[2] than a steady partner.

---

[2] A reference to the characters from Strange Case of Dr. Jekyll and Mr. Hyde by R.L. Stevenson. Dr. Jekyll is a respected physician who transforms into the violent, uncontrolled Mr. Hyde—his dark alter ego. They symbolize the duality of human nature and the capacity for sudden transformation from a composed individual into someone completely destructive.

MEMORIES AND REFLECTIONS FROM THE CHAMELEON MATRIX
The Prince Arrives – With Emotional Baggage

It felt like a celebration when Maciek finally came to visit me after a few weeks of messaging and talking online. Initially, he was supposed to stay for just a few days, but he extended his visit to two weeks since we lived quite far apart. My original plan was simple: we'd get to know each other a bit, then he'd go back home while I finished my last semester of college. During that time, we'd see each other a few more times and then decide what's next. Back then, reason was still guiding me.

But when he arrived, the magic became even more intense. All those already powerful feelings grew stronger still. Reason gradually gave way to emotion. And, as you've probably guessed, things were great in the intimacy department too.

The Rock You Could (Still) Sit On

One of the biggest illusions was that, in our first interactions and during those early weeks, Maciek seemed very grounded, composed, confident, and calm. A rock you could lean on. Only now do I realize the mastery of that illusion—because later, the reality was the complete opposite as the relationship moved through its various phases. Maciek turned out to be emotionally unstable, explosive, overly sensitive, anxious—and I ended up being the emotional foundation holding everything together.

Suitcases Of Hope And Snap Decisions

After a week of his visit, I thought—why wait another nine or ten months to finish school? I could just drop out and move in with him. I mean, THIS WAS IT, and I had zero doubts. The college I was attending wouldn't provide me with any long-term career opportunities anyway. I'd only enrolled to take a few courses I was genuinely interested in. So, in my rational mind, it didn't feel like a major sacrifice—especially compared to THIS moment that felt so monumental.

Maciek didn't object to any of it. He liked the idea just as much. After all, I changed everything and came to him, to his territory. He didn't have to change a thing. Truthfully, I found the idea of moving to the other side of the U.S. incredibly exciting. It felt like an adventure—something new to discover and explore. I had already done it once, leaving Poland for America. I was tired of big, bustling Lakeland and dreaming of something quieter. And voilà, here he came—like the perfect puzzle piece—strengthening the sense that I had met someone so ideal, it put fairy tales to shame.

He offered a smaller town that was peaceful and immersed in a culture of self-development and higher consciousness. It was a place where workshops and meditation groups were on every corner, and people lived with awakened awareness. Not even in my wildest dreams could I have imagined such a bonus.

Business Plan: Zero Testing, One Hundred Percent Faith

Pacifica was a place like that—full of events centered around spirituality, consciousness, and personal growth. Occasionally, we'd go to lectures, workshops, and gatherings. It was actually pretty good. We even came up with the idea of doing something together. He had his favorite energy work techniques, and at the time, I was just starting with EFT, so we decided to join forces.

I wanted to test things out first, to see how we worked together before officially launching anything or investing money. But he didn't want to go that route. He wanted to dive straight into the deep end without any trial runs—and that's exactly what happened. Looking back, it was an early sign that things always had to go his way, but I didn't pay attention to that then.

And just as I expected, after a few attempts at working together, it was not a good fit—and the money we'd put in never returned.

Sweet Life Before The Apocalypse

The enchantment lasted a year. During that time, we did many things together. We went on trips—to the ocean, the mountains, picked mushrooms and berries in the forest, took walks, went to the movies, attended workshops and gatherings, handled household chores, even cooked together, watched films and shows, went shooting at the range, visited his friends, and talked a lot. He had his own activities, and I had mine. I began to develop my professional life more seriously while he had the financial comfort of not needing to work and engaged in various pursuits as he pleased. Our intimate life was very good; in that first year, there wasn't a day we didn't enjoy that aspect of our relationship. Occasionally, there were some tensions in the relationship, but aren't there always? Besides, the sun that had returned to my body erased my negative moods. Each day felt entirely new and full of potential.

By the end of the first year, everything looked so good that we started talking about buying a house together, so we wouldn't have to pay rent. We toured many homes for sale, but nothing clicked. The idea arose that maybe we should change states. We both began to think that a house in the countryside, away from people, where we could establish a large garden and have our own harvest, would be good for us. Maciek said maybe we should go to the state of Westmont, as he had never been there. I had never lived in the countryside, so it was an exciting vision for me.

Welcome To Westmont – The Downward Slope

First, we took a trip to Westmont to see what it was like. He chose the region—I didn't have a strong preference. We went for a week and saw a few houses. None of them felt quite right, but at the last moment, the realtor called, saying they had one more to show us. As we drove up the access road through the meadow and looked out over the lake nestled in the valley below, tears welled up in both our eyes. It was breathtaking.

It was a small house on several dozen acres of land with a forest. A few months later, we moved in.

One month later, something happened that changed everything. It was a turning point—everything flipped, and from that moment on, the next ten years became a slow, steady slide downhill.

> **WARNING MAP**
>
> 7 SIGNS OF LOVE BOMBING
>
> 1. **Overly Quick Declarations**
>   a. "You're my home." "I've never felt this good with anyone."
>   b. If you're hearing fairy-tale-level declarations within days, watch out. Real connection takes time.

2. **Too Much in Common**
   a. It feels like you're exactly alike.
   b. A narcissist mirrors your passions, opinions, and way of speaking. They're not sharing your values—they're imitating them.

3. **Destiny-Like Resonance**
   a. You feel like you've known them forever.
   b. That's not intuition. It's your nervous system recognizing familiar emotional patterns, not necessarily healthy ones.

4. **Intense Emotional Storm from the Start**
   a. They hit like a tidal wave.
   b. Emotional intensity early on is a tactic to create quick dependency. Healthy relationships start slower and steadier.

5. **High Intimacy Intensity**
   a. You click instantly in bed.
   b. Sexual chemistry can be part of a trauma bond. Watch if the rest of the relationship matches that connection.

6. **Victim–Savior Dynamic**
   a. "I need you to survive."
   b. If they imply right away that only you can save them, they might be looking for a mother or caretaker—not a partner.

7. **The First Small Frictions Appear…**
   a. You said something "wrong"? Did something "off"?
   b. Subtle blame, sensitivity, and accusations start to creep in. It's not dramatic yet, but this is how your boundaries begin to shift.

CHAPTER 5

DEVALUATION – FROM PEDESTAL TO PAVEMENT

This act usually lasts the longest. It's the period when the narcissist starts making demands. In this phase, it becomes clear that during the love bombing stage, they weren't really loving you—they were investing. The conversations, gestures, sweet messages, and all that generously devoted time were a kind of capital the narcissist was depositing into your emotional system, fully expecting to collect interest—and then some. Now, it's time to cash in.

The Subtle Onset Of Devaluation

The withdrawal of what they once gave you happens gradually. They're no longer as open, as affectionate. They don't have as much time, and they're no longer eager to do things together. You often hear "no," or they're tired, not in the mood, that something is pointless or unnecessary.

You try to talk about it, but that too is "stupid"—and worse, it's seen as a personal attack, a lack of respect, or criticism. This becomes the perfect excuse for an emotional provocation, which, for covert narcissists, is literal nourishment. You become their emotional punching bag.

You hear more and more complaints and expressions of dissatisfaction. They blame you for the fact that the relationship isn't fulfilling. Classic narcissistic behaviors begin to emerge: gaslighting, stonewalling, silent treatment, projection, triangulation, dangling promises, love bombing when they want something, devaluation when they're displeased—in short, an emotional roller coaster.

The Effects Of Devaluation

Suppose you're an empath with weak boundaries. In that case, the devaluation phase will drain you emotionally and energetically to the point where you lose touch with your sense of self and start to believe you're worth nothing. Sometimes you're stripped of friends, your career, hobbies, and even your finances—because you tried to sacrifice everything just to satisfy that bottomless, sucking hole.

If you're an empath with healthy boundaries and you reflect their behavior back to them—refusing to internalize their tactics—you'll likely push the narcissist into what's known in psychology as "narcissistic depression." I think the term is too mild, because what happens doesn't look like any typical depression. It's like watching a crystal vase fall onto concrete and shatter into a million tiny pieces—a total collapse.

>  **REALITY CHECK**
>
> If you notice your partner becoming distant, irritable, grumbling, or saying hurtful things, it doesn't automatically mean you're dealing with a narcissist. Such behavior can have multiple causes. Sometimes, it's a sign that something is stirring within them, but they don't know how to name it or confront it.
>
> In emotionally healthy people, those phases pass–there's conversation, reflection, a shared effort to find solutions, and the relationship gets back on track.

> With a narcissist, that state doesn't go away. There might be a brief return to "love" when they need something or sense you might leave—but it's just a temporary tactic. Devaluation returns—not because something went wrong, but because that's how the structure of the relationship works.

MEMORIES AND REFLECTIONS FROM THE CHAMELEON MATRIX

It Was Magical—Until The Lights Went Out

We moved into a small house nestled on several dozen acres of forest. It was far from civilization and neighbors. To reach the nearest neighbor, you either had to drive or set out on a long walk. The land was breathtaking, teeming with wildlife, birds, the sounds of nature, and a diverse array of plants. However, it was neglected, as was the house, since the previous owners, an elderly couple, no longer had the strength to maintain it.

I took two months off work, planning to throw myself into fixing up the house and getting as much done as possible before winter. Maciek jumped into the work with great energy. And there was a lot to do—physically demanding labor, especially on such a large property. He worked tirelessly, and I helped in whatever way I could, focusing on the lighter but equally tedious indoor renovations.

A Tight Team: He Had The Hammer, I Had The Plaster

Before I get into what was happening between us on an emotional and personal level, we made a great team, at least when it came to physical projects. Whether it was renovating, building something, or organizing a big task, we complemented each other really well. I handled the more precise and detailed work, while he handled the heavier physical labor. I managed the finances; he took care of orders. For larger projects—such as building a three-car carport—he was the lead builder, and I was the assistant. Often, my job was checking the level and measuring distances.

When laying down flooring, I tackled the tricky corners and cut-outs around fixtures—being the more patient one—while he laid the main panels in the open space. He painted the walls, and I patched all the holes with plaster so seamlessly you couldn't tell there had ever been damage. And that was just the beginning—the list goes on. We worked together like a well-oiled machine.

After we moved to Westmont, we immediately found a beautiful patch of land near the house for a garden. Cows used to graze there, so the soil was wonderfully fertilized. At the time, though, it was overgrown with waist-high grass. He mowed it down, and I raked it up and hauled it to the compost pile.

We had to fence the garden in—there were plenty of deer and elk around, and bears, too. But we handled that as well: Maciek drove the posts into the ground and stretched the wire fence, and I secured it with a pneumatic stapler. We planted fruit trees and a few cold-weather crops for the coming winter. In the spring, I started an entire range of vegetables in small pots indoors, which we later transplanted into the garden. And so it went, year after year.

We lived in Westmont for seven years and established a beautifully landscaped garden over that time. We also had a good system in place for managing everything. He handled the watering, and I did the weeding. He took care of fertilizing, and in the fall, I made dozens of different preserves from our fruits and vegetables. I pruned the fruit trees, and he dug up the potatoes. Our garden had just about everything—even watermelons.

I also took care of shopping, the kitchen, and cooked different meals every day—Maciek loved Polish food. He handled more of the "man's work," like fixing things, building, chopping wood, and shoveling snow.

We were also very in sync when it came to finances. I managed the budget and ensured that all our shared expenses related to life and the house were split evenly. My mother had always told me to strive for financial independence, which has stuck with me. I didn't want to rely on anyone else if I could work and earn my own money. In this area, things flowed smoothly between us.

You might be reading this and thinking, what was the problem if things were going so well? That's exactly the typical dilemma in a relationship like this. There are genuinely good parts, and those are what keep you engaged. Because when the emotional roller coaster suddenly flips and you become the target of their emotional outbursts, your mind goes into cognitive dissonance and refuses to believe it's actually happening. You start rationalizing—thinking it's just a bad day, that they're tired, that they have trauma from the past—because there are all these other great things, right? This is especially dangerous for psychologists or therapists, who, with their broader understanding, often fall into the trap of overanalyzing and empathizing with the other person, instead of stepping back and simply thinking about themselves, which is exactly what happened to me.

Between Pickles And Psychological Abuse

When you're the narcissist's emotional punching bag and feel like throwing everything down and walking away, it's not that simple, precisely because of all those genuinely good things. Your mind gets stuck in a loop of hope, holding onto the good parts, believing the bad will somehow end, especially when you've spent a whole year in what feels like bliss, where 90% of the time, everything is truly great, and you enjoy the relationship. So when the switch flips and the dynamic turns dark, you still carry that image of this person as "good"—because that's who they were for a year—and you keep waiting for that version to return. If they could be that way, why shouldn't it return?

Your brain tells you it must be temporary, that it will pass, because surely, everyone wants to be happy in their relationship. But the truth is, in the case of a narcissist, things are never meant to be good. Their endgame is always destruction. The good times are just bait to pull you into their world, only to eventually rip off the mask and cast you in the lead role of their dramatic tragedy. But that realization only dawns on you much, much later.

In our case, the strong side of the relationship was the everyday stuff—day-to-day life, organizing our space, projects, business, and finances. In all of that, we really functioned like a solid team. In a relatively short time, thanks to our joint effort and smart decisions, we managed to get out of debt and make a good return on investment by selling at the right time.

That said, over time, I stopped enjoying working together on projects because nearly every interaction turned into an opportunity for him to vent his emotional frustrations on me—even though the practical tasks themselves always went smoothly.

He Suffered For Me, I Was Supposed To Suffer With Him

But let's go back to the relationship itself. After we moved to Westmont and immediately threw ourselves into work to get as much done as possible before winter, something suddenly changed. Maciek became tense, irritable, snappy, distant, and unwilling to engage or talk. The atmosphere turned unpleasant. He said he was exhausted, that an old injury was flaring up, and that he was in pain—and I was supposed to understand. Okay, I did understand. But at the same time, something needed to change—to slow down and avoid aggravating that old injury. Still, there was no getting through to him.

This was an early sign of what became a recurring pattern in our entire relationship. He would throw himself into intense physical labor, completely disregarding his body, pushing himself until he got injured again, and then that pain would ignite aggression and rage. And there I was, right next to him, his emotional punching bag.

I've lost count of how many hundreds of times I pleaded with him to stop, take care of himself, listen to his body, and show himself some respect. He always had two standard replies: either "It won't get done by itself," or "I have to kill time somehow, I'm bored." Whenever I suggested hiring someone to help with the heavy work, the answer was also always the same: "There's no one reliable enough—I have to do it myself."

Whenever I said that most of the heavy physical work he was doing wasn't really necessary—and that it only caused tension between us because he was always in pain, and it affected our relationship—I was accused of being ungrateful. He claimed he was doing it all for me and that I didn't appreciate it. When I said I didn't ask for any of it, and that if he truly wanted to do something for us, he could try taking better care of himself instead of running himself into the ground and having no time or energy for our relationship, it went right over his head. Any suggestion of doing something different or more constructive was labeled "wrong" and "against him." I became the enemy.

In Maciek's mind, all those physical projects were grand sacrifices he made for me. That he was suffering and exhausting himself for my sake—and how dare I expect anything else. However, the truth is that 80% of the things he took on were merely ways to kill time. They had nothing to do with me or the needs of the house.

It's worth noting that all this work and physical effort wasn't part of any job—Maciek didn't have to work. He was financially secure and had all the time in the world, so he filled it by constantly coming up with new projects to keep himself from getting bored.

The Dark Side Of The Mirror

Back then, I still didn't know that the covert narcissist's underlying goal is to play the martyr and the victim—and to feed off the emotions of the other person, including the negative ones. So all my efforts to end the emotional drama and restore harmony were doomed from the start.

What's more, just as in the love bombing phase, the narcissist carefully picks up on what brings you joy and mirrors it back to you, during the devaluation phase, they'll just as precisely sense what damages the relationship and hurts you, and that's exactly what they'll lean into. Constructive solutions are ignored. The script flips 180 degrees.

The more I tried to support him or make life easier so we could create more space for our relationship, the more he dug his heels in the opposite direction. I ended up being the one who didn't appreciate his efforts or was "clipping his wings."

It felt like talking to a concrete wall—everything I said bounced right back. I was stunned, especially remembering the first year, when he had seemed like a completely different person.

Eventually, I stopped wasting my energy on it and redirected it into growing my own practice.

Everything I'm describing—his anger, grumbling, criticism, dissatisfaction, blame, and emotional attacks—was exhausting for me, but thankfully not devastating. As I mentioned before, the Regenerating Sun in my belly always brought me back to the here and now, and the EFT Method instantly helped release any tension.

From Conversation To Detonation–In Under A Minute

There was one thing, though, that left me in shock for a moment. After we moved into Westmont and threw ourselves into the chaos of renovation and cleaning, he started walking around angry, annoyed, and dissatisfied with everything. That's when I also noticed something had shifted in our intimate life.

Back in Pacifica, that area had been at a super high level. But here—it wasn't. It wasn't about the physical part, because that was still okay. It was more that he was somehow… gone. Just as the charming Maciek had disappeared and been replaced by someone furious at the world, in intimacy too, he felt internally absent, as if he was treating me more like an object than a person.

That went on for a while. I kept watching, wondering what was going on. I thought it was exhaustion or pressure catching up with him. But nothing changed for a few months, and over time, I started liking it less and less, so I began avoiding contact.

Then came the day I decided to talk to him about it, because it really shouldn't have gone on like that. And that conversation turned out to be the beginning of the end, one that would stretch on for the next ten years.

We sat down and I asked him directly if we could talk about our intimate life—to improve it—because lately I'd been feeling a bit objectified. What I got in return was an outburst like nothing I'd ever experienced from anyone in my life. It shook me to my bones. He said horrible things to me—just vile—and then mocked me in this sneering, degrading tone that left me frozen, eyes wide like saucers. He added that if this is how I saw things and treated him, then he would never want anything to do with me in that area again (which, as life later showed, didn't turn out to be true). In that moment, I could feel it clearly—some inner part of me that had always felt close to him pulled back and said: No.

My logical mind and self-awareness told me that his reaction was completely disproportionate to the situation—that something had been triggered in him and he had no control over it, that it had nothing to do with me. And that I had absolutely done nothing to deserve it. But that didn't change the toxicity of the energy itself, so heavy with poison as it poured out of him and then lingered in the air.

Back then, still knowing very little about this disorder, I had no idea that a covert narcissist is completely unable to process anything that—according to his perception—feels like rejection. And it doesn't even have to be an actual rejection. Just one word, a gesture, or a completely innocent comment—and they fire back like an entire army's been unleashed in retaliation.

So I found myself in quite a situation. Far from civilization, surrounded by several acres of forest, family back in Poland, friends far away, alone in the house with someone like that… That disconnection from the world, the closeness of wild nature, and the sudden hostility from my partner turned out to be the most intense school of self and Self I could've asked for. You couldn't come up with better conditions for discovering the deeper layers of who you are. I'm saying it this way now, years later, because back then I wasn't fully aware of it.

What I did know, though, was that I wasn't afraid. Somehow, I was never afraid of where I was, what I was doing, or of him. I've always had this sense that whatever shows up on my path is there for me, and that my job is to unpack it and understand it. A kind of curiosity comes with it—a pull toward the hidden meaning, even if the packaging looks bad or difficult at first. Of course, if certain lines had ever been crossed—like physical violence or betrayal—I wouldn't have stayed even one minute. That second one happened ten years later, and it became the line that led to an immediate decision to end it, which is exactly what I did.

A covert narcissist constantly tests your boundaries—just to see how far they can stretch them without fully crossing the line. That's how they ensure a steady supply of narcissistic supply. It really adds up to a kind of emotional micro-torture—because it never stops. But it's never quite intense enough to destroy your system completely. Just enough to keep draining it for energy.

WARNING MAP

7 SIGNS OF DEVALUATION

1. **Withdrawal of Affection and Engagement**
   a. "I'm tired." "I need space."
   b. You spend less and less time together, they lose interest in the relationship, and emotionally disappear.

2. **Conversations Turn Into a Minefield**
   a. "You always want something." "You just don't get it."
   b. Every attempt to talk ends in conflict—you're to blame, and they're the victim.

3. **Growing Resentment and Criticism**
   a. "You're not giving me what I need." "You're always asking for something."
   b. More and more dissatisfaction with the relationship. You feel like you constantly have to explain yourself.

4. **The Silent Treatment and Emotional Distance**
   a. "I don't feel like talking." "Just leave me alone."
   b. Emotional connection disappears, they stop responding, emotionally isolate you, but they don't leave physically.

5. **Your Boundaries Trigger Their Rage**
   a. "You don't respect me." "You're hurting me."
   b. Any attempt to protect yourself ends in their attack, passive aggression, emotional punishment, or projection.

6. **Alternating Warmth and Coldness**
   a. "I missed you…"—right after they ignored you.
   b. This emotional rollercoaster keeps you in a state of uncertainty and naïve hope.

7. You Start Withdrawing Yourself From the Relationship
   a. "Maybe I just need to try harder?"
   b. Instead of setting boundaries, you begin to adapt to avoid "provoking" their reactions.

CHAPTER 6

DISCARD: TIME TO PUT ON THE INVISIBILITY CLOAK

Just like the idealization phase comes to an end, the devaluation phase eventually runs its course too. Emotional provocation no longer works as fuel for the internal emptiness, so the time comes for abandonment and turning toward a new source of supply.

Don't expect a dignified ending. They don't close the door—they vanish. At first, subtly, they withdraw emotionally, go silent, ignore you, become absent, and are irritated by your presence. Eventually, they disappear from your shared world altogether. Sometimes it happens through a sudden leap into a new relationship, sometimes by fading into the background of daily life.

A covert narcissist doesn't know how to end a relationship healthily because that would require authenticity, empathy, and responsibility. But responsibility doesn't exist for them, because it would mean having to see what they're really doing, and that's something they can't face. Since their personality structure can't process shame or guilt, they must escape into another illusion and shift all responsibility onto you. You're the one who doesn't fit. You're the one who has nothing to offer. It's "your fault" they feel so miserable and have to disappear quickly to "save themselves." They might even do it wearing white gloves, like in my case—telling me over and over how I'd grown away from him through the work I'd done on myself, how I'd outpaced him and was on a different level now, and how poor him, he just didn't belong anymore and were suffering because of it.

For them, any story works—as long as it leads to separation, detachment, and the release of any responsibility for their part in the relationship.

It also serves as a way to smear you and play the victim with the next person they're trying to lure in. Prepare to be painted as the evil "ex" who almost destroyed them. This is typical of covert narcissists—when they meet a new supply, they often start by telling dramatic stories about their "demonic exes." With those lies and manipulations, they trigger sympathy and draw in the attention of their new target, forming a trauma bond right from the start.

Closure? Never Heard Of Her

A breakup initiated by a covert narcissist gives you no chance for closure. There's no conversation, no explanation. And that's the hardest part of this phase—not just the abandonment itself, but how it's done. Deliberately, with indifference, and with a total lack of basic respect. You're not treated as a partner who deserves to be included in such a major decision, especially after years of life together. It becomes painfully clear that in this relationship, you were only there to be drained—they never really saw or respected you as a human being. You weren't part of their game as a person—you were just an object with an expiration date.

So you're left in shock, and your mind starts racing with questions—maybe you did do something so unacceptable that it made them react this way. You just can't believe your eyes that a normal human being could act with such ruthless coldness, without a shred of empathy, especially after a relationship that lasted for years.

A narcissist won't take responsibility for the mess they leave behind. Unfinished business, unresolved shared obligations— you're left to deal with it all yourself, while they've already moved on to seducing someone new.

As painful as this moment is, it's also your chance to break free from the chameleon's trap. Once your eyes open and you start seeing the symptoms one by one, you won't doubt what you're dealing with.

In their emotional ignorance, the narcissist will do everything they can to hide their true inner world—but the very behaviors they choose reveal everything about it. They expose themselves by acting the way they do, and it's almost tragicomic. The key is for you to be informed, because as long as you don't understand how this disorder works, you'll keep coming up with different explanations just to make sense of it. The mind will try to run from the simplest truth: there is no love here, only taking.

I hope that through this book, your eyes will open and you won't keep circling around the truth, trying to think your way out of it. You are worth so much more than being treated this way.

 REALITY CHECK

Not every painful breakup is abandonment by a narcissist. People part ways for many reasons—sometimes because they can't communicate, sometimes because their goals, needs, or values have grown apart. It can be painful, but it doesn't have to be traumatic. The difference lies in how the person leaves.

If someone disappears without a word, ignores your needs, dumps all the blame on you, avoids responsibility, and at the same time starts a "new life" with someone else, as if you never existed—that's not a mature ending. That's an emotional evacuation, leaving you standing in the rubble.

A healthy person ends a relationship with a conversation, with reflection, with some acknowledgment of the shared history. Even if they don't do it perfectly, they leave space for closure.

A narcissist closes the door without saying goodbye—because they can't bear to face their own inner world. And that's exactly how you recognize them.

MEMORIES AND REFLECTIONS FROM THE CHAMELEON MATRIX
First Exodus

In my case, the discard happened twice. The first time—when I still didn't fully understand the game—I got caught up in the emotions—the second time, I didn't, which led to a full-on narcissistic collapse on his end. The first time he disappeared behind my back was after seven years of the relationship. We were still living in Westmont, in the forest. Maciek occasionally traveled to the state of Deserta, because he had some old friends there. And this time was no different—he went for a few weeks. A few days after he came back, someone left a message on the answering machine (we still had a landline back then, so messages were for both of us). I didn't know who the message was for—I just saw the blinking light on the machine. So I played it, and a woman from the bank left a message for Maciek, saying he'd been approved for a mortgage and asking him to call back. Immediately, all my internal alarms went off—something was happening behind my back. When he came home, I asked him what the message was about, and he said he'd decided to buy a small house in Deserta and move there.

You can imagine my reaction. My brain was spinning in every possible direction, trying to make sense of what was happening. We were living in a house far from civilization; the mortgage wasn't even paid off yet. We had a huge garden, forty-three acres of forest, and a lifestyle that came with a lot of responsibilities—shared between two people. And now, out of nowhere, he announces that he doesn't want to live this way anymore. He said he didn't want this demanding lifestyle or to be with me, and that he was moving to a new house in Deserta, and I could stay here and do whatever I wanted.

Seven years of a relationship, a shared life with all kinds of interdependencies, an unpaid mortgage, unresolved matters—and he just decides to change everything because he feels like it. There is no consideration for what he's doing or the consequences for us as a couple. No respect for me, no acknowledgement of me as a partner with whom he built this life over the past seven years, as if I hadn't even been there. I didn't count as a person worth including in such a major decision about our life, or in tying up the loose ends. He just decided, because he wanted to, and—as always—I was expected to adjust to whatever he had chosen, without having a say in it.

And that's exactly what he did. He bought the house in Deserta, took half the things from the house, took the cat, and left me alone in the middle of the forest. We didn't have the dog anymore by then. He said he would continue paying the mortgage on this house, but that the rest was up to me.

Hermit Woman In Westmont

So I was left alone on this vast forest property, surrounded by wild animals and far from people. The area was slightly mountainous, so the winters were particularly heavy. There was no heating—you had to chop wood and keep the stove going. The road leading up to the house was a kilometer long and uphill. It was private land in the wilderness, so there were no snowplows. You had to take care of it yourself. Every year, he was the one who cleared the snow with a tractor and plow—there was that much snow. He would go into the forest and cut wood for the winter. If the snow wasn't cleared, we'd be completely cut off from the outside world for months—you couldn't even get to the store for a loaf of bread. Let alone if something happened and an ambulance needed to reach us.

I had no idea how to operate a tractor or any of the heavy equipment—that was his area. But clearly, it didn't matter how I was supposed to manage now, because—as always—what mattered was what he wanted or felt. A couple of times, snow did fall—thankfully, it was already the tail end of winter—and I got on that tractor and cleared the road. I had no clue what I was doing, and it was hard, but I did it.

After he left—or maybe more accurately, abandoned me—I had no idea what to do with my life. For the time being, I stayed there, taking care of everything in and around the house and the garden. There was a lot to manage, on top of my regular job.

Not Just Clearing Snow, But Clearing The Rubble Inside

On an emotional level, it was the first time in my life I had ever felt anything like this. The mix and chaos were so intense, especially with the uncertainty of "what now"—that it's hard even to describe. But as I mentioned, I don't know how to stay stuck in negative emotions. Either they pass on their own when my sun in the belly turns on, or I have to do something right away, because I can't just sit there, fall apart, or feel sorry for myself.

This time, though, the intensity and depth of the emotions were so strong that I needed support. On one hand, I worked through it on my own—using EFT and other deep-level tools I was already well acquainted with by then, since I had been studying and practicing them for years. On the other hand, I met online almost daily with my friend, a highly skilled therapist, and together we dove into the depths of that emotional pain. It was extremely intense work. Waves of emotion processed, dozens of beliefs released. With solid inner training and experience in self-work, I was able to contain the intensity of those processes without damaging myself. After about a week, I felt like the sun in my belly had expanded upward, and the sun in my chest had switched on. The darkness and emptiness were gone. A new space had opened up. A quiet joy of being appeared. Life had returned to my center.

After a while, the question started to surface: So now what? I wasn't going to stay there forever—it was too much for me. This was supposed to be our oasis, not mine. He bailed, claiming that living in such a remote area was too hard and demanding for him. I have no idea how he convinced himself it would somehow be easier for me, someone half his size and five times physically weaker. I couldn't sell the place on my own because the documents were in his name. I couldn't leave it all behind either—someone had to take care of it daily. So I was stuck. One thing I knew for sure was that I wanted to be gone before the next winter. And it was June. I began thinking about returning to Poland and purchasing a small house there.

To Be Continued…

So we started talking on the phone about what to do with the house. Additionally, because our personal matters had never been fully closed, explained, or resolved, the conversations began to drift in that direction as well. And you won't believe this (I can barely believe it myself now)—one thing led to another, and suddenly we were talking about giving it another chance. Maybe the lack of closure had been so overwhelming, and the sudden, brutal tearing of the relationship had left so many loose threads, that something inside me was grasping for anything that would make sense—something that could offer a sense of completion.

Over the next few months, I continued to manage the property and work my job, and he came by briefly in August. We decided to spruce up the place a bit, sell everything, and instead of returning to Poland, I would move to Deserta and live there with him. Holy Mary, Mother of God… clearly I hadn't had enough yet—I just had to tack on another four years in that relationship.

That's the price of not ending and resolving a relationship. When it's cut off so suddenly, you can't believe it's real—you think it's some kind of system error that needs fixing. Now I know it wasn't an error—it was a symptom. A clear sign of what this whole thing was, and that I had to end it myself, for my own sake. The second narcissistic exodus happened four years later.

Same Old Story

After an initial period of good fortune in Deserta, the old reality returned. Absolutely nothing had changed. Life became easy and physically comfortable. We lived in a spacious house in a beautiful neighborhood with lots of conveniences and amenities—no more hard labor like on the ranch. But even here, he found plenty of reasons to complain about everything. The same game, different props.

Looking at it now, years later, it seems that even though the relationship continued, something in me must have shifted after the intense emotional work I'd done following the first exodus—because now, even though everything had returned to the same toxic patterns, I felt different on the inside. As a result, I started setting boundaries on the outside.

I used to be understanding, tolerant, and forgiving, constantly adapting to his moods—because somewhere deep down, I held on to the hope that if he ever felt truly safe and at ease, something in him would soften, and he'd return to the way he was during that first year. Oh, blind naivety! Thankfully, my inner boundaries were never truly violated. Only a few times throughout the whole relationship did something reach a deeper level where I really had to sit with it or work through it with my friend, like during the first exodus. Most of the time, what I felt was calm. Which sounds good, and in a way it was—but on the other hand, that calm combined with the hope that he would eventually find his way into that same calm, feel what it was, and want it too, ended up dragging the relationship on far longer than necessary. Let's repeat the old saying: "Hope is the mother of fools."

Inner And Outer Boundaries

Let me explain what I mean by inner and outer boundaries. Inner boundaries are your sense of self-worth. You know who you are, you know yourself, you know your value—you know what is you and what isn't. In behavior, this manifests as an inner calm, regardless of how wild the storm outside may be. Even if someone says to your face that you're stupid or worthless, it doesn't mean anything—because when you know your worth, you know it's not true. You might even feel surprised to hear such words. At the same time, you understand that if someone says things like that to you, it's their problem—they're having a bad day, or they simply don't know how to express themselves differently. Often, when you genuinely don't absorb those words on any level—when they just bounce off your inner calm—the other person gives up, because the provocation doesn't land anywhere. There's no one to play the game with. When your inner boundaries are strong, you don't always need to set external ones through behavior. The calm you radiate becomes the boundary—without a single word.

By outer boundaries, I mean behavior—like verbally letting someone know that something's not okay or that you don't agree to something. Sometimes a person learns, almost mechanically, how to set outer boundaries, but it doesn't align with their inner boundaries—their calm and sense of self-worth. When that happens, the words aren't always taken seriously. The energy isn't aligned. Of course, even that kind of boundary-setting is better than not setting any at all. When I was still holding on to the hope that he would one day feel how great it could be to live in peace and calm together, I didn't set strong outer boundaries—because I thought it was my job to maintain harmony in the relationship, since he had lost his way. And I also didn't realize yet that I was dealing with covert narcissism—I was too optimistic, waiting for him to want that harmony too. But the truth is, a narcissist can't function in harmony because their inner system is based on chaos and fragmentation. Over time, even the calmest relationships become a battlefield for their inner conflicts. And inevitably, the result is destruction.

When we were still living in Westmont, a few times he said to me through clenched teeth, almost hissing, "I don't know why, but sometimes I just want to destroy you." At the time, I thought maybe it was a sign of trust—proof that he felt safe enough to reveal difficult emotions. Today, I see it completely differently.

Words like that aren't "difficult." They're abusive. Even when said as a joke, the goal isn't communication—it's control. And even though he never acted on it physically, the very idea of "destroying" another person is something that should never be brushed aside. In truth, it was one of the signs that the relationship I was in wasn't built on love—but on a need for control and destruction.

When we moved back in together in Deserta and things once again returned to the same old dysfunction, I started setting outer boundaries.

Some part of me must have realized that trying to create harmony and adjusting to his moods wasn't helping. It didn't improve the relationship—it was being taken advantage of. I began setting outer boundaries instinctively, without even thinking about it. Only years later, when I started studying narcissistic disorder and learned how to actually deal with a narcissist, did I realize I had done everything by the book.

A Lesson From The Desert

Let me tell you more about boundaries in Deserta, because there was an incredible synchronicity there. The place we moved to was in a semi-desert climate. For me, it was completely new—I had never lived in that kind of environment before, where the air was different, the plant life was different, the seasons moved differently, and the overall vibe was unlike anything I'd known. During the first month, I felt a bit out of place when I looked at the landscape; there was a strange kind of energy emanating from it. I often sat in silence, tuning into it, trying to understand what it was. Everything felt sharp, prickly, hard, unapologetic—like the cacti, agaves, thistles—even the weeds looked like something you shouldn't brush up against. The trees were stunted from lack of water, struggling to survive. I remember seeing the bleached bones of a deer, probably taken down by a puma. The bare hills were covered only in low, drought-adapted vegetation. At first, I felt uncomfortable with the energy—it felt gray, half-alive, raw, silent, focused on survival, unwelcoming, even threatening. It was so different from the forest where I had spent the last seven years, where around 45 different species of birds sang each day, and life overflowed in abundance. Still, I stayed with this new presence, letting myself get to know it.

I remember clearly the moment when, one day, the landscape seemed to suddenly open itself to me and reveal its best qualities. I saw the life pulsing within it, the determination, the incredible will to survive—and most of all… the strongest boundaries I had ever seen in anything. I remember looking at a cactus growing out of the ground near the house, with its long, stiff, razor-sharp spines—sharp enough to really hurt you—and I was suddenly flooded with awe for this plant. I thought, "This cactus has such clear, well-defined, and uncompromising boundaries…" I was in absolute admiration of that purity.

In a semi-desert climate, where lush vegetation is scarce and water is limited, everything that exists becomes a potential food source for something else—or risks dying from the heat. That's why the defenses against being wiped out are especially well-developed. I looked at those cacti and other sharp plants, and I kept thinking how they have no trouble setting strong boundaries. They don't let anyone cross those lines, and they have no guilt when someone tries—and gets stopped by a thorn. The deeper realization was that they not only know and value their own worth, but they also communicate it clearly to other organisms: "Here I am—but if you want to know me or form a relationship with me, it will not happen without respect." Direct hit.

Back then, I had no idea how all of it was connected—how it all resonated, formed a whole, and taught me how to live, as long as I stayed open to learning. Now, looking back with the benefit of perspective, it's

truly incredible how everything came together. But at the time, the only thing I had was my trust—that whatever appeared on my path was there for a reason, there to teach me something. The understanding always comes later. The more unfamiliar or difficult the thing is, the longer it takes to unpack and get to the essence. Back then, it was clear that my higher self—the one with the wide, elevated perspective—made sure that the lesson of boundaries would come at me from all sides: from the environment, from my inner journey into awareness, and from the relationship where testing and pushing my boundaries had become a daily routine.

Boundaries Are The Answer–And The Medicine–For You

Boundaries are something a narcissist doesn't have. I'll write more about that in the next chapter, along with how I set mine. That's why, on one hand, they constantly cross other people's boundaries, and on the other, when you set boundaries with them, they experience it as a personal injury. Consistently setting boundaries will eventually force a narcissist to confront their own inner world—which they hate—and that leads to narcissistic collapse. A narcissist doesn't want to learn how to live. They'll sabotage any sign of healthy functioning and accuse you of being against them.

After four years in Deserta and after setting boundaries, this started to happen. His masks began to fall away, one by one, and I became more and more certain of what I was dealing with. And still, I held on to the hope that once all the masks were gone—when the real inner Self would finally show, and I wouldn't be scared off or turned away by it—he would finally wake up. But no. Nothing of the sort.

The deconstruction of reality began when we decided to sell the big house in Deserta and move to the state of Palmara—to a smaller house, in a milder climate, with an even easier lifestyle. He also had some old friends there from his younger years. It was my last hope—but already a half-hearted one—that maybe a change of scenery, a softer climate, and reconnecting with old friends would bring something positive into his life.

Turns out, it was part of his second exodus. This time, he actually informed me—telling me a fairy tale about how he needed space and was going away for a year of "solitude," because he had to spend time with himself and sort things out, and that I could stay in Palmara. Of course, there was no discussion—just a done deal I was expected to adapt to.

After we moved to Palmara in early January, the relationship was already in its death throes. It lasted another three months, and in April, I ended it for good. And when it comes to a narcissist, that ending has to take one form only: zero contact.

Second Exodus

What happened during those three months was the most intense period of my life. On one hand, I saw the full spectrum of narcissistic disorder—because by the end, Maciek had entered full-blown narcissistic collapse. I witnessed every sign, every symptom, every behavior, leaving absolutely no doubt about what I was dealing with. Chaos, hatred, mind games, lies, betrayal, manipulation, verbal aggression, emotional blackmail, triangulation, blame-shifting, intimidation, the silent treatment, playing the victim, and creating emotional scenes where all responsibility was dumped onto me. A complete lack of empathy. Exploiting my kindness. Ignoring the fact that all of this affected me, too—there was only him, and what he felt. Nothing else existed. The bombardment was massive. And yet, at the same time, I was diving—live, in real time—into the deepest recesses of conscious darkness, uncovering new layers of reality. The more chaos and pain he hurled at me from the outside, the deeper I went within—and the more grounded and steady I became from the inside out. I discovered beautiful corners of my Self I hadn't known before.

The second exodus deserves a chapter of its own, so I'll return to it later on.

 WARNING MAP

7 SIGNS OF ABANDONMENT BY A COVERT NARCISSIST

1. **Emotional Withdrawal**
   a. They shut down, become absent, and are already living in another world.
   b. Your presence starts to feel unnecessary.

2. **Disappearing Instead of Breaking Up**
   a. They don't end the relationship—they vanish.
   b. There's no conversation, no closure—you're left with emptiness and questions.

3. **Shifting the Narrative—It's Your Fault**
   a. They make you feel like you're not enough.
   b. They say things like "we're just not a match" or "this doesn't make sense anymore."

4. **A New Relationship Before the Old One Is Over**
   a. A new person enters the picture.
   b. They tell them how deeply they were hurt by their "diabolical ex"—you.

5. **Lack of Empathy for the Consequences**
   a. They don't consider your situation, shared responsibilities, or what you built together.
   b. They leave you with the mess to deal with—while they've already moved on.

6. **The Emptiness After the Illusion of Closeness**
   a. You realize you weren't seen as a person—only as a source of narcissistic supply.
   b. Their choices show you clearly: you never really mattered—you were just part of the game.

7. **Shock and Cognitive Dissonance**
   a. The breakup makes no sense—it defies logic. You can't believe someone could do this.
   b. You feel tempted to make excuses for them or blame yourself.

CHAPTER 7

WHEN EGOCENTRISM STOPS BEING INNOCENT AND BECOMES A LACK OF RESPONSIBILITY

In the previous chapter, I offered my working definition of a narcissist: a three-year-old child without a parent, trapped in the body of a physically grown adult. Let's take a look at some behavioral mechanisms typical of a young child.

When a small child enters the world, even though they are physically separate and independent from the mother, they are absolutely helpless when it comes to survival. A newborn can't even roll over in the crib on their own. Everything has to be done and thought of for them—otherwise, they won't survive.

The life of a very young child is constantly on the edge of fear of death—it's in a constant fight for survival. Of course, the child isn't consciously aware of this, but it shows up in their behavior. The moment a caregiver disappears from sight, there's helplessness and crying—the world falls apart. In the instinct of a small child, just like in any animal, there's a drive to stay close to the mother, because she means survival, and to raise the alarm the moment she's gone.

When a child is born, they know nothing about the world. The rational part of the brain hasn't developed yet—they can't speak, they don't know what they want, they don't know what they need, and they don't know what to ask for. All they have are basic, animal-like reflexes, wired into their biology from birth. And the primary goal is survival. The brain learns quickly—in fact, up until around age six, it functions in a kind of hypnotic state, absorbing everything from its environment and storing "life instructions" deep in the subconscious.

The whole world revolves around the child at home. The child is the center of attention, because they need that not only to survive, but also to grow. They absorb enormous amounts of information about how the world and life work.

Because a child is completely helpless when it comes to survival, and because their life depends on the care of adults, being the center of attention is absolutely essential for their development. Instinctively, the child knows that when they receive attention, they are "under watch" by their caregivers—and therefore safe. Their needs are noticed and met, and when they get stuck or can't do something, the adult steps in to help. Being the center of attention equals a sense of physical safety, while being outside the adult's focus triggers panic, akin to facing extinction. We're talking here about physical survival.

But attention is also crucial for developing the child's self-awareness. When an adult reflects on the child's behavior, talents, personality, and who they are, it helps build the structure of the Inner Parent—something that later becomes a healthy boundary, giving the person inner strength and independence. Through the caregiver's attention, the child develops an internal sense of worth, importance, and usefulness. They begin to develop confidence and trust that everything is generally okay, even when faced with challenges. So in this way, caregiver attention directly supports healthy personality development and emotional maturity.

As a person grows up, they gradually become independent—both externally and internally—and come to know who they are, provided that the conditions for optimal development have been met.

Now let's take a look at the world and communication style of a child during the first months and years of life, and compare it to the tactics of a covert narcissist. Since a child's brain is still developing, it doesn't yet have the capacity to think rationally, process reality, or express needs through language. Therefore, the child must rely on a basic system of emotions. They cry or raise the alarm when they feel any kind of discomfort, and they're calm or happy when they feel comfortable. They form a strong emotional umbilical cord with their caregivers. This basic emotional language is the only communication channel a small child has, so they use it constantly.

The emotional development of a narcissist is frozen at the level of a two- or three-year-old, though occasionally you might see flashes of behavior more typical of an older child.

In the following sections, we'll look at some specific behaviors of a narcissist. You'll see how closely they resemble the strategies of a small child who hasn't yet developed a mature emotional system.

Expectations And Entitlement

To a covert narcissist, you are a source of supply—a form of nourishment that fills their inner emptiness (narcissistic supply). They are dependent on your attention and love and can't function without it. They draw from you whatever resources they need: not just attention and love, but also admiration, validation, sex, money, time, favors, and more.

A child does the same thing. They take everything they possibly can from their parents. It's no coincidence people say parenting is the hardest job in the world—it changes your life completely and pulls you into the child's world, where you give your time, money, effort, energy, care, problem-solving, protection, and more. Of course, in the case of a child, this is natural—they need that for their development. And when parents choose to have a child, they willingly agree to this level of effort and the act of giving everything that's needed.

A covert narcissist—though an adult in age—is emotionally stuck at that early developmental stage and will expect the same things from you. In their inner belief system, they feel entitled to it, and you're supposed to give unquestioningly. They don't understand that when you give something, it's a gift—an act of free will. They want you to be their parent—someone they can constantly draw from. However, the key difference is that in an adult relationship, neither party is the parent, nor is either the child, so the whole dynamic is doomed to fail from the start. What's more, when a child is still young and hasn't yet developed an Inner Parent, their system is naturally open to receiving from the outside—this is what allows for growth and development.

In the case of an adult, the structure of the Inner Parent is supposed to be already formed—there's nothing left to build. But because that structure is unconscious and dysfunctional, it creates the illusion of a need to keep taking. That's why the narcissist keeps drawing and drawing—and gets nothing from it. Everything disappears into a bottomless pit. For an adult, only the Inner Parent can give the Inner Child what it truly needs. No one on the outside can do that. Which is why, if you try to take on that role, at some point you'll notice that it's never enough. And the more you give, the worse it gets. It's a never-ending, sucking hole.

 **REALITY CHECK**

If there are expectations in a healthy relationship, it doesn't mean you're with a narcissist. For a relationship to be healthy, it has to be built on certain fundamentals that make it so. In addition to love, there must be trust, respect, the ability to compromise in a healthy manner, empathy, openness to communication, collaboration, autonomy, and friendship. These qualities aren't just okay to expect–they're necessary. Though in healthy relationships, they're often so natural and present that you don't even have to think about them.

But be mindful of special treatment that's expected from you, especially when it starts to feel like you're caring for a child. I'm not talking about exceptional circumstances, like illness, where someone genuinely needs extra care. I mean everyday life, where this kind of dynamic is simply demanded. If what's expected of you starts to feel like parenting, fixing, rescuing, or serving–run.

MEMORIES AND REFLECTIONS FROM THE CHAMELEON MATRIX
"Where's My Reward For Ignoring You?"

Before we go any further, I want to show you what narcissistic supply looked like in practice in my relationship, and how it affected me.

Looking back now, I can say that for Maciek, the main source of narcissistic supply was sex, and second to that, my emotional stability. As you may remember, during the first year of our honeymoon phase, our intimate life was genuinely great. But after we moved to Westmont and he transformed into a walking aggressor, intimacy no longer felt okay to me. And after he tore me down when I tried to talk about it—and refused to discuss it at all—it became something I no longer wanted. The fact that he had no respect for me didn't mean I had to stop having respect for myself.

It's incredible to realize that the core drive of a covert narcissist is destruction. If intimacy was the most important thing to him—and our first year together was great, nothing lacking—then wouldn't it be logical to take care of that, not sabotage it?

At the time, intimacy was something sacred to me. That's exactly why what happened after his verbal attack and refusal to talk about it left a mark.

People have different philosophies about this, but for me, it was an area I could only share with someone I was truly connected to, where there was love, trust, respect, and friendship. I couldn't share that part of myself for the sake of sport, convenience, or fear of rejection. Unthinkable. When two people share that space, the experience is multidimensional, not just hormonal. That's why, for me, the connection had to be real in order to experience that kind of closeness on every level.

When Maciek tore me down for trying to talk about it, I felt myself pulling back internally from that part of the relationship, taking several steps back. For him, everything was suddenly back to normal the next day, as if nothing had happened, so there was no "conversation to finish." Our intimate life never returned to the quality it had in the first year. I absolutely refused to allow a situation where he could treat me like an emotional punching bag—because it was convenient for him—and then expect physical closeness, also because it was convenient. Trying to talk with him about these things felt like walking on thin ice, so I eventually stopped trying. From then on, intimacy became rare, limited to moments when, for whatever reason, his energy was lighter and there was some kind of flow between us.

When I tried a few times to point out those good days he had—that he was genuinely a great person then, and that I naturally responded to him differently—it usually ended with him accusing me of saying things he didn't understand, or that I was expecting some vague, unreasonable things from him. Anything but harmony—covert narcissists can't handle it.

Instead of talking with me about it and trying to bring back the way things were in our first year, Maciek started complaining about me more and more. Eventually—this was already in Deserta—he began threatening to buy himself a separate bed and move into the other room. He talked about it constantly for about a year. I couldn't take it anymore, so I finally said, "Fine, do it—I just don't have the energy for this anymore." And so he did. Then, of course, that became one of his favorite stories: that I had "kicked him out of the bedroom." So much energy spent on manufacturing drama… when all it would have taken was a conversation, some willingness to meet halfway—and we could've had that "first year" again.

The truth is, he was the one who kicked me out of bed. One of my favorite things to do in the morning is to make myself a cup of coffee and get back into bed to sip it while reading or watching something. I wake up early—between 4 and 5 a.m.—so I have time for that. Suddenly, in Westmont, it started bothering him that I'd come back to bed with my coffee in the morning. Apparently, I was "drinking it too loudly." For the record, I don't slurp anything. Just the sound of me swallowing was too much for him. After one of those mornings when he glared at me and irritably told me it was bothering him, I stopped going back to bed with my coffee.

Winters in Westmont were freezing cold in the mornings— there was no heating, just a wood stove. Overnight, the fire would die down, so in the morning, you had to light it again and wait for the house to warm up. It would've been nice to crawl back under the covers with a hot cup of coffee while the house heated, but I preferred wrapping myself in blankets on the couch and enjoying some peace and quiet, rather than dealing with his displeasure again.

Of course, it wasn't the end of the world—I adjusted and found a way to make it work for myself. Still, it's those dozens of little comments about how much you're bothering them that slowly eat away at the relationship from the root, until eventually it collapses.

The reversal in a covert narcissist is extreme. They'll destroy the very thing they care about most, while feeding energy into what they supposedly don't want. Because for a covert narcissist, losing that role—the victim, the martyr, the one who's always wronged—would be like the death of their internal myth. That myth is the one thing they will protect at all costs… so they can start it all over again with someone new.

The Need For Constant Validation

Because a young child hasn't yet developed the structure of the Inner Parent—that inner voice that tells them who they are—they rely on feedback from their caregivers. That feedback helps them learn about themselves and supports their Inner Parent's growth. That's why children often look at their parents with an expectant gaze, waiting for confirmation that what they're doing, thinking, or wanting is good or not. When they receive attention in the form of some kind of response, they feel seen, important, and safe. When they're ignored, they're left in a state of confusion and disorientation. Beliefs begin to form within their developing Inner Parent, like: "No one wants me," "I don't matter," "The world is unsafe and unkind," "I don't know who I am or what I want," "I can't handle anything," "Nothing ever works out for me," and so on.

For a small child who's being ignored, the absence of parental attention feels like an internal sense of nonexistence. That's why children fight so hard for attention and understanding from their parents—they genuinely need it for their development.

In a covert narcissist, whose emotional growth stalled at this stage, the need for validation is one of the core drivers. Without constant praise, acknowledgment, and appreciation, the narcissist can't locate a sense of existence within themselves. There's only emptiness and despair, just like a child who's lost in a big, overwhelming world with no caregiver to orient them. That's why the narcissist is so driven in their demands for recognition and so punishing when they don't receive it.

Remember: no matter how much praise and validation you give them, it won't change anything, because it's a never-ending story. For a child, attention, appreciation, and validation help build the structure of the Inner Parent. For a narcissist, it's just a temporary patch over a bottomless void—an unfilled, sucking hole that only wants more and more, until you collapse from exhaustion. This emptiness comes from the disconnect between their Inner Parent and Inner Child. Only deep personal work on rebuilding the Inner Parent can begin to fill that void.

So free yourself from the illusion that you can do it, because not only can you not, but you'll also be punished when you finally run out of strength. You are not their mother.

 REALITY CHECK

If someone enjoys hearing a compliment about themselves (which is basically everyone), don't automatically assume you're dealing with a narcissist. In a healthy relationship, people naturally notice and appreciate each other, offering kind words. But when you notice that praise becomes a requirement, and if you don't always give it–or forget once in a while–and you're punished for it, be careful. If someone does things mainly to get a compliment, be careful. If they lose motivation for life because they're not being praised, be careful.

MEMORIES AND REFLECTIONS FROM THE CHAMELEON MATRIX
Deserved Silence For Offending The Holy Driveway

As I've mentioned before, I was constantly accused of not showing him enough praise, admiration, appreciation, and respect. When I offered validation, I did it "wrong." When I occasionally expressed more appreciation, he would immediately reject it or dismiss it as trivial. But with Maciek, the need for validation eventually reached a whole new level—something I would've never imagined. I'll give you one example, because it stuck with me—I was in such shock. This was back in Westmont, in the forest. The access road to the house was long, partly through the woods and partly across a meadow. It was a gravel and dirt road. In spring, when the snow melted, it would turn into a giant muddy mess, so every year Maciek worked on it: leveling it with a plow and tractor, hauling in rocks to firm it up, and once he even ordered a truckload of gravel to improve it.

We had lived there for about six years by then, which also meant six years of him working on that road. I suggested that I had the money, so we could hire professionals to lay a proper, solid road. I intended to spare him the hard labor each year, because it really was a physically demanding job. He didn't say anything—just made a strange face.

That day, we were headed into town for a big shopping trip, which was about an hour and a half drive. Right after that conversation, we left—and he didn't say a word to me the entire drive. He stayed silent in the store and all the way back home. I had no idea why I was being punished with the silent treatment.

The next day, he told me that I had disrespected him by suggesting we hire professionals to do the roadwork because he had worked on it every year.

It would never've occurred to me to treat a dirt road like a monument to someone's personal legacy—something sacred you're not allowed to touch. But a covert narcissist, who has no clear boundaries of Self and identifies with everything like a child does, is fully capable of treating a road as an extension of themselves.

Even the gravel road—and my attempt to make his life easier— had to be used as a weapon. With a covert narcissist, you don't stand a chance: say "yes," you're the enemy; say "no," you're the enemy.

The lesson here is that it's not about what you do—it's that you will always be the one he resents. Because you're not his mother, and his Inner Child has never stopped waiting for her.

Panic Fear Of Rejection

For a small child, rejection by their caregivers equals death, not metaphorically, but literally. A child's biological instinct is wired to stay close to their parents and to be seen by them. Even a newborn "knows" this and will scream at the top of their lungs when they can't sense the caregiver's presence. A slightly older child—around age three—might be able to play on their own for short periods, but they still need to check that a parent is nearby. That presence gives them a sense of safety.

Emotional development that's frozen at this stage causes narcissists to live in a constant fear of rejection. That's why control over the close partner becomes a primary defense mechanism. In the initial love-bombing phase, this shows up as a need for constant contact and uncertainty about whether the other person is still truly "there." Like a child checking if their mom is still nearby, the narcissist will keep asking: "Are you sure you'll still want me?" "Am I the only one in your life—there's no one else, right?" If you don't reply quickly enough, they're flooded with anxiety and obsessive thoughts, urgently needing reassurance that you're still there.

In a child, this is normal, and they eventually grow out of it. A narcissist never does. They have to keep checking you, controlling your presence, your loyalty, your devotion. In later phases of the relationship, this manifests as jealousy, tracking your whereabouts and who you're with, cutting you off from family, friends—and even from yourself—so they can keep you exclusively for their own purposes.

In a child, the desire to have their parents all to themselves is not only normal—it's accompanied by deep trust in those caregivers. In a narcissist, this same need is not only dysfunctional, but there's also not an ounce of trust in you. From the start, you're seen as someone who could potentially abandon or hurt them, so they have to control you.

If, in the early phase of the relationship, you're charmed by how often they reach out, how much they "worry" about you and what you're doing, how they say they can't live without you—pause and consider whether you might be dealing with a child looking for a mother and emotional dependency. That kind of person will never be a real partner to you. In adult relationships, this is a recipe for relational drama.

> **REALITY CHECK**
>
> When we're emotionally invested in something, it's natural to feel afraid of losing it. And nowhere do we invest more emotionally than in relationships, so the thought of losing the person we're with can trigger fear. If your partner gets upset because you're late coming home one night, don't jump to the conclusion that you're with a narcissist.
>
> But if you start noticing that they're making you feel guilty for spending time with your friends–meaning there's jealousy involved–take a closer look. Same thing if you express a different opinion during a conversation, and they react like it's a personal rejection or a sign of disrespect–then it's worth asking yourself what exactly you're dealing with. ·

MEMORIES AND REFLECTIONS FROM THE CHAMELEON MATRIX
"Leave Me, But First Promise You Won't"

One thing that showed up regularly from the very beginning—even during that first idyllic year—was him telling me that I would definitely leave him. That once I left, or once he died, it wouldn't even take me two days to forget about him. Why say something like that to your partner over and over? Why program the relationship from the start as something fleeting and meaningless? Why send the message that, in his eyes, I wasn't capable of loving him or committing to the relationship? Now I understand—it was a projection of how he saw the relationship.

Back then, I would engage in those conversations and reassure him that I wasn't going anywhere—that I was here, and I'd stay. But over time, after a few years, I noticed that my reassurances didn't matter. Neither did the actual facts—that despite the way he treated me, I was still there, patiently waiting for "the first year" to return.

It's the same tactic as a child checking to see if the caregiver is still in the room—just translated into an internal emotional game: fear of abandonment kicks in, so they trigger a conversation where they can be reassured that you're still "there."

On the flip side, he regularly told me that he was thinking about ending the relationship—and that he really meant it this time. Another provocation. After the hundredth time, I stopped reacting—because how far can you go with that? Eventually, my only response was: "OK, if that's your decision, then do it."

Guilt And Projection

Because a child hasn't yet developed the structure of the Inner Parent—the part that gives them perspective on the world and helps them distinguish between "what's mine and what's not"—they are completely merged with their environment. They can't tell what's real from what's imagined. They don't yet understand that others—especially the adults closest to them—have their own reasons for acting the way they do. Without a boundary between their inner and outer worlds, a child feels as if they are the cause of everything. When their mother has a bad day and becomes emotionally unavailable, the child immediately feels like they must have done something wrong and that it's their fault.

A child's instinct tells them they have to be the way their parents want them to be—because only then will they avoid rejection, which their nervous system equates with death. When a parent doesn't respond with enthusiasm to the child's presence, red flags go off internally, and the child's defense mechanisms kick in to try to regain that attention. They don't understand that Mom is just having a bad day—that she has her own reasons for feeling the way she does. For the child, this is a matter of survival. "I must be doing something wrong, and that's why Mom isn't interested in me—so I have to fix it." They take it on themselves. They become well-behaved, overly sweet, and try to win her back.

Three things are happening here. First, the child isn't yet capable of taking responsibility for anything. Second, they try to take responsibility for the situation. Third, they try to take responsibility for emotions and behaviors that aren't theirs to carry. There's a fourth element: the child's internal drama—based entirely on illusion and a lack of self-awareness—generates the accusation, "Mom doesn't love me." The mother is blamed for something she hasn't actually done, and often isn't even aware of. What the child needs at that moment is reassurance that they are loved and clear information that what's happening isn't their fault. That helps restore their internal sense of order, and usually, that's enough. Over time, the child grows out of this phase and develops a sense of self-awareness.

A narcissist who's emotionally stuck at this developmental stage keeps replaying the same internal pattern over and over. Their Inner Parent doesn't function properly, so they can't distinguish between what's theirs to take responsibility for and what isn't. They take everything personally, and because that's distorted and can't be processed in a healthy way, they project it onto you. You're the one to blame. You're doing things wrong. You don't love them enough. You don't give them the warmth and attention they need. You're the reason they're not happy or fulfilled in the relationship. You're the one they can't stand to be around anymore. The list goes on and on.

Meanwhile, you're left confused because you're actually doing things to keep the relationship functioning, and not only does he take those things for granted, but he'll also tell you you're doing nothing for him. Then, when he pushes too far and senses you've had enough—meaning you might reject him—he shifts into charm mode, like a child trying to win the parent back. That's the love-bombing phase. It's not a sign that things are improving—it's a sign that he's afraid and using manipulation to regain control and access to narcissistic supply. Step out of that game.

A covert narcissist, lacking a functioning Inner Parent—the part that processes and regulates emotions—can't take internal responsibility for what they feel. This turns into a chronic sense of guilt: "I am bad." They also can't take responsibility for themselves as a member of society, someone who contributes through their life and actions, which turns into chronic shame: "I am worthless." Because these emotions remain unprocessed, they must be discharged somehow, and more often than not, they fall on the people closest to them.

 REALITY CHECK

We all experience feelings of guilt or shame from time to time. That doesn't automatically make us narcissists. Usually, when a person feels these emotions, they see them as information about themselves, the world, or a situation, and try to do something to resolve the discomfort, often by taking responsibility for their part. And if those emotions can be processed and used as an opportunity for growth, that's a great outcome.

A narcissist, however, doesn't have the capacity to process these emotions. Because they're disconnected from their true sense of Self, they can't take responsibility for themselves, pushing those emotions outward. Other people, the world, life itself, even God–someone or something else will always be responsible for how they feel and what they're going through. Never them. They will never look inward to examine the source of their dissatisfaction. Someone must be blamed. It's a constant condition–and it doesn't change.

MEMORIES AND REFLECTIONS FROM THE CHAMELEON MATRIX
All Roads Lead To… His Ego

Maciek lived in a constant, unconscious state of guilt. You couldn't see it outright in his behavior, but his micro-reactions and subtle responses gave it away. I couldn't say or do anything—even something totally neutral—without him twisting it into something personal about him. I'd say, "I'm so tired today," his first response would be, "It's not because of me, is it?" Or I'd say, "I can't find my phone," and he'd snap, "I didn't take it."

These might seem like small things, but when this is the pattern day in and day out, it wears you down. It becomes distancing—everything ordinary and neutral has to somehow be rerouted back to him. There's no room for real dialogue when you're in that for years, and he constantly sees only himself, when every little thing gets reframed to be about him. You can't talk about anything simple just for the sake of connection. Everything became a personal offense. And later, I'd get told that we "had a communication problem."

This showed up in other areas, too. Whatever I said—even if it had absolutely nothing to do with him, like when I came up with an idea or felt like doing something—he would take it as if it somehow revolved around him. For example, I might say, "I feel like visiting a friend," and he'd respond with, "Of course—because you don't want to spend time with me."

In the narcissist's system, there's no space where you're allowed to exist independently from them. You can't want to spend time with a friend simply because you want to spend time with a friend. That desire has to be a reaction to him. He must be the reason behind your decision, not you.

Hot Springs And A Cold Shower – The Full Package

There was a time we had planned a trip to Silverland, to the sulfur hot springs. Now and then, we'd go there to "soak and unwind." We were going to take my car. Before we left, Maciek was checking the oil. The car was already packed, and I happened to be walking by to take out the trash. I noticed the car was parked on the driveway, which had a bit of a slope. A red flag went up in my mind because I remembered the first time I took a solo road trip in the States—several days, around three thousand miles—and I had to check the oil myself. Not being very experienced at the time, I checked it once while the car was on uneven ground, and the reading was off. I ended up overfilling the oil based on that bad reading. I drove the rest of the trip with my heart in my throat, worried something would go wrong from overfilling. Thankfully, everything turned out fine, but that fear stuck with me, especially when you're driving across hundreds of miles of empty American landscape where there's absolutely nothing around.

As I walked past Maciek and saw the car sitting on the sloped driveway, I had a flashback of that earlier experience and instinctively said, "Maybe it'd be better to move it to flat ground." Oh, holy saints—what a scene he made. He exploded, accusing me of treating him like garbage, like a worthless idiot. He raged that I was lecturing him about something he knew better than anyone—he'd been changing oil in cars for ages—and how dare I suggest otherwise? I had no respect for him, and all I ever did was try to control him.

I was stunned—frozen—trying to make sense of how my simple comment could have triggered such a violent reaction. What I said had come from my past road trip experience, not from any desire to undermine or question his competence. But he spiraled so far out that he finally said he wasn't going anywhere with me, that he couldn't take it anymore. He pulled his bags out of the car and said he could reimburse me for the hotel, since I was the one who had paid for it.

I was left with the dilemma: should I go on the trip alone, or head back inside and try to defuse the situation somehow? I sat in the car for about half an hour, deeply debating with myself while also trying to calm down, because after a tirade like that, your emotions aren't exactly in vacation mode. You need a moment to settle. Eventually, he came out of the garage and, with full sarcasm, said, "What, you won't even come inside because I'm in there? I can leave if I'm such a problem for you."

This is a perfect example of how, in the narcissist's mind, everything revolves around them. It never even crosses their mind that you might be doing something for your own reasons—that maybe you're just sitting there trying to calm down and make a decision for yourself. What is evident here is a complete lack of empathy—and an inability to foresee the consequences of their own actions (which I'll discuss further later). First, their mind simply doesn't register that their behavior creates consequences in the other person, consequences that person now has to manage. Second, even if they did register for it, they wouldn't be able to feel it. Because if they did feel it, they would fall apart.

For them, everything begins and ends with them. Every decision you make is somehow about them. If you're thinking about something, it couldn't possibly have originated in your own mind or from your own initiative—it must be connected to their presence in some way. In their world, you don't exist without them.

At that moment, I really didn't care whether he was in the house or not. My dilemma was whether I should go on the trip alone, because the whole plan, including the hotel and everything else, had been set up for the two of us. And both options felt heavy in different ways: if I went and left him in that emotional state, who knows what I'd come home to? If I stayed, the tension in the air would be so thick it would feel unbearable.

In the end, I decided I wasn't going to let him ruin a trip I had been looking forward to for months with genuine excitement. He's an adult, and I'm not responsible for his behavior. This time, I chose myself. I started the car and left. I soaked in the hot sulfur springs, which probably pulled a few toxins out of me in more ways than one.

And the next day, when I got back, he was surprisingly calm. He even apologized for how he'd acted. Don't be fooled—when a narcissist apologizes, it's rarely sincere. When someone truly sees the damage their actions caused another person and feels bad about it, they apologize to show that they're committed to not repeating that behavior. A narcissist apologizes because they fear the "punishment" of rejection. Once they sense that you've let it go and they've regained control of the situation, they revert to their old behavior because it was never really about you.

Emotional rollercoasters are the norm with a covert narcissist. The most important thing is not to take responsibility for their actions or start convincing yourself it's your fault. These people are deeply dysfunctional, and their behavior stems directly from that.

Emotional Provocation

Picture a two-year-old with a need they don't yet know how to express with words or logic. What they do have is an emotional communication channel. So they draw attention to themselves through crying, screaming, anger, or even laughter. When a mother sees her child in strong emotion, she instinctively gives them attention. That's natural. When children get their parents' attention, they feel safe. So they learn to provoke emotion—because it's the only way they know to stay connected.

A covert narcissist, stuck at this emotional stage, does the exact same thing: they provoke your emotions. At first, it's positive emotions—through love bombing, they trigger awe, admiration, tenderness, gratitude, acceptance, and more.

But once the love-bombing phase ends and the devaluation begins, they start provoking negative emotions. They pick fights. They gaslight you until you're irritated or angry. They play the victim to trigger your guilt and make you explain yourself. They belittle you until you feel sad or even cry. And so on.

One of the more insidious tactics covert narcissists use is that, once they get to know you and figure out your sensitive spots, they'll deliberately use that knowledge to provoke an emotional reaction. For covert narcissists, any emotional reaction from you—positive or negative—is fuel. Because it brings your attention, and when they have your attention, they have control. That gives them a false sense of security and power.

 REALITY CHECK

If your partner occasionally drives you crazy–or vice versa–it doesn't mean one of you must be a narcissist. Everyone, at some point, ends up triggering someone else's emotions. Maybe something happened, you're overwhelmed, and you need compassion to feel grounded again. Maybe you're furious about something and venting to a friend, hoping for understanding and calm. Maybe a tragedy struck, and you just need someone to sit in the sadness with you. All of that is normal.

With a narcissist, though, this isn't occasional or situational. It's a regular tactic that deliberately exploits this human tendency to evoke emotion to pull your attention toward them and feed off of it.

MEMORIES AND REFLECTIONS FROM THE CHAMELEON MATRIX

Gaslighting And Other Soothing Sounds Of The Evening

One thing I absolutely can't stand is when someone raises their voice at me for no reason. I have no problem with someone yelling at me if I've really messed something up, and I deserve it. But yelling for no reason? Zero tolerance. Maciek picked up on that pretty quickly. Once the devaluation phase began, he started speaking to me in a condescending, commanding tone more frequently. It wasn't exactly yelling, but his voice would be slightly raised. I don't even know how many thousands of times I said things like, "Stop talking to me like a sergeant barking at a recruit," or, "Stop ordering me around," or, "Don't yell at me."

Every time, I got some kind of gaslighting response, like, "I'm not yelling—you don't even know what yelling sounds like," or a dumb excuse like, "That's just how I talk, I'm used to working with guys, and that's how you have to speak to them."

You hear something like that and just blink, wondering if you actually heard it right. Wait, are you seriously telling me I've been demoted from being your partner to one of your construction site coworkers? Of course, he had an answer for that too—he'd reference A Course in Miracles, saying that expecting "special treatment" was toxic, and if I wanted to be more evolved, I should read the Course. I never asked for special treatment. I just wanted to be treated normally—in a way that fit the situation. And raising your voice at me for no reason didn't fit.

Near the end of the relationship, he changed the tune to: "That's just how I am—I don't know how to be any different." Which, of course, was also manipulation—because in other settings, with other people, or when he wanted something from me, he had no problem being calm and polite. But whenever he needed to fill his inner emptiness, he'd default to his go-to method for getting a reaction: raising his voice at me for no reason.

Facts Don't Register

Back then, I didn't realize that this was the whole point for a narcissist—to provoke emotion. They don't know how to communicate on the level of facts. A covert narcissist doesn't want harmony—they want emotional chaos. If you reveal your sensitive spots, they'll use them to destabilize you. That's their method of control. Because the moment you get irritated, you're giving them attention. And for a narcissist, attention—especially charged, emotional attention—is better than peace. Peace offers nothing to feed on, so they won't give up the game. They'd rather blow up the relationship than lose their dysfunctional sense of control. Facts are like a red flag to a bull. You'll never be able to have a calm, factual conversation with them, especially about your relationship. The moment you refer to anything concrete, the gaslighting starts: they cut you off, change the subject, make excuses, or twist your words until you're in an argument. Facts would lead them straight to the truth—and a covert narcissist runs from truth like the devil from holy water. Facing the truth would require taking off the mask. And that's something a narcissist will never do.

A covert narcissist is so desperate and relentless in pulling attention toward themselves through emotional chaos that they can practically move mountains to do it. It still amazes me that Maciek actually managed to get me to yell at him a few times during our relationship. I honestly can't remember ever raising my voice at anyone—except maybe at a dog running into the street. In my family growing up, my parents never yelled or argued. If there was tension, it usually came out as a bit of sulking, but that passed quickly, and things returned to normal. On top of that, I've always had a pretty stable emotional baseline—and even more so since I began working with EFT and emotional intelligence.

But Maciek? He was a master. He could talk in circles, poke and prod endlessly, ignore every request to stop, until I felt like I couldn't take it anymore. Eventually, I learned to tune him out and just nod along, because I saw the game for what it was. I'd simply say, "Yes, of course," which only led to more accusations—this time, I wasn't listening or taking him seriously. Just know this: with a covert narcissist, you'll always be the one at fault—especially when you start setting boundaries.

"Stop it!" – The Secret Word To His Zen

I still remember three times when I completely lost it—once I slammed a door so hard it almost flew off the hinges, and twice I yelled at the top of my lungs for him to stop. I don't think I've ever screamed "Stop it!!!" as loudly as I did then. I honestly thought the windows might crack. And that's when I noticed something strange for the first time. Maciek, who had been pacing and complaining and dumping his unhappiness on me nonstop, suddenly went quiet. But not just quiet—peaceful. I was bracing for backlash, but instead, he went soft. Serene, even. Like all was suddenly right with the world. It wasn't the silence of fear. It was a kind of eerie calm, as if my outburst had finally given him what he needed. It was unsettling to realize that my screaming made him feel safe. This wasn't a relationship. This was a child reenacting an old emotional drama.

At the time, I was frightened by my own reaction. It didn't feel like me. I didn't like myself in that moment. But years later, after studying how narcissistic personality disorder works, I finally understood: in that moment, he had reached a genuine inner calm. Like a baby who managed—through intense emotion—to pull all of mom's attention back onto himself and, in doing so, regained a sense of safety. He'd regained control. And when he feels in control, "everything is fine."

That was the most extreme example of how he actually got to me. Other attempts at emotional provocation—which were a regular tactic—usually ended in tension, where I would pull back and remove myself from the interaction. But even that was a win for him. For a narcissist, conflict is still a form of control. Chaos, not harmony, is what keeps the dynamic alive.

> *A covert narcissist maintains control in a relationship by injecting chaos and division into it.*

Lack Of Empathy

This might sound harsh, but the truth is—small children don't have empathy. Not because something's wrong with them, but simply because their brains haven't yet developed the neural networks needed to process things on a deeper level. They're just not wired for it yet. Empathy begins to emerge gradually as the brain matures and the child becomes more able to process the world with awareness.

So What Is Empathy, Really?

The kind of human empathy I'm talking about here goes beyond just sensing someone else's emotions, which even animals can do. Animals can feel fear or calm in others. Infants, too, can sense the inner states of their caregivers. When a mother is anxious, her baby will often feel that energy immediately and begin to cry. Let's call that a biological mechanism—a starting point from which true empathy can eventually grow.

Healthy empathy isn't just the ability to feel someone else's emotions—it's also the ability to understand that person and their situation. That requires a deeper level of cognitive processing, a kind of awareness that takes time to develop.

The next stages of mature empathy extend beyond merely feeling and understanding another person's perspective. They also include the ability to stay grounded without being triggered by one's own unresolved pain.

The highest form of empathy encompasses all of this: feeling and understanding someone's difficult state, remaining calm within yourself, and allowing their struggle to evoke love and compassion within you. Not fear, not discomfort you're trying to get rid of, not a need to be praised or admired, not guilt, just the genuine desire to offer something good, whether anyone notices or not.

Another aspect of the highest form of empathy is this: when you see someone going through something difficult—you feel it, you understand it, you hold calm and love inside you, and genuinely want to help—but for whatever reason, you can't. And even that… is okay. You have full trust that this person will receive the help they truly need, at the moment that's best for them, from the people most equipped to give it. In the meantime, you can create a calm and positive energy within yourself and send that energy their way, quietly supporting their process.

Why Don't Children Have Empathy Yet?

Very young children simply aren't capable of it yet. They lack conscious depth and perspective. The only thing that matters to them is their own needs, regardless of whether their mother is sick, busy, or dealing with something that requires her attention. The little "dictator" demands absolutely, and if that need isn't met, they throw an emotional storm until someone comes and gives them attention. Nothing else matters—only themselves. The family exists as a source of survival. And that's natural—their system is just beginning to learn and absorb. The giving part comes later.

As the child gets older, the first signs of empathy begin to show, like feeling deep sadness upon seeing a dead animal. But that kind of empathy still lacks internal distance—there's only pain. They may also start experimenting with doing kind things for others, but even that is still primitive, often driven by the desire to be noticed, so it's not entirely selfless yet.

The Narcissist Without Empathy: Needs Instead Of Relationship

A narcissist who's emotionally stuck at the developmental stage where empathy hasn't yet formed—and whose main goal is to draw attention in order to survive—does exactly the same thing. Everything has to be for them, about them, and because of them. Other people's needs don't matter, and their weaknesses often trigger contempt. If you see a narcissist being kind, helpful, or showing compassion, understand that it's a calculated move, driven by self-interest. Usually, they want something from those people; they're a form of supply. Watch closely because the kindness disappears once those people are no longer useful. In fact, criticism begins. They gave what was needed—now they can be tossed aside, even stepped on.

If a covert narcissist does something for you, it's not truly for you. They do it to be noticed, to receive praise, recognition, or appreciation. Sometimes they do it out of fear—afraid that they'll be criticized or rejected if they don't meet some expected norm. But it's never really about you. Whatever a narcissist does, at the beginning and end of it, it's always about them. They're unable to step into your shoes, sense your perspective, or even validate it as different without feeling threatened. They can't see a situation through your eyes and do anything for you selflessly, without feeling like they've lost something if there's no personal gain involved.

Empathy As A Tool For Manipulation

It's important to point out that narcissistic personality disorder isn't the only condition marked by a lack of empathy. Autism is also characterized by difficulty in processing and understanding emotions. And while people on the spectrum can be extremely self-focused, there's a key difference that sets them apart from narcissists: they are brutally honest. Despite the challenges this condition can bring—often straining family dynamics—there's a sense of purity in their way of being.

Narcissists, on the other hand, also can't process emotions and lack empathy, but they have the intellectual capacity to understand emotional nuances, and they know how to manipulate them. They lie, play the victim, twist stories, and distort facts. They manipulate people's emotional states. They manipulate empathy itself, even though they don't truly possess it. They know how to emotionally destroy someone or win them over with sympathy. That's where the game becomes deeply dishonest.

> *A covert narcissist doesn't have empathy–*
> *but they know how to use your empathy*
> *to gain acceptance.*

> **REALITY CHECK**
>
> Not showing empathy all the time doesn't automatically mean you're incapable of it—so no, that doesn't make you a narcissist. There can be many reasons for struggling with empathy in a given moment. Sometimes your own problems are so overwhelming that there's simply no energy left for anyone else. Or maybe you grew up in a home where showing emotion wasn't allowed, and now you feel shame when you try to express it. Or you might be highly sensitive, and empathy becomes so intense that it feels too heavy to carry. However, in all of those cases, the capacity for empathy remains present. You can still feel what another person feels, and that naturally translates into not wanting to cause them harm. Because if you can feel how painful something is, you won't want to do it.
>
> A narcissist doesn't have this ability. They feel very hurt when someone does something upsetting to them, but in the next breath, they'll turn around and do that same thing to you without even noticing. Once you point that out, a healthy person will feel a little awkward or embarrassed—they'll see it. A narcissist won't. They won't register it even if you point directly at it with your finger. That basic mechanism of reciprocity simply doesn't exist in them, because the structure of the Self is so deeply impaired. They genuinely don't see it.

MEMORIES AND REFLECTIONS FROM THE CHAMELEON MATRIX

One-Way Empathy – Exclusive Rights Reserved

This was probably one of the hardest things for me in that relationship, because it made mutual understanding and connection nearly impossible. I only noticed it when we moved to Westmont, where the devaluation phase began.

When everything started irritating him, he'd often tell me I wasn't treating him right, that I was speaking to him in the wrong tone, or even that my energy was attacking him. By the end of the relationship, he even accused me of attacking him in his sleep, because I supposedly hated him so much. At first, I tried to talk through it. I'd explain that it must be a misunderstanding, and perhaps we should sit down and talk it out. But over time, I realized that the very things he couldn't stand, he was constantly doing to me. So I began to confront him. Whenever he criticized something about how I spoke or acted, I'd hold up a mirror and say, "But you just did the same thing to me a minute ago." Eventually, I started adding, "It's not fair that you get to do this and it's okay, but the moment it happens to you, you're offended." I naively hoped that he'd reflect on this at some point and realize how unfair it was. He held constant grudges against me for things he had no problem doing himself.

None of it worked. My attempts at holding up a mirror only led to more accusations. He began lashing out, saying I was constantly blaming him, deflecting responsibility for my own behavior, making him the bad guy to make myself look good, and the best part? That I was using psychological manipulation on him. Honestly, it's hard to imagine a bigger case of projection. For him, the simple desire for mutuality and being seen by each other was a form of manipulation. Because the only one who was ever supposed to be seen… was him.

I couldn't even count the hundreds of situations like this that there were. Only now do I truly understand how damaged the sense of Self is in someone with NPD. They are simply incapable—on a mechanical level—of seeing and feeling in both directions. There's no empathy. There's only one direction: toward their own ego. Everything else is outside their perception.

A narcissist doesn't respond to the mirror. They don't see themselves in the mirror—they see a threat to their self-image. Their response will be either an attack or a projection.

Testing Boundaries

If you're a parent, you probably remember those moments when your child tested your limits and pushed your buttons. It's one of the more difficult parts of parenting—when your child is coming at you full force and you have to hold your boundaries just firmly enough not to crush their spirit, but also not let them walk all over you and lose your mind.

That's natural. A child doesn't yet have an Inner Parent, meaning they don't have internal boundaries. That's why they're impulsive, unfiltered, lacking in restraint, directionless, and don't yet know how far is too far. Since children aren't intellectually mature enough to grasp reality, they learn about boundaries through experience, through behavior. When parents sense that something isn't right about a child's behavior in any way, they step in and set a boundary, providing feedback that the behavior needs to stop.

Because this kind of learning happens through behavior and emotion, it can feel like a power struggle. And in a sense, it is—but when boundaries are set in a healthy, respectful way that meets the force of a child's energy, no one really loses, no one dominates, and both sides actually win. It's simply a clash of elements that ultimately leads to wisdom and self-regulation.

A child might resist boundaries at first, but their internal system is open to learning, and slowly starts to take shape. As a result, the child's behavior becomes more mature and responsible. Their Inner Parent begins to form and gradually takes over the job.

A narcissist who is emotionally stuck at this stage will constantly test your boundaries and push against them. The problem is, unlike a child who is still forming those inner structures, the narcissist already *has* an Inner Parent—just a dysfunctional one. Which means your attempts to set boundaries won't have the same effect as they would with a child. Their system is closed to outside learning, so any boundary you set will be interpreted as an attack, a lack of respect, rejection, control, or domination.

At the same time, because they don't have a healthy internal boundary themselves, they'll keep crossing yours until they break you down. With a narcissist, you can't afford to let harmful behavior slide in hopes they'll come around. When you draw your first real boundary, prepare for the script to flip and for them to accuse you of attacking them.

> **REALITY CHECK**
>
> If you're in a relationship that's still going through the rough patches and feels like two strong forces clashing, don't assume right away that you're with a narcissist. That kind of friction is common in new relationships—people test each other, figure out what works and what doesn't, and explore each other's boundaries. This process leads to mutual understanding in a healthy relationship, and things gradually become easier and more harmonious.
>
> But in a relationship with a narcissist, that never happens. The "figuring it out" phase only leads to more distance, deeper division, and ultimately the collapse of the relationship.

MEMORIES AND REFLECTIONS FROM THE CHAMELEON MATRIX
Beta Love - It Never Leaves The Testing Phase

That was my mistake—believing I was dealing with an actual adult, someone capable of self-awareness and reflection. I thought that if I just stayed grounded, kept letting things go, and tried to nurture harmony, he'd eventually calm down and stop stirring up emotional drama. If I had known back then what I know now about narcissism, I wouldn't have even tried.

I'll never forget something he said to me—not once, but a few times. The first time was after we moved to Deserta, so about seven years into the relationship. He said, "I don't get it. I've tried everything to make you give up on me, and you're still here. I'm out of ideas." Well, he did come up with one final idea—four years later—when he started secretly declaring his love to another woman behind my back. My reaction was immediate. That crossed a line. And if I had tolerated it, it wouldn't just have been him crossing my boundary—it would have been me crossing my own. That would've been me betraying myself.

With his other behaviors, I allowed my boundary to be stretched, but it never snapped—it was flexible, which meant I didn't lose my inner integrity. But this time, there was no room left for stretching. The only option was to remove him from my space entirely. You could say he finally achieved the goal he had been pushing toward all along by repeating to me thousands of times: "You're going to leave me, I know it."

Confessions Of A Chameleon – Limited Edition

Let me remind you that a narcissist's manipulation lies in the way they mirror you during the initial love-bombing phase. They copy who you are, what matters to you, and then later use it like a chameleon. For me, it was important that a relationship be a space where both people are self-aware and committed to growth through the connection. Maciek knew this perfectly well, and every now and then, he'd drop a line that seemed like a brilliant sign of awareness, like the time he said, "I don't know what it is. I've tried everything to push you away, but you're still here." It sounded like a truly self-aware observation.

It took me years to realize it was just manipulation. He was feeding me, in words, what I valued most—self-awareness—but only as a way to keep me hooked. Every time I heard something like that, which happened regularly, I was floored. My jaw would drop, and I'd immediately feel a rush of hope that maybe this time he actually wanted to talk about us, about the relationship, about what we could do to make it grow.

Imagine this: every single time, without exception, it was just words. Nothing ever followed. It was the classic hidden narcissist fantasy, one that always stays suspended in the realm of illusion and never crosses over into reality. The only goal was manipulation—to keep stringing me along and siphoning off more narcissistic supply.

My only real enemy was my own ignorance about this disorder, and my complete disbelief that there are people out there who don't want to be happy, who are driven mainly by destruction. I believed that with enough acceptance, support, and understanding, the other person could start to feel safe, especially if they had painful experiences in their past. And in healthy relationships, that's usually true. But not with a narcissist. Forget it.

One-Way Dialogues – Monologues With Consequences

As I mentioned earlier, after we moved to Deserta and I saw that everything was slipping right back into the same old patterns—and that being understanding and letting things slide wasn't getting me anywhere—I started setting verbal boundaries. I began confronting a lot of his behaviors, holding up a mirror so he could see himself in it. I thought that if he wasn't aware of the impact of his actions, maybe if I stopped allowing them, it would make a difference.

Well, it did make a difference: it brought a flood of new accusations that I was hurting him. That we were no longer a good match. I was clipping his wings, not supporting him, rejecting him, giving him nothing, just using him—and on and on.

Narcissists won't confront their behavior because they're incapable of taking true inner responsibility. They'll run from it. And in that escape, they'll choose damaging behaviors and make destructive decisions—ones they'll later feel ashamed of, though they'll never admit it. Eventually, all of it gets dumped back on you.

Lack Of Responsibility And Awareness Of Consciousness

This is a classic trait of childhood, and it persists into adolescence. That's why they can be held legally responsible only when they reach adulthood. Before that, the brain simply isn't developed enough to anticipate the consequences of behavior, so a young person can't be judged by the same standards as an adult.

For a child, the fact that something can be done or obtained in the moment is reason enough to act. They'll jump in with both feet if it seems fun, exciting, rewarding, or appealing. They have no ability to visualize the longer path of that choice or where it might lead. So they can't take responsibility for it. That's why it's so important to be present and involved in a child's life—to help protect them from harm and patiently explain consequences so they gradually build perspective. Children often rebel and feel misunderstood or unhappy, but that's part of learning how to relate to life. It's the parents who are responsible for their child's behavior—and who bear the consequences of it.

The covert narcissist does exactly the same thing. They believe they have the right to do whatever they feel like in the moment. They're not interested in consequences—neither for their own life nor for anyone else's. They can't see past their own ego. If they're involved in something and others are counting on them—whether it's one person or a group—they won't hesitate to walk away overnight if they're no longer enjoying it for whatever reason. The fact that others will have to deal with the fallout? "Not my problem."

They can be engaged, active, even hard-working—but only as long as there's something in it for them: praise, appreciation, a sense of importance, or just the buzz of novelty. The moment that fades and the excitement wears off, they drop it all and move on, leaving others high and dry. It no longer feeds their ego, so they search for the next thing that will.

They're convinced they have the right to behave this way—and technically, they do. But the way they exercise that right—completely disregarding others and serving only their own impulsive whims—is deeply selfish and, in many cases, downright disgraceful.

 REALITY CHECK

I don't think there's an adult on this planet who hasn't, at some point, done something out of carelessness, poor judgment, lack of awareness, or because the thrill of risk made them deliberately ignore the consequences. That doesn't mean they have NPD. Healthy people, when they face the unpleasant consequences of their choices, usually learn from them, so that next time, they can avoid or at least minimize the damage. They register the consequences, and their brain starts to anticipate them moving forward.

> But the narcissist doesn't learn. They repeat the same patterns like a horse with blinders. Even if they've already suffered the fallout of their own actions, that experience never really registers in their behavior. They might remember it intellectually, but they'll still do the exact same thing again—and then blame someone else for the outcome. That's why they don't change. To grow, you must first take responsibility.
>
> And really, in a relationship, it's not even about both people having to know everything or be perfectly skilled. In my view, if one person lacks a certain ability or struggles in an area, and the other is stronger in that area, the two should be able to lean on each other and let those differences support the relationship as a whole. But with someone who has NPD, everything becomes a battlefield—and what's being fought for is blind, rigid control.

MEMORIES AND REFLECTIONS FROM THE CHAMELEON MATRIX
Full Throttle Enthusiasm, Strategy In A Coma

I often saw this kind of behavior in Maciek. The moment he came up with an idea, he would dive into it headfirst, investing time, money, and a tremendous amount of energy and effort. But it never had a purpose. It didn't lead anywhere. It was just a temporary distraction, something that seemed exciting in the moment and then lost its shine just as quickly.

On its own, there's nothing wrong with that kind of behavior. The problem arises when he becomes involved in something that actually requires consistency, long-term effort, and commitment to achieve results, especially when it involves other people. He simply couldn't grasp that actions like this need a plan, a bit of foresight, a strategy. In his mind, things were just supposed to happen. He had the idea, so that meant it should automatically become real.

My brain struggled to understand this approach. I just couldn't believe someone could treat complex things so carelessly and still expect results. At first, I thought maybe he had some kind of special talent, that maybe he didn't need to operate like a regular person. But eventually, it became clear—he simply lacked the ability to develop a broader perspective around his actions.

Every time I tried to offer a wider view, to suggest that yes, things are possible, but they'll require some thought, some planning, some actual strategy—especially when we were talking about bigger decisions or projects—it always ended the same way. He'd brush it off and say, "That's your way of doing things. I have my way. I'm not going to do it your way." He just couldn't grasp that it wasn't about mine or his—it was about the fact that certain things demand a certain kind of approach, or they're just not going to work. No discussion. Later, it would always turn out that, actually, yeah—maybe thinking it through would've helped. At the end of the day, the consequences still had to be dealt with, but now they came with extra costs in all sorts of forms.

And that was the most unbelievable part—every single time he also saw that maybe, just maybe, it would've been better to talk things through first, and even admitted it out loud, I would get my hopes up again. I thought, "Okay, if he sees it now, then surely next time we'll be able to actually build something together, without that obsessive need for control." But after dozens of these moments, it wasn't until the very end of the relationship that it finally started to sink in: he was saying all those things just to create the illusion that we were moving in a good direction. In reality, they were nothing more than sweet-sounding empty promises, designed to keep the same old dysfunctional patterns going just a little longer.

Lack Of Sense Of Self And Changing Ideas Of Who They Are

When we look at small children experimenting with life and all it has to offer, it's a joyful sight. They're full of energy and enthusiasm as they try new things. First, they're curious about the world around them. Second, they don't yet know themselves very well, so they learn who they are and what they like through experience. That's why they dive into various activities and often change their preferences. It's a fascinating and creative process. They also fantasize about who they want to be when they grow up, usually based on whatever currently fascinates them. Occasionally, you'll see a child who knows from a very young age what they want and who they're going to be—and that never changes—but that's rare.

Over time, as people mature, they usually develop a clearer, more conscious understanding of who they are, their strengths and preferences, and what they'd like to do in life. They start to pursue education in that direction, or if it's a hobby or passion, they begin to develop it.

A covert narcissist who has no real connection to their core Self doesn't know who they are or what they're truly passionate about. That's why their behavior is chaotic, inconsistent, lacking in follow-through, and full of randomness. They start many things but rarely finish them. This often translates into financial loss, as they invest money in a project they never intend to complete, or one that hasn't been thoroughly thought through and is expected to succeed solely on the strength of their intention.

 REALITY CHECK

Just because you like change and variety doesn't mean you're a narcissist. It's not about the fact of change itself – if you're in a phase of life, or going through circumstances that naturally lead to a new stage, or if you just want to refresh your inner or outer world, then by all means, make that change. Usually, though, there's some kind of continuity or underlying coherence.

With a covert narcissist, changes are compulsive, random, and driven by whatever they happen to think is important in the moment. They can flip their entire life upside down just because they overheard something in a store and suddenly decided it was a great idea. They dive in, invest time, energy, money – and then,

> poof, it's over. It's no longer exciting; they're bored, and it's time to chase something new. That's why covert narcissists usually don't accomplish anything meaningful – they start, quit, start, quit, over and over again. What's missing is a steady inner Self that could guide those changes. Their life looks like someone took a thousand random scraps of fabric and stitched them together into something where nothing matches, flows, and harmonizes – just a patchwork of chaos with no cohesive thread.

MEMORIES AND REFLECTIONS FROM THE CHAMELEON MATRIX

"Take Care Of Me—But Don't Make Me Take Care Of Myself"

When we moved to Westmont, deep in the woods, and Maciek morphed into someone irritated by absolutely everything, he started complaining that I wasn't giving him enough time and attention. I was too absorbed in my own things instead of focusing on him. First of all, I never had any intention of giving up "my things," and second, interacting with a walking time bomb isn't exactly anyone's idea of pleasure. I could stay calm, not provoke him, give him space, and not take it personally — but trying to manage his emotional state, pacify him, and make him my personal "project"? That was way too much. In my view, creating harmony in a healthy adult relationship doesn't mean controlling the other person's emotions — it means taking responsibility for your own, so you don't get dragged into their emotional storms.

During one conversation — again, he was accusing me of making the relationship unbearable by not giving him enough attention — I suggested that if he had a passion of his own to dive into, he might feel more fulfilled. He snapped back that he didn't have any passions, that it was all stupid, and that he never knew what he wanted — only when he tried something could he tell if he liked it or not.

This kind of state is perfectly normal and characteristic of a child, but in someone who's already past the halfway point of life, it becomes a serious problem. And if what he said had been true, there might still be some hope that he'd eventually find his passion. But in the case of a covert narcissist, who lives in chronic anger and self-loathing, the main driving force is destruction and unhappiness. So there's no chance he'll be able to embrace anything that might bring him fulfillment truly. And even if he does find something… he'll abandon it anyway.

Identity: Temporarily Borrowed

Another thing I didn't understand about Maciek for a long time was his constant need to belong to something and his tendency to change identities frequently. When your sense of Self doesn't actually belong to you, you can never truly feel at home with yourself. You're always searching, always trying to change something, never content anywhere for long. But the search happens in the wrong direction—outward. Ultimately, the problem lies within.

A covert narcissist gets easily fascinated with whatever is new and mistakes that rush of fascination for confidence. But the unraveling begins after a while when the "new" isn't new anymore. Because a narcissist has no interest in truly getting to know anything as it actually is — flaws, difficulties, and all. He wants to reject whatever feels uncomfortable and live inside an idyllic illusion. That illusion is only briefly sparked in contact with something shiny and untouched, still unknown.

That's why, once a narcissist starts to get familiar with something — once the layers begin to show — he becomes internally uneasy and craves change. He chases that pleasant rush, but it only lives in the early stages of discovery, when everything's still new and untouched by reality. When fantasy can still fill in the blanks, he longs to belong — but keeps looking in all the wrong places.

> *This lack of belonging to his own Self is what makes a covert narcissist unable to find his place in the world.*

The Chameleon On The Catwalk

Another thing I never understood about Maciek was his constant changes in appearance. Sure, someone might say, "Why not? People can change how they look." Of course, they can. But in his case, it always seemed driven by a strange kind of motivation. When he got fascinated by a new group of people and spent time getting to know them, he'd suddenly announce that he was going to look like them now, or start living like they did. He'd change his hairstyle, grow a beard, shave it off, trim it differently just to match, buy the signature clothes, hats, sunglasses — the whole package. He'd basically style himself to fit their mold.

This wasn't a one-time thing — it was constant. Then it would pass once the fascination wore off. Kids or teenagers do that when their identity is still forming and they're eager to belong to a group. That kind of belonging helps them define themselves in the world. But for someone with NPD, this is just a performance — it never leads anywhere. Because what helps a child grow naturally stops working for an adult. In adults, only deep inner work, especially on the internal Parent structure, can complete the emotional development that got stuck in childhood.

That's why, in a narcissist, all these strategies end up being just borrowed identities — superficial imitations of others, with no real impact on what's happening inside.

Only Praise Allowed

You probably know how a child reacts when they're told "no" or criticized for something. The emotional reactions may vary, but one thing remains consistent: the child feels hurt. And it's not because the child is spoiled or poorly raised, but because their psychological system isn't yet developed enough to process difficult feedback in a healthy way. To truly process that kind of message, a person needs a sufficiently mature internal system that includes emotional independence. The more emotionally dependent someone is on others, the less capacity they have to cope with challenge or adversity internally.

A child's system, being emotionally dependent on others, is wide open to receiving. It takes everything in without filters or critical judgment. That's why only supportive, encouraging, accepting, and comfortable things can be taken in directly by the child. Anything difficult, uncomfortable, or perceived as negative is experienced as harm because the child doesn't yet have an Inner Parent structure that could create distance and help process such information in a healthy way.

That's why it's the parents' job to deliver difficult truths in a way that doesn't undermine the child's sense of safety or love. The message needs to be clear: "You are still loved and safe. This challenge doesn't mean rejection — it's just something that has to be addressed." As you may recall, rejection is a threat to survival for a child.

A covert narcissist, still stuck in that emotional child state, perceives the world in the same way. They can only tolerate praise and approval, and respond with panic — often masked as anger or an attack — to criticism or opposing views.

 REALITY CHECK

Don't assume you're a narcissist just because you enjoy compliments. Compliments are naturally pleasant. A healthy person, aside from appreciating praise, can also handle criticism. They don't have to like it, but they can take it in as useful feedback – a sign that something might need improvement. In a healthy relationship, people don't seek confrontation, but don't avoid it either. When it does come up, they work through it together. The world doesn't fall apart because of it.

For someone with NPD, the world does fall apart. So pay attention to people who react explosively, disproportionately, or irrationally to even the slightest thing they perceive as criticism – even if it's not actually there. If you find yourself being punished for that, it's time to step back and take a closer look.

MEMORIES AND REFLECTIONS FROM THE CHAMELEON MATRIX
Approval By Narcissometer - Measured In Doses

I remember exactly the first time Maciek said I didn't praise him enough. It was in the kitchen in Westmont. I looked at him kind of confused, because every time he finished a project, built something, got something done, I acknowledged it with, "Great job!", "That looks really nice!", "I'm so glad!", "That turned out great!", "You really nailed it!", "Well thought out!", "Good idea!" — things like that.

Turns out, in all my noticing… I wasn't really noticing him. Apparently, instead of saying, "Well thought out," I should've said, "You're so smart and creative!"

I was stunned. Talking to a grown man like he's five years old — just to prop up a fragile ego — felt degrading. What self-respecting man wants his partner to treat him like a child in order to make him feel like a man?

If only it actually meant something… Because whenever I did happen to say something that stroked his ego directly, he'd immediately reject it. He'd downplay it, brush it off, act like it didn't matter. He couldn't genuinely take it in. It was just a quick fix to plug that gnawing internal emptiness — never about real self-recognition. I didn't want to play those emotional games.

But the moment I tried to point out anything that could be improved or done better, the attacks started. Accusations and deflections — no space for reflection or room for actual thought. That's when the original lie began to unravel — the one where he'd promised that what mattered most in a relationship was facing things together, bringing into the light all that still lived in shadow. I still have that exact sentence saved in an old email. A perfect chameleon performance — mimicking just enough to blend in and keep anyone from seeing who he really was underneath.

Always Wrong, As Long As He Controlled The Narrative

The biggest surprise hit me near the end of our relationship. There was a moment when we were supposed to go on a vacation to Europe together.

I went ahead a bit earlier, and he was supposed to join me later. While he was alone at home, he kept texting me about how awful he felt, like he was going through some kind of hell, saying he didn't want to live anymore. To distract himself, he stayed busy with work around the house.

But when he finally arrived and I came to pick him up at the airport, I was stunned — he looked ten years younger and visibly lighter. My first thought was that he must've released something heavy, like he'd let go of a burden and felt better. I told him outright how great he looked, how different and lighter his energy was. It was remarkable. And surprisingly, he actually seemed happy to hear it.

The first two days of that trip were amazing. I was almost enchanted by who he was being — I even said to him, "Where have you been all these years? I really like this version of you."

You won't believe it, but it didn't last. Just a few days later, he threw it back at me with contempt, saying how terrible it was to hear that, in my eyes, he'd been "absent" all those years. I was speechless. It was like watching someone chase a goal for years, finally reach it, and then completely reject it, complaining that the path to get there wasn't the one they wanted.

Get ready for this, because with a covert narcissist, it's the norm: they always have to be the victim. You're the bad guy if you don't praise him like a child at every turn. But if you do praise him, you're still the bad guy — because you said it wrong, or at the wrong time. With a covert narcissist, you can't win. He has to control the narrative; in that narrative, he must be the victim — even if it costs him his happiness, relationship, or life.

Fantasy Life

Children have incredibly vivid imaginations. They can weave elaborate stories or invent imaginary friends, and they also tend to mix real-life facts with pure fantasy.

Imagination is a beautiful human trait — it's the source of creativity, and those who manage to stay in touch with it into adulthood often lead much richer inner lives. However, in children, because the boundary hasn't yet formed — that is, the structure of the Inner Parent that helps distinguish between external reality and internal experience — facts and fantasy blend together and coexist on the same plane.

For example, a six-year-old watching a scary movie filled with monsters, evil, or violence might scream, cry, run away, hide their face, grab onto the person next to them, or even climb into their lap. Their brain doesn't fully grasp that what's on the screen isn't real, even if they know on some level it's "just a movie."

Children believe everything they see or imagine. That's why it's so important to give them clear information about what's real and what's not — to protect them from developing anxiety disorders later in life.

It's exactly the same with a covert narcissist. Granted, it's no longer about movies or imaginary friends, but the same mechanism moves inward — into the world of self-fantasy — and spills over into relationships and intimacy. If it were just harmless daydreaming that served to inspire novels, that would be one thing. But it turns serious when fantasy becomes a tool for manipulating and misleading others.

A narcissist paints beautiful visions of the future for you — visions carefully tailored using your own values, mirrored back at you. And they do it so convincingly that you believe them. But the narcissist has no grounding in reality because they have no real connection to themselves. They don't know their own preferences, strengths, or limitations — so their promises are, by nature, false. There's no intention or ability to follow through.

These visions may sound entirely realistic — and that's what makes them so deceptive. But they're not meant to be fulfilled. Their sole purpose is to intoxicate you, to win you over, or, once the relationship is underway, to keep you hooked.

> ### 🧠 REALITY CHECK
>
> If you have a vivid imagination and have managed to hold onto it from childhood, that's a gift—it doesn't make you a narcissist. Imagination is beautiful. It expands the boundaries of awareness and fuels creativity and visionary thinking. Healthy people are grounded in reality. Their sense of Self is stable and solid, and their imagination enriches and enlivens their lives.
>
> With a covert narcissist, imagination becomes a tool for escape — a way to flee from the Self and create a false reality, an illusion they live inside. Their core Self is nonexistent, so they constantly adopt new masks to fit into the latest illusion. That's why they're so inconsistent and can lie easily—because fantasy is truth in their inner world. They blur the lines between reality and imagination, turning facts into fiction and fiction into fact.

MEMORIES AND REFLECTIONS FROM THE CHAMELEON MATRIX

When depth becomes threatening, it's easiest to dismiss it as being "out there." What struck me most was how often Maciek accused me of living in "la-la land." I honestly don't know a more grounded, pragmatic person than myself — someone who thrives on facts, thinks in systems, and connects the dots across all areas of life into one coherent whole. I'm direct, practical, and precise.

Yes, it's true that my passion lies in delving deeply into consciousness, exploring the laws that govern it, and perceiving the complex structures that underpin our reality. But that's not some escapist fantasy or spiritual bypass — quite the opposite. I aim to understand reality's deep mechanics and bring that insight back up to the surface, so I can live more consciously and help others do the same. That kind of exploration anchors me more deeply in reality and in myself.

Now I see how threatening that is to a narcissist — someone who would sacrifice their own happiness and entire life just to avoid encountering their hated, buried Self. Fantasy becomes the substitute.

There were times—especially toward the end of the relationship, when I was increasingly exhausted from tiptoeing around his moods—when I'd say during our conversations that thoughts are just thoughts. They only become real when they're turned into action and take physical form. He'd argue with me, insisting that he didn't see it that way at all. Thinking, he claimed, was his strong suit, and for him, his thoughts were reality, not the kind of grounded, tangible world I was describing.

Yet another example of the narcissist's inverted system: fantasy equals reality, and reality is treated like fantasy. No wonder he saw my pragmatism and practicality as "la-la land." And of course, in those moments, he never missed a chance to accuse me of not understanding him or respecting his perspective.

Control

A small child enters the world with zero control over anything. They can't even manage their own physiological needs. The brain gradually develops awareness: first of the body, then of the external world, and eventually of the Self and its inner landscape. The greater this awareness becomes, the better the capacity for self-regulation.

In the early stages, children express this through primitive forms of control: when something doesn't go their way, they cry, scream, or get angry. They also try to manipulate their caregivers into doing what they want. It's all part of the learning agency.

You can watch, for example, a one-year-old who picks up a cookie from their plate but drops it on the floor. The look of fascination on their face when they notice it is priceless. Especially when their mom picks it up and places it back on the plate so the child can eat it, the child, utterly captivated by their new sense of influence—first by making the cookie fall, and then by making mom bend down—grabs it again and throws it to the floor. This time, intentionally. They realize: "I made this happen."

It's a fun game—maybe not so much for the mom who's now bending down for the fortieth time.

This has nothing to do with malice. Children at that age aren't yet capable of that. It's simply a moment of discovering agency and learning the skill of influencing reality, what we eventually call control.

Over time, our sense of agency becomes more refined. It begins to take into account multiple layers of experience and operates in resonance with reality. The highest form of control is actually surrender—complete trust in the life force that creates and moves everything. Primitive control, by contrast, is the imposition of one's will on reality without any awareness beyond personal interest.

A covert narcissist operates entirely through primitive control. They see nothing beyond themselves, and everything must happen on their terms. Even when they do something for you, they don't ask what you might want or need. In the early love-bombing phase, they might act thoughtful, but it's all about manipulation. Later on, they'll come up with their own version of what you "should" need—and you're expected to accept it.

It's like a child making a drawing for their mom and expecting her to gush over it and declare it the most beautiful thing in the world. That's perfectly sweet and developmentally appropriate when a child is learning how to give, receive, and engage in emotional exchange. Even in adult relationships, spontaneous gifts or gestures are lovely, on occasion.

But when it becomes a tool for control—when only what they think is good for you is allowed, and your actual needs or preferences are completely disregarded—that's not love. That's erasure. And it is absolutely not okay.

A small child also needs to check that their caregiver is nearby constantly. Their survival literally depends on adult care, so knowing that an adult is nearby is crucial. That's why a young child left alone in a room where they can't see their mother will often panic. As the child grows older, they begin to tolerate longer periods of being alone, but still need to call out occasionally, just to hear the adult's voice and reassure themselves that someone is there. Eventually, they gain enough independence to stay at preschool for a few hours because they trust that Mom will come back.

A covert narcissist, emotionally frozen at that early developmental stage, needs the same kind of reassurance in relationships. During the initial love-bombing phase, this shows up as obsessive levels of contact—constant texting, calls, checking in, asking, "Are you still here?" or "Do you still want to talk to me?" If there's a silence for even a short while, they spiral into panic, just like a small child terrified that their parent has vanished.

Once you're caught in the chameleon's web and they've gained more control over you, that initial panic about being abandoned gradually morphs into jealousy.

A more insidious and cruel form of control is when they start chipping away at your confidence, pulling you down so subtly and persistently that you begin to lose faith in yourself and feel worthless. At the same time, they plant the belief that your survival depends on them. This happens most often to people who already have weak boundaries, low self-worth, and an ingrained tendency to over-give.

They need to control you and the relationship because they have absolutely no control over their own inner world. As I've written before, they exert that control through emotional provocations, creating chaos, imposing their will, dictating your actions, changing their mind on a whim, playing the victim, sulking over nothing, picking fights, issuing emotional threats, threatening to leave, and using many other manipulative tactics.

 REALITY CHECK

If you struggle with a strong need for control, it doesn't mean you have NPD. That urge can stem from many places: trauma, anxiety, OCD, a lack of trust in life, or patterns learned in childhood. A healthy person, once they notice that their need for control is starting to sabotage their life, will try to do something about it.

A narcissist, on the other hand, absolutely won't. They would rather burn their entire life to the ground than surrender control.

MEMORIES AND REFLECTIONS FROM THE CHAMELEON MATRIX

Every "Yes" Went Unseen, Every "No" Was Unforgivable

Looking back now, I honestly can't believe I made it through all of that without falling apart—and with so much patience. I can see clearly that I owe it to my innate optimism (that sun in my belly that keeps rising), the constant support of EFT, and my deep, unshaken belief in the goodness that people are capable of. I believed in that goodness in Maciek, too. Without that, I think I would've been reduced to a wreck.

From the very beginning—even during our blissful days in Pacifica—I took on the role of the one who went along with things. Maciek made most of the everyday decisions, and I usually just agreed. I didn't have strong preferences, and honestly, I was fine with most things: where we went, what we did, which restaurant, what kind of trip. I'm flexible like that—each option still feels like an adventure with life. Occasionally, I did have a preference, and sometimes even a firm "no" if something crossed a boundary.

That's how it was throughout the entire relationship. If I suggested something simple—like going out for lunch the next day—his typical response would be, "I'll see how I feel tomorrow and let you know." There was never any consideration for the fact that maybe I wanted to go out. It was always his decision. But honestly, those kinds of things didn't bother me much. If we didn't go to the restaurant, it just meant I had two extra hours to do something else. No big loss. And there were hundreds of examples like that.

What's most interesting is this: if I look back and compare how often I said "yes" to something versus the few times I said "no"—because saying "yes" would have meant going against myself—the ratio would probably be 80 to 20. But he only ever saw that 20%. The rest was invisible, as if it had never happened. When I think about how much I adapted myself to accommodate his preferences, it honestly blows my mind.

Don't get me wrong—it's actually a joy for me to do those little things that help create flow rather than tension. I don't need recognition for it. Just being able to create ease for someone I care about is rewarding in itself. But the thing is, a covert narcissist only focuses on what supports their inner narrative—that they're the perpetual victim, and the world is always against them.

So the only moments he seemed to remember were the ones when I firmly disagreed—when I had my own opinion that wasn't up for negotiation, or when I clearly expressed a personal preference. Those were the times when he couldn't control me. And for a narcissist, a lack of control feels like the collapse of their entire world. Almost every time, he'd respond with irritation in his voice: "Just do what I say!"

And almost every time, my answer was either, "You've got to be kidding," or, "If I think it through and it makes sense, then sure—I'll do it. But I'm not doing something just because you told me to."

The Dish Rack – My Personal Power Move

One time, I came home from a trip and found several things in the kitchen rearranged — a couple of canisters for coffee and tea, the water filter, the dish rack, and a few other things. He told me outright that this time things were going to be the way he wanted them because he liked having those items in the new spots, not where they'd been before.

The kitchen had always been my domain — I did the grocery shopping, the cooking, sometimes the baking, and most of the dishwashing. I had everything arranged to be efficient and comfortable, with the whole flow of kitchen work set up in the simplest, most practical way. He had no problem with that for years — he used it and benefited from the setup without complaint.

I just stood there, dumbfounded. I knew exactly what this was—another tactic, either to provoke a fight or to assert dominance. There was no practical reason for moving anything; it was just a demonstration of control. Honestly, the new placement of the water filter and the dish rack was awful—it wasted a ton of counter space, and just filling a glass of water now required more awkward steps. The whole setup was clumsy and inefficient.

The house was big. If he really felt the need to rearrange things, couldn't he have done it in some other area? Did it have to be the one space that was clearly my domain — and the very items I used most often?

After two days, I told him I didn't care about the coffee and tea containers — they could stay where he'd put them; that didn't mess with my flow in the kitchen. But the dish rack and the water filter — no, I couldn't agree to those. They were now right in the way and cluttering the space. Cooking had become awkward and uncomfortable.

He answered, with satisfaction in his voice, "Ha! I knew you'd say that. You're such a control freak. Everything always has to be your way. Nothing can ever go how I want it."

Completely forgetting, of course, that most things were always the way he wanted. I constantly asked what he needed, how he wanted something done, what I should make for dinner, where he'd like to go for a walk or lunch, what time worked best for him, and so on. I never checked up on him — he did as he pleased, went where he wanted, traveled, bought and sold what he pleased, and changed things at will. He had total freedom in his life. I said "OK" to everything, as long as it didn't cross my boundaries.

That's when my arms dropped in defeat — again. It was yet another emotional game, designed to set me up to fail, just so he could turn around and prove how awful I was, and how he was the poor victim. It was done deliberately, with full intention. If he had put even half the energy and creativity into building this relationship as he did into tearing it down, we probably would've been one of the most aligned couples on the planet. I'm only sharing isolated examples here for illustration, but these tactics were regular.

The One And Only In The Entire Universe

Jealousy was also a part of daily life. On one hand, he had no problem openly complimenting other women. When we watched something together, I often heard how beautiful some woman was, how amazing, and how spiritual. Sure, he said similar things to me, too—but only when he was in a good mood. When he wasn't, I'd be compared to an insect, or lumped in with the entire lineage of women, which, according to him, was "bad" by nature.

I wasn't allowed to say anything positive about another man. Actually, it wasn't even about saying something positive—*any* comment at all was already too much. There was this one situation after we moved into our new house. A neighbor named Greg came over to welcome us. I looked at him and froze—he looked exactly like an older version of a guy from my teenage years named Darek, who had once had a crush on me (though nothing ever came of it). I said to Maciek, "Wow, he looks just like Darek! I'm shocked! Darek was a friend from high school who liked me." Big mistake. I can't even tell you how many passive-aggressive, snide remarks I heard about it afterward. For example, when I was trying to hook up the garden hose to the outdoor faucet, Maciek said sarcastically, "Why don't you go ask Greg to help you? I'm sure he'd be thrilled." Unbelievable. A high school friend from Poland, thirty years ago, who was just that—a friend. For me, the resemblance was just a funny coincidence. For Maciek, it became ammunition. How dare I get excited about something that wasn't him…

The Research Team Vs. The Suspicions Committee

There was one thing he kept throwing in my face until the very last day of our relationship. In the second year of our time together, when I began to grow professionally, I joined a consciousness research group for two years. I met with them either as a group or individually with different members, always online. I had a very good rapport with the group director and sometimes had one-on-one sessions with him, too, just like everyone else on the team, to discuss the structures of consciousness. I was absolutely fascinated by the methodology, and what I learned there was invaluable to my work. I even took Maciek with me to visit the director in person once so that he could meet him himself. Another time, we invited the director over to our house.

Maciek absolutely hated him. To me, it was absurd—my relationship with this man was purely professional. But now I understand that it couldn't have been any other way. For a covert narcissist, even the smallest bit of attention given to another man feels like a death sentence to their fragile inner world. Maciek called my collaboration "a betrayal." And as I mentioned, he brought it up again in the very last week of our relationship—over ten years later—right after I discovered he'd been having an online affair with another woman—classic projection and shifting the blame for his own actions.

A covert narcissist keeps playing the same tired play over and over, always with the same script, always casting themselves as the victim. The supporting cast may change, but the roles they assign never do—they're always the villains. No wonder life feels so boring to him when the script inside never evolves.

Name Games

When a child begins to play more consciously—creating worlds, acting out scenes, assigning roles—their imagination runs wild. They give names to dolls and animals and make up new words to describe the parts of their play world. Their mind, still unanchored in reality, simply goes with whatever suits the fantasy in the moment.

With a covert narcissist, something very similar happens, but in the realm of relationships. One distinct pattern is the way they call their partner by all kinds of names—everything but their actual name. It might seem sweet at first, even charming. You might think, "Aww, I must be special if I get my own nickname." But underneath it, there's a subtle erasure happening. The narcissist doesn't want to see the real you. They don't want to meet your authentic Self. These alternate names, no matter how cute or poetic, serve to keep you in a role of their choosing. It's not about intimacy—it's about control through fantasy.

> **REALITY CHECK**
>
> If your partner calls you "babe" or "sweetheart," don't panic—you're not necessarily dating a narcissist. Terms of endearment are perfectly natural in a warm, affectionate relationship.

> The red flag appears when your partner rarely or never uses your actual name. That's when something deeper is at play. Avoiding your name can be a subconscious way of not acknowledging you as a whole, separate person. Saying your name would mean recognizing your individuality—and for a covert narcissist, that's far too intimate.
>
> Using someone's name in a relationship is a quiet yet powerful way of affirming, I see you. In narcissistic dynamics, individuality has no place. You're not a person; you're property—something they believe they own, manipulate, or rename as they please, depending on their mood. You're meant to merge completely with them, lose your boundaries, and let them decide who you are, even down to your name.

MEMORIES AND REFLECTIONS FROM THE CHAMELEON MATRIX

When I dove into professional literature after the relationship ended and learned that narcissists rarely—if ever—use your actual name, I was stunned. For over ten years, not once did Maciek call me by my name in a normal, everyday conversation.

No Name–No Face

A couple of times, he did say "Kasia," but only as a joke—mimicking my friend who used to pronounce it in this exaggerated, funny way. Then there were the reprimands. That's when he used my name in a stern, scolding tone, exactly like a parent disciplining a toddler. The way a mother might snap, "John, if you don't calm down right now, you're going straight to your father!"—even though she usually calls him Johnnie. Maciek would say something like, "Kasia, I am not going to tolerate this!"—his tone sharp, authoritative, like he was talking to a misbehaving child.

Sometimes he'd even call me "Katarzyna Dodd," again mockingly or jokingly. Now, all of that would have been fine—if he had also used my name in everyday, ordinary moments. But I'm not exaggerating when I say he never once used my name in a simple, neutral conversation. Not a single time. If we were just going about our day, talking about dinner or making plans or laughing about something, my name was never part of it. There was always some kind of role-playing or power dynamic attached to it. It's as if using my real name meant seeing me, and that was something he simply wouldn't do.

A Masquerade Of Names

Here's a list of the "names" Maciek gave me throughout our relationship. I'm sharing them in the original English, since that's how they were used:

Lover, PG (Polish Girl), Monk, Monkey, Roommate, Mermaid (used in poems), Alien, Alien Nation, Woman, Stranger, Amber Eye, Friend, Witch, Polish Witch, Cowboy Girl, Slavic Queen—and probably a few more I've forgotten by now. There were also some negative ones, but let's skip those here.

A person with NPD lives inside an illusion of their own mind, and they assign names to people based on the roles those people are meant to play in their fantasy script. The name has to match the scene.

Interestingly, he didn't want to be called by his real name, either. He changed it to something that sounded different in another language, and that's how he expected to be addressed. One time, I slipped and called him by the name his mother used when he was a child, and I genuinely thought he was going to incinerate me on the spot. I never dared do it again. And that, honestly, explains a lot.

Vacation That's Anything But

Going on vacation with a small child means the entire trip revolves around them. You can't just leave them to do your own thing — someone has to stay with them, or you need to arrange care. Your mind never really relaxes;

you're constantly checking in, wondering if everything's okay. Activities are planned around their needs and rhythms. While vacations with kids can be exhausting and full of logistics, many parents look back on those moments with fondness. Especially when they see their child laughing and squealing with joy as they run from the waves crashing at the shore.

Going on vacation with a covert narcissist feels remarkably similar, only much less joyful. The whole trip revolves around them. Constant complaints, nothing is ever quite right. The people are rude, the service is lacking, this is boring, that's beneath them, and everything could have been better if it had been done their way. Arguments are a given. And God forbid you dare to actually enjoy yourself. They'll shut it down when you show real happiness, excitement, or peace. Instantly.

 REALITY CHECK

Don't stress too much if you've ever had a vacation like this with your partner – it doesn't automatically mean he's a narcissist. Sometimes people go through rough patches or aren't feeling well, and a trip doesn't turn out how you hoped.

As always, it's the pattern that matters, not a one-time event. With a covert narcissist, once the love-bombing phase is over, every trip becomes a test of endurance. You won't come back rested, because your energy will be entirely consumed by their moods, their needs, and the latest installment of their emotional drama.

MEMORIES AND REFLECTIONS FROM THE CHAMELEON MATRIX

Vacation From Hell

You could say that trips with Maciek were "exotic"—but not in a good way. They weren't from this world because, at times, they felt like they came straight from hell.

The first year, every trip was amazing. I loved traveling with him—wherever we went, I came back with great memories. But the vacations from hell began the moment the cycle shifted into the devaluation phase. From that point on, every single trip was filled with tension, complaints, and arguments over the most ridiculous things. Twice, he threw such a dramatic tantrum that he claimed he was buying a ticket home and leaving immediately. He never actually did, because, of course, that was never the point. The point was control. And getting my full attention.

Our last trip to Poland, in the final year of the relationship, was probably the worst. We had planned a short visit to the seaside to find a place we liked enough to return to from time to time for longer stays. Our main base was Kraków, where I'm from. From there, we took a few days to explore the Baltic coast.

Maciek wanted to visit the Hel Peninsula, so we took the ferry over. On the way, we grabbed coffee and some pastries—they were delicious. As we were walking, I asked him if he liked it here and whether he could see himself spending more time in this place one day. He snapped. With an irritated tone, he said it was too early in the morning to ask him things like that, that I was pressuring him for an answer he didn't have, and just like that, he launched into an argument.

We got on the ferry. I stood by the railing, taking in the view. He went to the opposite end and sat on a bench alone. When we arrived in Hel, still in complete silence, we found a restaurant and sat down for lunch. That's when it started. He began unloading all his frustration—how miserable he was, how he couldn't take it anymore, a full-blown tirade of complaints and blame. Then came the climax: he said that once we got back to Kraków, he was buying a ticket back to the States. Because he wasn't going to spend his vacation "in this kind of atmosphere."

I didn't let myself get pulled into it—I can't even tell you how exhausted I was from this constant drama, invented out of thin air just to ruin anything remotely positive. Sure, I responded, but it was always along the lines of, "Okay, do what you need to do."

After lunch, we went down to the beach. That's when he fell apart. It usually happens like this—when you stay grounded in your own boundaries, when you don't step into the drama or take on the role he's casting for you, when you refuse to feed that emotional black hole by dragging yourself down in the process, the narcissist begins to unravel. He cried, sobbed, and said how much he hated himself. As usual, I sat beside him in silence, holding his hand. Then he got up, ordered a coffee from a beach kiosk, and just like that, everything was fine again. The only downside? He had a nightmare memory of our trip to Hel. Needless to say, he never bought that plane ticket to the States.

Even My Dad Fell For It

A week later, back in Kraków, we visited my dad. He was incredibly warm and accepting toward Maciek, and Maciek clearly felt safe in his presence. When we returned to the apartment that evening, Maciek wrote a letter to my dad. Since he wrote it in English, he asked me to read it to my dad after Maciek had flown back to the States—and not to open it until then. Maciek was scheduled to leave a few days before I did, so I kept my word.

The day after Maciek left, I went over to my dad's place and brought the letter with me. I opened it and began to read it aloud. It was filled with praise and gratitude, thanking my dad for raising such an incredible daughter and acknowledging that both he and my mom had done an amazing job. He wrote that being with me was the greatest privilege of his life, that he would do everything to be the best partner I could possibly have, that he would support me always and help me in everything, and on and on it went.

Maybe you're thinking, "Wow, something must have shifted in him during that meltdown on Hel. Maybe he finally came back to the center." If that thought crossed your mind, welcome to the False Hope Club.

My dad, of course, was beaming with pride, nearly choking up as I read. He had no idea—and neither did I at the time—that he had just been love-bombed by a covert narcissist—the same man who, just six months later, would start an online affair with another woman.

Next Episode Of The Soap Opera

A year later—after we had already broken up—I found myself back in Kraków, sitting on the exact same stool in my dad's kitchen where I had read him that letter. And at that very moment, while I was sitting there in that quiet kitchen, Maciek was parading his new conquest around Kraków (!). He took her to all the places I had once shown him—where I grew up, where I used to go to concerts, where I sang in the choir, and where our favorite architecture and historic sites were. Kraków was the only city in Poland he knew even remotely well, and only because it was my hometown and we had spent quite a bit of time there together. Now, there he was, playing the charming tour guide for another woman, posing as some kind of cultural insider. I was sitting at the kitchen table with my dad, holding that same letter in my hands.

My dad was so disgusted he nearly spat. He said no man had ever treated him with such deceit and disrespect. Of course, it hit him twice as hard—because it was his daughter who had been used. I was furious, too, but not because of what was happening at that exact moment. What enraged me was that Maciek had dragged my father into his web of lies. A covert narcissist has no honor. Everything and everyone is just a resource to be used in the service of the illusion. That was just one example of a vacation trip straight to hell. I could write a whole book on them.

The Mole Cricket

It wasn't just the big blowups that chipped away at the relationship—it was also the constant stream of little things, like a mole cricket silently gnawing at the roots. For example, we boarded a train from Kraków to the seaside. I had the window seat, and he had the aisle—just the way he liked it. I always asked him which seat he preferred when booking the tickets.

We sat down, and the train pulled away. After a few minutes, he noticed the empty seats across the aisle and suddenly decided he wanted a window seat. So he got up and moved. A moment later, he gestured for me to switch seats, too. I told him I was staying where I was—I preferred the window. Usually, I would've just switched. But after ten years of constantly bending to what he wanted, I decided to do what I wanted at that moment.

Of course, the passive-aggressive remarks came soon after. "What kind of vacation is this if we're not even sitting together on the train?" The blame was on me because I didn't switch seats; I had supposedly ruined the trip and rejected him.

If he really cared about sitting together, holding hands on the train, he could've stayed in his original seat. But that was never the point. It wasn't about connection. It was about controlling the narrative. If you don't go along with it, you're the enemy.

You might think it's just small stuff. But that's exactly what covert narcissism is. It's not the big, dramatic moments — it's the hundreds of tiny things that happen every week. It's like water slowly dripping on stone. One drop doesn't do anything. However, if it continues to hit the same spot repeatedly for years, it will eventually carve a hole. It can even crack the rock open.

That's why a relationship with a covert narcissist can last for years. Because those little things, on their own, are never quite enough to leave. And in between, there are good stretches. Only when you reach the point of total exhaustion — or something truly outrageous happens — can you finally say, "Enough."

Sulking And Silence

Young children often go silent when they feel hurt, scared, or frustrated. This quiet protest can show up after being told "no," after a boundary is set, or even when a need goes unnoticed. A child doesn't yet have the language for their emotions, so silence becomes their only way to express what's going on inside—an unspoken plea saying, "see me, notice that something's happening in me." At this age, sulking isn't manipulation. It's a defense mechanism—a way to cope with inner chaos they can't yet name. A child's silence isn't empty—it's full of emotion. Underneath that withdrawal might be anger, disappointment, fear of losing connection, or even a test: "Will you still love me if I pull away?" The child doesn't know how to come back into contact—they're waiting to be "found" by the adult.

A covert narcissist operates in the same emotional pattern. When overwhelmed by feelings, they cut themselves off. The only difference is that they do it consciously, and they do it to manipulate and control the relationship. As an adult, they have every resource available to handle their emotional states, but they won't make any effort to do so. Instead, they'll punish you with silence. They'll display their "hurt feelings" and wait for you to come apologize or somehow soothe them. They want to be "found" like a child does. But in adults, this behavior is no longer innocent—they aren't helpless like children. They could choose to talk, meditate, walk, clear their head, and ask for support—anything.

But instead, they'll turn their discomfort into emotional blackmail, making sure you feel responsible for their pain. So when you try to "find" them, you're really giving in to their power play.

> **REALITY CHECK**
>
> In any relationship, there are sometimes what we call "silent days." If you've experienced something like that, it doesn't automatically mean you're in a relationship with a narcissist. Most often, when people argue, both retreat into their own emotional corners and just need a break from each other. Sometimes, if they're more emotionally aware, they do this intentionally–to pause communication so they don't make things worse, and come back to talk when they've calmed down. In both cases, both people usually feel uncomfortable about the silence and are willing to talk it through later.
>
> In a relationship with a covert narcissist, however, silence is used as a form of punishment and control. They deliberately withdraw their attention to punish you. They don't explain anything, they disappear or ignore you, because they want you to feel like the "bad one" who caused harm. It's a way to create a sense of threat around losing the relationship. And don't expect them to want to talk about it later. They won't.

MEMORIES AND REFLECTIONS FROM THE CHAMELEON MATRIX

He Changed His Face—Literally

I got the silent treatment for the first time in the second month after moving in with him, in Pacifica. I don't think I'll ever forget it—partly because it was the first time anyone had ever treated me like that, and partly because something happened during that moment that felt almost surreal.

It was still the "butterflies in the stomach" phase—just a month had passed since I'd moved in. Everything had been truly great. One evening, we were sitting in the living room. It was dimly lit, just a bedside lamp glowing softly. He was in the armchair, and I was sitting across the room on the couch. We were talking about something. I was looking at his face, and suddenly… something changed.

It looked like a special effect from a sci-fi movie. His face shifted—its shape, features, everything distorted unnaturally, as if made of rubber. For a few seconds, it was the face of someone else entirely. Then, just as quickly, it contorted again and turned back into Maciek's face.

It genuinely scared me. I remember curling up, pulling my legs under me, and sinking deeper into the couch. I told him what I'd just seen, and he responded, "I am a shapeshifter." That answer didn't seem all that strange at the time—we'd been talking a lot about energy, shamanism, Native American traditions, and various spiritual concepts. I even thought for a second that maybe he had some kind of gift in that realm. But I couldn't shake the feeling. Whatever had just happened had hit me deep—it lodged in my body and wouldn't let go.

A moment later, he walked over and sat beside me on the couch. I instinctively pulled back even farther. He reached out, trying to touch me, and asked what was going on—my whole body tensed, sinking even deeper into the cushions. At that, he got annoyed, stood up, and went to the bedroom to sleep.

Operation: The Invisible Woman

As I always did, I got up early in the morning and went to the living room. I made some coffee, read a little, and watched something. He got up later—I could hear him getting ready. I was sitting at the table when the bedroom door opened, and he walked out. I looked at him and was about to say "hey," but he walked right past me, head held high, didn't even glance in my direction, as if I were invisible, said nothing, and left. I heard the car start a moment later, and he drove off. He was gone for over half the day.

When he came back, he acted like nothing had happened—talked normally, didn't say a single word about the cold, theatrical way he had ignored me that morning, as if I hadn't even been there.

I couldn't wrap my head around how someone could treat a loved one like that, especially when nothing had even happened. Of course, now I understand: in his mind, my reaction the night before was rejection, and rejection calls for punishment. It didn't matter at all that I'd been scared—it was only his bruised ego that counted—and bruised by what, exactly…?

Warning: Identity May Distort At Any Time

Eleven years later, when I finally dove into the literature on narcissism, I came across something that stopped me in my tracks: in everyday language, covert narcissists are often referred to as shapeshifters! That's because they don't have a true inner Self or a stable identity, so they constantly shift who they are, what they do, where they live, and how they look. They borrow identities from others and try them on like costumes. If only my logical brain had known this back then…

To this day, I still don't fully understand what happened in that moment. I explain it now as a powerful intuitive flash that goes beyond the logical mind, drawing information from layers we don't fully grasp and delivering it in an unconventional way. I just didn't know how to interpret it at the time.

What's certain is: he wasn't lying. That one statement—"I am a shapeshifter"—was probably the most accurate thing he ever said. If only everything else he said had been as honest and spot-on.

The Mirror Of Silence

Over the next ten years, the silent treatment would show up from time to time. But when it came to this particular tactic, I was unshakable. Not once did I go in to pacify him. Not once did I take the bait. For me, it was a blatant violation of my boundaries. So I held up a faithful mirror. If he didn't speak, I didn't speak. If he holed up in a separate room for three days, I simply stayed in my own space and quietly did my thing. I had zero interest in "finding" him. Emotional blackmail is something I don't tolerate. If there's a problem, I can talk it through. I can compromise when needed. But these kinds of games? Absolutely not. So it was always he who ended the silence.

Toward the end of the relationship, he once told me with a kind of pride that maybe he was finally improving emotionally. He said he didn't get as swept up in things anymore, because where he used to stay silent for days, now he just needed ten minutes in another room before it passed. This is exactly where the hooks are. A statement like that, so seemingly self-aware, really gives you hope that maybe he's finally getting better. Only to realize later that it was just a string of borrowed words, lifted from somewhere and designed to match your values. The reality? Still the same. The silent treatment faded because it lost its power—no one else in the house wanted to play that game anymore. So I encourage you: log out of every emotional game.

There are many more traits typical of young children that show up in covert narcissists in almost exactly the same form. The difference is that, in a child, these behaviors are simply part of growing up—things they eventually outgrow. In an adult, they become dysfunctions that don't go away. I hope I've given you enough examples to help you see the full picture.

CHAPTER 8

NO MAN'S LAND BETWEEN 'I' AND 'WE'

Continuing the look at narcissistic identity disturbance through the lens of early childhood development, it's worth highlighting a critical developmental milestone that typically occurs around the age of two. Margaret Mahler and Otto Kernberg explored this concept.

The Birth Of Psychological Separateness

When a child is born, they finally achieve physical separation—they're no longer physically connected to the mother. But on a psychological level, that separateness doesn't yet exist. The brain isn't developed enough to register the child as a separate being. In their early experience, they're still fused with the mother—there's no "me" and "you," just an undivided "us."

It's as if you were sitting next to someone and could feel their arm as if it were your own, like when they moved, it felt like you were the one moving.

It's only around the age of two that a child starts to notice a crack in their perception—and suddenly realizes, with amazement, that the "big object" in front of them (a.k.a. mom) is actually something separate. This is a monumental shift in the child's inner world, opening the door to a whole new level of independence. The child begins to pull away more and more—running off, climbing on furniture—and they're usually delighted by it. Discovering that kind of power is exhilarating.

The Conflict: I Want To Be Close, I Want To Be Free

But this breakthrough comes with an intense inner conflict. On one hand, the child is fueled by their newfound power and drive for independence. On the other hand, their survival still completely depends on their mother or other adults. Internally, the child is in a borderline state. They want freedom, yet they also need dependence. They haven't yet learned how to hold both at the same time. They swing from one to the other.

At this stage, a child also begins to form a basic understanding of the new situation. When they aren't yet able to regulate their own freedom—and their mother steps in to do it for them, setting boundaries, stopping them from running off, or saying "no" to something—the child begins to see the mother as "bad." But when she allows them to do something, or when they need closeness and she welcomes them, then she's "good."

It's absolutely critical that the child navigates this developmental conflict in a healthy manner. The brain needs to learn that mom is both "good" and "bad" at the same time. This is how the mind begins to integrate extremes into a whole. So when the child separates—physically or emotionally—it's essential that they still feel the mother's presence. That way, they get to be in their own independent power while also feeling safe, knowing there's still a connection. This teaches them that being yourself, making decisions, trusting your instincts, and following your ideas is not only allowed but also safe.

When a child begins to separate, but the mother isn't emotionally present, they fall into a kind of helpless panic. They want to be independent, but they're still not capable of it—they need to rely on their mother to survive. So internally, they abandon themselves in order to stay connected and safe. Later in life, this can manifest as a fear of being oneself or a deep resistance to expressing one's true Self.

If the mother punishes the child for separating—for example, if she's displeased by it or finds it inconvenient—the child starts to feel guilty for doing things their own way. Again, they abandon themselves on the inside, choosing to please the mother in order to survive. This becomes the foundation for deep self-rejection, and sometimes even self-hatred. The child may grow up believing they don't deserve to be who they are, or that being themselves makes them a bad person.

In both of these cases, the child never learns how to truly be with themselves. So they seek relationships to fill the void, and yet—even in a relationship—they still feel profoundly alone.

When Separation Hurts – A Stalled Development

A child's brain is faced with quite a riddle. When they separate from their mother, they still crave closeness. And when they're close to her, they feel the need to pull away.

If this separation conflict isn't resolved in a healthy way—if the two extremes don't become integrated—the system remains split, and emotional development stalls. This developmental arrest is characteristic of both borderline personality disorder and narcissism.

This split is particularly evident in close relationships. A person with this kind of wound feels lonely, unfulfilled, anxious, and empty when they're alone, desperate for connection and emotional dependence. But once in a relationship, they merge with the other person and begin to sabotage the bond, driven by an equally intense craving for independence. This is the mark of a split psyche and an unintegrated personality.

When the personality is sufficiently integrated, a person can be in a relationship—that is, in a certain kind of emotional dependence—while still maintaining their inner independence and personal boundaries. Both poles—dependent and independent— can coexist in the same emotional space. There are no wild swings from one extreme to the other, no "I love you–I hate you" cycles. The brain can perceive the partner as a whole person— someone with whom you're sometimes emotionally close and sometimes emotionally separate.

Of course, this is a simplified explanation. For a full-blown personality disorder to develop, more factors are involved than just an unresolved separation conflict at age two. Still, this particular moment is critically important in personality development—it marks the birth of inner independence, and often shapes the trajectory of a person's entire emotional life.

In people with NPD, the internal split is obvious and severe. I have a sense—and I'm not sure if this is objectively true, it's just my impression—that the split in narcissism runs even deeper than in borderline personality disorder. With BPD, emotions are more on the surface—raw, intense, dramatic—because despite the fragmentation, there's still some thread of connection to the Self.

In narcissism, it often feels like that thread is gone. The Inner Parent treats the Inner Child with cold hatred, as if they want nothing to do with it. Inside, there's just… emptiness.

An Adult Without Boundaries

When you're in a relationship with a covert narcissist, you're on a constant emotional roller coaster. One moment you're close, needed, loved, and good—and the next, they're pulling away, talking about leaving, because now you're bad. One day, they'll tell you that you're the only person in the world who truly understands and supports them—and then, flip, they're in the opposite extreme, seeing you as someone who tries to control them, clip their wings, hurt them, and completely miss the mark.

This cycle doesn't end, and it doesn't change, because their emotional system is stuck at the developmental stage of a two-year-old in the middle of a separation conflict. Good mommy—bad mommy. I want closeness—I want independence.

Shame That Must Not Be Felt

Another developmental theory worth mentioning here is Freud's theory of psychosexual development. What's fascinating is that in narcissism, the one emotion that absolutely cannot be processed or integrated is shame. For a covert narcissist, this also includes guilt.

In Freud's[3] classic model, the anal stage occurs between roughly 18 months and 3 years of age. This is when the child begins learning to control their bodily functions—and with that, their expression, sense of control, and personal boundaries. It's also a stage marked by an intense struggle between autonomy and dependence.

To sum it up briefly, here's what happens during this stage:

- The anus becomes the primary erogenous zone, and the child starts consciously controlling their elimination.
- It's the first real confrontation with external expectations—for example, during toilet training.
- Key elements start to emerge: autonomy, agency, control, ambivalence, and defiance.

What happens when this developmental stage doesn't unfold properly?

Pathological shame becomes ingrained. When a child is shamed for their body, for going to the bathroom, for their emotions or impulses, it can lead to what's known as core shame—a deep sense that "something is wrong with me," rather than "I did something wrong."

This creates a split between the need for control and the ability to express oneself. As an adult, this may show up as intense anxiety around losing control—emotionally, physically, or in relationships. It can also manifest as compulsive or controlling behaviors, or body-based habits like perfectionism or obsessive rituals. Boundaries become distorted, and the very act of "letting anything go" becomes difficult.

For a two-year-old learning how to control their body and emotions during the anal phase, any act of giving—whether it's a bowel movement, anger, or a need—can feel like a risky form of exposure. Later on, this may show up as difficulty giving of oneself in relationships, discomfort with

---

[3] Sigmund Freud (1856–1939) – Austrian neurologist and founder of psychoanalysis. His theories on psychosexual development, the unconscious mind, and defense mechanisms had a profound and lasting impact on the fields of psychology and psychiatry.

sexual openness, avoidance of emotional honesty, or resistance to receiving help. All of these can feel like revealing something "dirty."

Since the body stores the memory of the anal phase, this may manifest physically as digestive issues, tightness in the lower belly and lower back, difficulty letting go (both literally and metaphorically), or over-control of bodily functions and emotional release.

Projection-Dumping Toxic Waste At Someone Else's Expense

People with NPD don't process shame—they disown it, deny it, and project it onto others. They never learned that you can make mistakes and still be worthy of love. Where a healthy psyche transforms guilt into responsibility, a narcissist escapes into attack, control, or victimhood. Each of these roles is just a mask—a desperate attempt to distance themselves from a deep sense of humiliation that was never spoken aloud but has been stored in the body since they were too young to understand it.

In a relationship, this unprocessed "emotional waste"—when it can no longer be contained—must be dumped on someone else. Instead of saying "this is mine," they say "this is yours." This is how narcissistic projection works: a psychic purge at someone else's expense. But every emotion that isn't consciously owned and processed multiplies like mold in a sealed jar.

MEMORIES AND REFLECTIONS FROM THE CHAMELEON MATRIX
Foundations On Shifting Sand

Around the second year of living in the woods in Westmont, I began to realize that what was happening with Maciek wasn't just about a bad day, a rough season, or simple exhaustion. The most striking pattern was the emotional whiplash—going from "I love you" to "I hate you" in a flash. The extremes were jarring. It took only a little over a year to realize that these were not isolated incidents triggered by specific events. They were a constant pattern.

For someone with NPD, anything new and still unknown—with all its qualities yet to be discovered—exists inside a romanticized fantasy. That fantasy allows them to project whatever they want onto the situation, object, or person. However, as reality starts to reveal itself—as the thing or person becomes real and exposes aspects that no longer fit the fantasy—they flip to the opposite extreme: devaluation and rejection.

I saw this clearly for the first time when we moved to Westmont. After our first year of bliss, we made a big move—relocating and buying a house in the woods. That new chapter was intoxicating for him: full of potential and novelty.

Blinders On, For Real

It took us two days to drive from Pacifica to Westmont. Maciek came in his pickup with a large trailer, and I drove separately with the dog. When we finally arrived in Westmont, we stopped at a restaurant in town to grab something to eat. While we waited for our meal, we chatted. Maciek said everything here had a different vibe—something about it was amazing, almost perfect. Nothing bothered him here the way it did in Pacifica. That was the first time I raised an eyebrow, because my brain was struggling to make sense of what I was hearing.

Sure, the air was different, the atmosphere had its own feel—but everything else was pretty much the same. The people looked just like in Pacifica. The restaurant we were in actually looked like it had a lower standard than the ones there. And several other things Maciek had constantly complained about back in Pacifica? They were present here too. So I asked, just to be sure, about those exact things that used to irritate him—didn't he see them here? And he said no, not at all, none of it bothered him. Everything felt nearly perfect.

I remember feeling relieved, like the move was a great decision. Sigh. That was just my ignorance talking. In the years that followed, I observed the same pattern repeating itself over and over again: jumping from one extreme to the other.

After some time, Westmont became a place he absolutely loathed. The way he spoke about it practically oozed venom—you could almost feel the hatred seeping through his skin. He hated everything: the property, the weather, the people.

When he eventually moved to Deserta and we were still talking on the phone for a few months, he was completely enchanted by it at first, constantly comparing it to Westmont. He'd gush about how polite everyone was—"Yes, sir! No, sir!"—how calm the people seemed, how beautiful the sky was, the endless sunshine, the wide-open spaces—it was paradise. Knowing the pattern by then, I said, "I wonder how long before it all changes and it's not so wonderful anymore." As usual, he bristled, rejected the truth, and clung tightly to the fantasy. It didn't take long.

All it took was someone being late to a meeting, working too slowly, not looking him straight in the eye, messing up a service, or simply walking down the street looking dirty, and the fantasy came crashing down from its pedestal straight onto the pavement. After that, everything was hated. The whole "Yes, sir! No, sir!" charm went right out the window.

Plow Horse, Not A Mustang

This is the typical pattern of someone with NPD: a perfect illusion that brings euphoria—a fresh, unblemished fantasy about something new that hasn't yet been "tainted" by the reality of facts. Then, reality starts to seep in—details that don't fit the idealized image—and that becomes threatening, because they can't emotionally process the mismatch. So the defense mechanism kicks in: growing devaluation, which eventually turns into such intense hatred that escape is the only option. And then the cycle restarts: new illusion, euphoria, and so on.

It applies to everything—romantic relationships, friendships, places, endeavors, and projects.

A narcissist, lacking any grounding in themselves or a stable sense of Self, can't be grounded in reality either. That's why they live in fantasy—and the moment reality begins to surface, they must escape into a new illusion. If they kept that to themselves and lived in isolation, it might not be such a big deal. But when they start pulling others into their delusions and using them like puppets in their private theater—lying straight to their faces—it becomes a dirty game.

The problem is, a narcissist doesn't know how to process or release their internal waste. So all they can do is wrap it in shiny foil—and serve it up as "chocolates with a surprise filling."

The Loud Silent Whisper

I remember it as if it were yesterday. It must have been around the third month of our honeymoon phase in Pacifica. I said to him, "You know, I had this strange feeling today that made me uneasy—that one day you might get bored with me." He quickly denied it, reassuring me profusely.

But I remember that moment with absolute clarity: where we were, what time of day it was, what we were wearing, where I was standing, where he was sitting. It must have been one of those moments that leaves an imprint—maybe a whisper from my higher Self that sees in all directions, forward and backward, or perhaps a nudge from the future me trying to send a message back through time.

Today I know not only to hear such a whisper, but to follow it. Each of us has that quiet intuition that offers hidden truths as if served on a silver platter. Yet we often don't listen to it, because the loud and colorful visions driven by our dreams completely drown it out. It's only later, when we face the consequences of our choices, that we realize our intuition knew all along.

The Leaky Container: Always Empty

There was another moment—this one in Westmont, maybe in our third year of living in the woods—when I seriously began to suspect that Maciek had a personality disorder. At the time, I thought it might be borderline, because the swings from "I love you" to "I hate you" were straight out of a textbook.

It took just the tiniest thing—barely the size of a speck—that he interpreted as "rejection," and suddenly our life would shift into another dimension, or it would be "over." The reactions were wildly disproportionate to reality.

One day, I drew it all out—the mechanics of it, I mean. I even made some silly little sketches to illustrate that critical moment of separation crisis around the age of two. I sat down with Maciek at the table and said I wanted to share something with him that I felt might be going on. I told him that maybe if he saw it visually, it would help things click into place. He listened very attentively, and by the end, he was beaming with absolute delight. He said everything suddenly made sense, that it was such a relief to realize he wasn't going crazy—there was actually an explanation for it. He looked blissful, and I was over the moon that he felt so understood.

But because I never intended to be his therapist or his savior, I gently suggested that maybe he could talk to someone about it or read more, because this kind of thing doesn't just go away on its own. I could share an observation, sure, but real work needed to be done with someone outside the relationship. My role could only ever be to offer support in the process. He was so happy in that moment that he even seemed open to the idea.

The Hunger For Attention Knows No Fullness

Alongside my joy at how good he felt, there was this quiet feeling deep inside me, and a thought that whispered: "This happiness isn't about some deep realization. He's happy because his sucking hole just got filled with my attention."

Now I see how prophetic that thought really was. A few days later, the void emptied again, and he was back to being a walking aggressor. The whole "borderline" project? Gone in a puff of dust—he dropped it and moved on without a trace.

Everything, and I mean everything, in Maciek's world seemed to follow the same pattern: when the sucking hole was filled—with someone's attention or the thrill of something new—he'd feel euphoric, happy. But when the void went empty, when no one was feeding it, or the illusion of newness faded, he'd turn to hate. Hate for the world, for me, for life itself.

And reality? It sat untouched somewhere in between.

CHAPTER 9

ARMAGEDDON – THE FINAL ACT IN THE THEATER OF ILLUSION

The last four months of the relationship were the most emotionally intense time of my life. So much happened, and it reached such deep layers of awareness, that now, as I sit in a comfortable chair and look back, it almost feels unbelievable.

Still Together

Finger On The Map, Chaos In The Heart

After we returned from vacation—the same one where Maciek wrote that letter to my dad—we started discussing selling the house in Deserta and moving to the state of Palmara. The decision to move to Palmara came after a real emotional ordeal for me. At first, it was his idea, and I wasn't entirely convinced. Then, once I warmed up to it and started getting on board, he suddenly changed course and said no—Savanash would be better. He pushed and pressured me until finally I said, 'OK.' So I shifted gears, researched Savanash, looked up towns, neighborhoods, houses, and prices. Just as I started settling into that idea and shaping plans around it, he flipped again—nope, we were going back to Palmara.

Inside me, the resistance was building. I was getting fed up with the emotional whiplash, so I started confronting him about it. That's when the gaslighting kicked in: he claimed he never said those things, or if he did, so what? He had every right to change his mind—yesterday was yesterday, and today is today. And my refusal to go along with it? That was just my need to control him. As usual, my preferences didn't matter, because why would they? Once again, there was no grounding in reality—only emotional manipulation designed to create chaos.

In the end, it was Palmara. We listed the house with a realtor and started packing. When it came to logistics, Maciek was incredibly efficient—he handled the packing like a pro. We got the house ready to sell, and he did about 80% of the work.

In the middle of all that, Maciek announced that he had an opportunity to spend a year in solitude—at someone's unoccupied house out in the middle of nowhere—where he could focus on himself, recharge, return to meditation, and so on. He was already making plans and arrangements. The idea was that once we got to Palmara and settled in, he'd leave me there and head off on his own for a year. There was no real conversation about it, no consideration for our life together. He wanted it, and that was that. I was expected to adjust. I didn't even bother trying to open the discussion—whatever I said would've been twisted into me clipping his wings or trapping him. So I said, "OK." It was a clear sign that Exodus 2.0 was already underway.

Once most of our belongings were packed, the house was listed with a realtor, and we'd already chosen the area in Palmara where we'd start looking for a new place, Maciek came home from the hardware store one day with an announcement. He told me he'd had a long conversation with a clerk there, and the guy had raved so much about the state of Maryline that Maciek had decided we were moving there instead. I thought I was going to explode.

Some random man's opinion at a store mattered more—not just more than our shared plans, but more than a conversation with me, his partner of ten years. He simply decided. His stubbornness and need for control were so absolute, so impossible to reason with, that in the end, once again, I had no choice but to say "OK."

It was December. The chaos unfolding around us felt like part of a dissolving old reality. I recall that month as being filled with strange internal states—an unmistakable sense that a significant chapter was coming to a close. But it didn't feel like just any life phase, like "ending our time in Deserta and starting fresh in Palmara." No. It felt like something much bigger. As if an entire era of my life, stretching all the way back to birth, was drawing to a close. In its place, something entirely new was beginning to unfold.

I could literally see it in my inner space—like walking from the center of a circle to its outer edge, feeling myself arrive right at the border, about to cross over. Just beyond that edge, a new circle was waiting—a whole new dimension. I truly believed Palmara would be our new beginning—a fresh life together, on a higher frequency. I was certain that something old was coming to an end. And yes, something new did begin, filled with a different energy and vibration. Just not with Maciek. But I'm getting ahead of myself.

The house sold beautifully, and we hit the road. We arrived in Maryline, and it was the proverbial Sodom and Gomorrah. The vibe was so awful that neither of us had to say a word. We both just knew—this wasn't it. We stayed a few days and then went where? To Palmara, of course, wasting time, money, and energy on that ridiculous detour. Three days later, we found a house in Palmara and made an offer.

Deep down, I knew this was my final attempt. I told myself: if this move—this change of scenery, the warm weather, the easy lifestyle, the proximity to his old friends from years ago—if all of that didn't breathe life back into this relationship, I was done. The plan was to buy the house in Palmara and then use the remaining money from selling our previous home to rent an apartment in Poland. Maciek had always loved Europe and wanted to travel around. The idea was to live six months here, six months there. I even started working on the documents he'd need for residency in Poland.

Everything was tailored to him, so he wouldn't have to do physical labor anymore and could live the way he wanted—traveling. I could make it work because with the kind of job I have, I can work from anywhere. And I do like to move around, too.

The Dream Home: Anywhere, As Long As It's Uphill

Back when we were still deciding where to move, I got an earful again. After years of hearing him complain about how hard physical labor was and how his body was ruined (by his own doing, despite my repeated pleas for him to stop), my goal became to help us shift into a lifestyle that wouldn't keep destroying him. He told me—accusingly—that he was done with houses and all the work they required, that he wanted an easier life.

Honestly, I feel perfectly fine in a regular apartment. I don't need a house. That would have been the simplest and most lightweight option. But for him, that was absolutely unacceptable. He had to have a house.

So I started suggesting that maybe we should consider a newly built house—something move-in ready, with nothing to fix or renovate. His response? That I didn't appreciate him enough. Because for him, older homes that needed work weren't a problem at all. Right. Except that they were ruining his health, and he constantly complained about how much he hated it. But that didn't matter—end of discussion. I just didn't appreciate him.

When I then proposed we look at a used home, but something smaller, without acres of land and a little closer to civilization, I was accused of thinking only about myself—and not about him at all—because he needed to live far away from people and have lots of space. OK… but that lifestyle was precisely what had wrecked his body. Didn't matter. Suddenly, I was the selfish one who always thought of herself, and he—according to him—did nothing but make sacrifices to fulfill my wishes.

With a covert narcissist, there is no such thing as a conversation. The gaslighting is masterful. They'll steer every discussion into the same endless loop, and the center of that loop is always the same: they are the victim, and you are the abuser. Everything must orbit around that narrative. Rational thought and facts aren't even allowed in the room.

> *A conversation with a covert narcissist has one purpose: to throw you off balance and keep you disoriented.*

The house we found in Palmara struck a perfect balance. It was close to town, nestled in a charming neighborhood, surrounded by lush greenery that offered privacy from neighbors, with a thick patch of forest right behind it. The place gave a real sense of seclusion, yet had every modern convenience. Each lot in the area was generously sized, so there was no feeling of crowding.

Before He Even Signed The Papers, He Was Already Living In A Different Reality

Let's rewind for a moment to the time just after we arrived in Palmara, when we had signed the preliminary agreement to purchase the house and were waiting a few weeks for the closing and for the previous owner to move out. That's when the final phase of the "apocalypse" began.

We rented a small apartment in a nearby town for the interim. I had the sense that Maciek was feeling good in Palmara—the weather was beautiful, he was reconnecting with old friends, writing poetry, and finally taking a break from the constant physical labor he always imposed on himself. We talked a lot during that time, often about deep and meaningful things, including what we wanted going forward.

The whole idea of moving to Palmara was rooted in starting a new phase of life—one with no more grueling work, where we could live lightly, travel, and relax. I remember telling him that in this new phase, I didn't want to be the emotional rock of the relationship anymore. It was just too heavy a burden if only one person was carrying it, and I simply didn't have the strength for that anymore.

One morning—I'm always up early—I noticed my phone needed an update. In our relationship, it was always my responsibility to handle any electronic devices, including laptops, phones, software, and apps, as well as paying bills online. Maciek couldn't stand dealing with that stuff. So I updated my phone and then picked up his to do the same. I ran the update, and that's when a message popped up from someone named Anastazja, full of little hearts.

In my entire life, I had never looked through someone else's phone. But this time, every red flag in my system shot up and started flapping. I tapped the message.

And there it was—he had written to her that he was leaving me next month, that he already had a place lined up to go for a year, and that he was inviting her and her daughter to join him there. He even added that her daughter could do homeschooling so she wouldn't miss school. As I scrolled, I saw love declarations, money transfers—everything. The exchange had started a few weeks earlier.

Amazing. Some random woman on the other side of the world already knew he was planning to leave me, while I had no idea. Facts: Anastazja lived halfway across the globe, in Europe, and after just a few weeks of messaging, he was inviting her to bring her child and come live with him. Nothing ever came of it, but the sheer manipulation was enough to knock the wind out of me. At the time, I was shocked from head to toe. Now, I just shake my head in disbelief that someone could do that. But today I know—this was the start of yet another narcissistic cycle of love-bombing and seduction.

I had packed my bags during the love-bombing phase and moved in with him quickly, but I was already a U.S. citizen living here. I wasn't on another continent. I didn't have a child or a family life I'd need to leave behind. It was just me, my adventure, and the freedom to choose—no consequences for anyone else, just myself.

Today I laugh at myself, realizing that even the Universe must have stepped in at that point, arranging a perfect synchrony between a phone update and that message popping up—because I was still half-in, still hanging on. What I needed was shock therapy. Well, I got it. A wake-up call better than a bucket of ice water over the head.

After reading that exchange, thank goodness I had EFT and my emotional processing tools at my fingertips—otherwise, it would have been brutal. I dove into them with passion and intensity because deep in my soul, I know there is nothing more important than staying centered and integrated, especially when the world outside is falling apart. Experiences this shocking and profound catapult you into the deepest recesses of your inner Self, and that marked the beginning of an incredibly intense period of inner work for me.

The deeper you go, opening parts of yourself that have never been touched before, the more inner pain starts to emerge. Those deep places within us tend to be "born in pain." But you can get through it—if you don't lose your center. Beyond the pain lie such beautiful parts of you that it's worth the struggle, no matter what's happening around you. Your conscious Self becomes richer, fuller, and expanded by those once-lost pieces. And with that comes peace. Of course, this is a process, not something you can accomplish in a single afternoon.

> *When something knocks you flat emotionally, reach for help right away—don't sit there feeling helpless.*

Crouching Tiger, Hidden Dragon

For a few days, I didn't say a word. My trust in him had completely evaporated, and I needed time to figure out what was actually going on. That meant observation and distance. Clearly, he had started planning a whole new life behind my back, while still planning a life with me, waiting to sign the papers on a house we were buying together. My brain just couldn't connect those dots, so I watched to see how it would play out.

Inside, I knew this was the end. If there had been even the tiniest thread of hope left when we moved to Palmara, this moment severed it completely. All that remained was empty space.

But because I was hyper-attuned to my inner world—my emotions, my distance, my center—I gave myself time for the right solution to emerge.

I knew, down to every cell in my body, that I absolutely could not act from a place of emotion. It took everything I had to stand in the middle of the chameleon's matrix of manipulation and stay grounded in myself. It wasn't easy. It drained a ton of energy and focus. But it was necessary.

At that point, for the first time, it became solely about me—about my survival. On the inside, it was over. But on the outside, there were still things that needed handling. The only way to handle them was without falling into despair or emotional destruction. That was a matter of survival.

When All The Lights Go Out–Light Your Own

If you've ever been through something like this, you know the kind of emotional tidal waves that crash through your entire system. Your mind won't stop spinning, your heart races non-stop, sleep disappears, you cry, you despair, your life feels shattered, and the big question looms: What now? I went through all of that too.

But as I've said many times before, I just don't know how to stay in that place of collapse. Something inside me—probably that little sun in my belly—immediately pushes me to take care of it. So I sit with it. I stay present. I ask myself, 'How do I feel? What's really going on? Where did this come from? What does it mean? What am I supposed to see here? Which part of me is hurting? What does that part want from me? What does this remind me of? What do I need to tend to? Where is this taking me? What space is opening up?'

At the same time, I engage in emotional work—exercises and techniques—so the whole process stays alive and doesn't just spiral around in my head. I won't stop until harmony returns and I feel reconnected to my integrated Self.

If you're reading this, I want you to know—no matter what's happening in your life or how terrifying the emotions feel—don't give up on yourself. Get support. Start practicing EFT. Take care of yourself on the inside. That's where everything begins, and that's where everything ends.

If you've forgotten about yourself somewhere along the way, it's time to remember. Turning your attention inward is something you can always do, and no one can take that from you. The more you reconnect with yourself, the stronger you'll feel. You'll gain perspective. Solutions will begin to appear.

I'm sharing all of this as living proof that it's possible. Tending to your inner world, holding your boundaries, and consistently asking how you feel and what this means can protect you even from the destructive chaos of a narcissist. I can testify to this not just because I lived through it, but because for over thirty years, I've lived and breathed emotional awareness and inner work. That's what helped me come out of this intact.

This isn't theory. It's not a feel-good quote. When you truly take care of your inner world, it doesn't just feel better; it becomes a more fulfilling experience. It saves you. And then you thrive.

You Don't Leave The Matrix With Your Feet—You Do It With Your Heart

If you haven't been working with your emotions for thirty years, which is totally understandable, and you're currently stuck in the narcissist's matrix—feeling lost, powerless, and confused—then this is exactly why I'm sharing all of this: to tell you firsthand, it works.

Due to my passion, ongoing inner practice, and profession, I had a stronger foundation to navigate it with greater clarity. However, I know most people aren't immersed in this kind of work, which is why I don't suggest you go it alone. What I am saying is: start looking for solutions that turn your focus inward. Begin with EFT—it's free at the basic level and will strengthen you from the inside. Or find a therapist who can walk you through this.

Wherever you are in your relationship with your inner world, it is essential that you begin or continue deepening that connection. That's the only real way out of the narcissist's matrix: through your own inner center. Because even if you physically separate from them and finally feel "free," you might still feel emotionally and energetically trapped—if you haven't broken free inside. The path runs through your inner world—through a deep, steady connection with yourself and your true Self. Emotional work is the key.

> *The only way out of the chameleon's matrix is through that inner connection.*

A Deep Breath Before Moving On

Maciek turned out to be a master of camouflage. He spoke to me as if everything was fine, and we were handling things around the new house—everything seemed perfectly normal.

From the outside, using plain logic, you might ask: if things were already this tangled, why didn't you just leave right then and there? And sure, when you're not in the middle of it—when you're not tied together by dozens of shared responsibilities and tangled emotional and logistical threads—it's easy to say. Yes, acting on impulse can sometimes feel like the bold choice. But more often than not, you end up paying the price for those impulsive decisions, because they weren't thought through, and they leave everyone worse off.

I had just landed in a new state, three thousand miles from what I knew. I didn't know anyone. I couldn't trust him anymore. I had no clear vision of what was next. There are too many unknowns to start piling on even more. For now, I just wanted to settle into the move and catch my breath. Then, once I had a clearer sense of where things stood, I'd figure out the next steps.

"I Be You Now"

By that time, I was already convinced that Maciek had NPD. Alongside my own emotional work, I also dove deep into professional literature on narcissism to make sure I wasn't drawing the wrong conclusions. I had never specialized in this disorder—I had only gained a general understanding from my university studies. But at that point, my eyes opened all the way.

One small thing proved with precision that Maciek had entered a new narcissistic cycle and was closing the previous one.

As you may recall from earlier chapters, when a narcissist starts their cycle, they use love bombing and mirroring, faithfully reflecting you to gain your approval and become "just like you." They read between the lines to figure out what you like and shower you with gifts that match your preferences. They imitate what you do, say they love what matters to you, and promise to give you what you value. Sometimes they'll even change their appearance for you or genuinely believe they love what you love. They do this to create perfect resonance, to win your admiration, and to make you believe you've literally met YOUR soulmate.

Suddenly, I noticed that Maciek had started speaking in an ungrammatical manner. Every now and then, he made mistakes, as if English were his second language. But Maciek was a native speaker, born and raised in the States, and had never spoken like that before. He had always chosen his words carefully—after all, he wrote poetry. There were no signs of a stroke or neurological issue, so it caught my attention.

I noticed it was a handful of the same words he kept messing up. And then it hit me—the distortions he was making were characteristic of someone whose native language is Slavic and who speaks English with that kind of influence. My eyes widened because Anastazja was from Eastern Europe. The words he was misusing sounded exactly like something a person from there might say when their English is slightly off.

There were a few terms he began misusing regularly. Two stuck in my mind. One was "changement", and the other was "I wait you." The first one he used when he meant to say "a change," and the second instead of "I will wait for you."

Just to be 100% sure, I asked him once, right after he used the word "changement"—"Why do you say 'changement'? Is that a real word in English that I don't know about?" And he replied after a short pause, "No, it's not. It just came out that way."

But it didn't "just come out." It was a regular occurrence, and he wasn't even aware of it. It was a clear sign of mirroring—when a narcissist starts copying you during the love bombing phase. I never imagined that mirroring could go so far as to alter his native language—something so deeply ingrained in the human brain. The instability of the Self and the inability to just be oneself were stunning. It's a serious indication of how deep NPD runs that the deficits are almost biological, because the emotional brain stopped developing at the level of a three-year-old who mimics and copies everything. Especially parents, the people with whom they form emotional bonds.

That's why I urge you not to throw around the term NPD lightly. In relationships, a person with NPD truly regresses developmentally and begins to act like a child, emotionally attaching to their partner and expecting to be treated like a good little boy by mommy.

So, no wonder that when I refused to play that role and wanted him to behave like a grown man, a partner, not a child, to him, that felt like another injustice. But the truth is, the only person who was hurting him was himself, by refusing to take responsibility for his inner world, his emotions, and his past. It's the narcissist who abandons his own Self and his own needs, not you. He's an adult. You're not his mom.

No matter how much you might feel compassion for the narcissist or understand them, you need to know that this disorder, at its core, is wired to destroy relationships. So, don't wander too far into that empathy—stay grounded in your own integrity and boundaries. In the end, it's up to them whether they turn inward and choose to heal. And there's a 99% chance they won't. Sadly, nothing else will help them but themselves.

> The covert narcissist doesn't actually want help.
> What they want is to feed off your attention—
> disguised as asking for help.

The Savior From Across The Ocean

One day, I noticed that he had posted something on one of his social media profiles—something I had shared with him for personal use only. It was a video that included a series of drawings, part of a therapeutic method I'd been developing for seven years with my friend. I shared it with him because he was interested in that kind of thing, and I thought it might be helpful to him.

I was a little pissed when I saw it posted. First, it was part of an original method that hadn't yet been published, so sharing it publicly was, at the very least, inappropriate. Second, he shared the results of my years of work as if they were his own, without any explanation of what they really were.

I asked him to take it down. And of course, I got accused of not trusting him. I mean… what does that have to do with anything? My concern was about intellectual property rights and the potential difficulties I might face in securing them later if the material had already been posted online under someone else's name.

But a covert narcissist has to twist everything to suit their narrative, where they are always the victim. So, once again, the facts didn't matter—and once again, I got cast as the bad guy who was hurting him.

Under that post, I noticed a heart reaction and the name Anastazja. I clicked on it, and her profile opened. That's when I had a bit of a shock—because right there in the header photo of her profile were the wire figurines I had personally made for Maciek as a gift back when we were still living in the forest. That was too much.

I messaged her, introduced myself, and asked about the header image, explaining exactly what it was. She was caught off guard because she had given me an explanation and promised to take it down right away. Not long after that, I saw that I had been blocked.

I shared all of this with Maciek. He gave me a long-winded explanation, saying she was just a friend, that she was going through a tough time, and that he was her "lifeline." He actually used those words. But by then, I already knew what I was dealing with. So I held my observer stance—pretending I knew nothing and believed everything he said.

I didn't question anything, nor did I want to. The game had flipped—the narrative was mine now. The first point of contact in this triangle he had constructed had been made. At that point, the only thing that mattered to me was getting out of all of this in the most optimal way possible.

With that level of deceit and manipulation, I had no reason to trust that he'd be honest about anything else—and there were still many practical matters we needed to agree on and sort out before going our separate ways.

The House Of Cards Began To Tremble

After that confrontation, his narcissistic facade started slowly cracking. He began acting in ways that were totally out of the ordinary. At one point, he told me he had received an email from her, stating that I had reached out to her, and that she didn't want me to contact her again because what they had together was special and didn't need any "jealous energy" from his partner.

I thought to myself, Wow, he really met his match, because that made absolutely no sense. He was the one who had brought up Anastazja in the first place—I had simply followed his lead. At that point, I wasn't trying to fight. I was focused on watching, listening, and understanding what I was dealing with.

Inside, I had already let go of any desire to fight for the relationship. Now it was all about surviving the endgame. And because I always strive to maintain integrity with myself, it was essential for me to come out of this with a clear conscience. No matter how he treated me, that wasn't a reason to lose my own values. I wasn't interested in making any decisions that would harm another person, because I would have to live with the consequences of that decision. And keeping that inner clarity means everything to me.

Diamond Mine

I'm writing this now with calm and distance—and in a heavily condensed version. But back then, it was nothing like this. The emotions that were surging through me were enormous. After all, I was in the middle of dismantling over a decade of my life with this man—years of experiences, highs and lows, dreams, hopes, health crises, deep bonds, and everything else that comes with a long-term relationship.

I walked around with a constantly elevated heart rate—my pulse racing from stress, sleepless nights, my mind spinning nonstop, and waves of emotion crashing through me. I was doing the work in real time, not on emotions tied to the relationship itself anymore, but on the grief of letting go of everything that had once been woven together.

I was meeting regularly with my therapist friend, working through the deep inner process we had developed together. What happened during those sessions felt like magic. The emotional wreckage caused by Maciek was pulling me into profound inner depths—depths where real transformation could occur. As I moved through the process, breathtaking layers of reality started to unfold—deeper, more expansive, and more beautiful than anything I had ever experienced.

Paradoxically, the emotional turmoil and inner deconstruction were leading me to a stronger, more grounded connection with myself. In a single session, I could transition from the rawest emotional pain and darkness to a radiant inner light and open space so powerful that tears streamed down my face from joy. It took a huge amount of energy, but it was worth every ounce of it. Because of this work, I never lost the solid core inside myself, no matter how much chaos he was stirring up on the outside.

Two-Faced Man

Through it all, I didn't forget about my body. I kept moving, doing some light exercise and walking on the treadmill. For some reason, the treadmill is where I often get flashes of insight or even visions—maybe it's the oxygen boost to my brain from increased circulation.

I remember one particular moment clearly. I was deep in thought, in the thick of everything that was happening, when a vivid image suddenly washed over me. I saw myself and Maciek standing face-to-face. Between us, there was an energetic connection. Through that connection, I was transmitting my energy of sharing to him. It flowed directly between our faces.

But then I suddenly noticed—he had a second face on the back of his head! Two faces. One in front, the one receiving my energy, and one in the back. The front face absorbed what I gave and passed it on to the face in the back, which then radiated it outward to someone standing behind him. A woman. Probably Anastazja. And my immediate thought was, *He's taking the best of me and handing it over to someone else.* It felt awful—sickening, even.

I remember consciously closing that channel of giving and cutting the energetic connection. I disconnected from that vampire.

A New Dimension

Another time, again on the treadmill, I had a different kind of vision—this one about my future. Amid all the wreckage, I kept wondering what was next. Suddenly, I saw it: I was lifted above the clouds. It looked just like when you're flying on a plane and it breaks through the cloud cover into clear blue skies. In the vision, I was literally standing in that open, luminous space, looking down at the earth, at life, at physical reality. The feeling of freedom was so overwhelming that I nearly dissolved into it. At the same time, I knew with absolute certainty that everything was okay. That I didn't need to worry. All I had to do was trust—and in the meantime, "clean up the rubble" left behind after the collapse, so I could step into that new space unburdened and clear.

There were other visions, too—insights so deep into the fabric of reality, human connection, and the principles of life that they felt like pure gold. All of it, without a doubt, came from the deep work I was doing on myself, and from not being afraid to do it. My higher Self and subconscious were working in harmony, bringing me clarity and understanding through visions, insight, and sensation.

> *Never give up on yourself—especially when it gets hardest.*
> *Your inner world will repay you a hundredfold.*

Truth That Burns Through The Mask

Meanwhile, Maciek was getting ready to leave for his planned retreat in the middle of nowhere. Before his departure, he continued to message Anastazja, still insisting she was "just a friend." Never mind the love declarations flying back and forth between them. I decided I was done staying silent. I didn't feel like swallowing any more of it. So I began confronting him—openly and calmly telling him how it all made me feel, what it was doing to me, and how I saw it from my side. He disagreed with almost everything, but I could see he was starting to tense up.

Finally, I said, "Listen, what you're doing is a straight-up betrayal. You cheated on me." He instantly denied it, repeating the same line—that she was just a friend, nothing more. But I didn't back down. I calmly said it again: "You cheated on me." He denied it again. I repeated it. This went on maybe five times.

And something interesting happened. He suddenly froze, like the words had finally landed. Up until that moment, it was as if he'd been floating in some fantasy world, completely disconnected from reality, untouched by the weight of what he was actually doing or the consequences of it. But my calm, steady repetition seemed to break through. He didn't say anything after that. That's when I said, "I want to separate. I'm not doing this anymore." He walked out.

> *A narcissist doesn't see or feel the consequences of their actions – others are "not affected," others "don't suffer." Only they do.*

When he came back that evening, he completely fell apart. It was his first *narcissistic collapse*. I had never seen him like that before. He was sobbing so hard, gasping for breath, shaking with grief. It wasn't fake—it was real. It was painful to watch. I didn't say anything. At some point, I simply walked over and laid my hand on his shoulders. After a while, he calmed down.

The next day, he said he had broken down, that he really had emotionally betrayed me, that he was now going to do everything he could to regain my trust, and that he was ashamed of himself beyond words.

For the first time, I didn't believe a word he said. Years of emotional manipulation had made me an expert in this field. Of course, I nodded and told him I understood. He pulled himself together, got stronger, and probably thought everything was going back to normal.

The King Is Dead, Long Live The King

If you think that collapse changed anything in him—or that he'd now genuinely try to repair the relationship, think again. Just a few days later, his correspondence with Anastazja was in full bloom again. Luckily, I was expecting it, so I wasn't surprised.

The vision of me leaving him triggered the narcissistic collapse. As you might recall, a narcissist's greatest panic is rejection. When I told him I wanted to end things, I struck right at the core of his worst nightmare. That's why all the masks and illusions fell away, and he had to face his deepest trauma.

But here's the thing with narcissists: they don't use that collapse to heal. If they ask for a second chance, it's not because they truly want one. They ask for it just to pacify you, to gain your sympathy or support, to feed off it, rebuild their false identity, recharge with your energy, and rise like a phoenix—only to continue their games. And that's exactly what happened. The only difference was that I didn't fall for it. I knew better this time.

Being that clear-headed didn't make the whole thing any less emotionally intense. It was still heavy. However, I kept myself in check, and in my inner world, I continued to do my work.

When The Curtain Of Illusion Fell

When he resumed his correspondence with Anastazja, the truth of it all started to stand bare. There was nowhere left to run or hide. He could see that his illusions, lies, and masks no longer worked. He had been fully unmasked—and I was watching. There's nothing worse for a narcissist than being truly seen. Their whole life is built around illusions and wearing masks, because the last thing they want is to see themselves.

At that point, he even gave up on maintaining the illusion. He started to be blunt, as if he no longer cared. He said to me outright: "Yeah, I'm a liar,

I'm a cheater, I'm a thief. So what?" And honestly, it was all true—even the thief part. Not of money—he was actually very honest with money—but he stole my ideas, my insights, my identity, my words. More than once, after I'd share something with him—some deep realization or personal insight that truly moved me—he'd tell me how powerful and meaningful it was. Then later, I'd hear him on the phone saying, "You know, I had this thought today…" and repeat exactly what I had told him, claiming it as his own. He'd pass it off to impress someone else.

Same thing on social media. Once, he saw a quote of mine—something really thoughtful and sharp—and said, "This is brilliant, I'm going to post it on my page." I said, "Fine, just credit me by name." He gave me a sideways look and ended up posting nothing. If it wasn't his, it couldn't get him the praise. The likes and hearts would go to the real author, not to him.

These are just a few examples, but they weren't isolated. This was the norm.

Best To Step Aside

The agony of the relationship dragged on. We both already knew it was over—it was just a matter of sorting out reality. We had just bought the house, and now we were already talking about selling it. I told him I wasn't going to live there alone, that I'd figure out another way to set up my life. He was about to head off for his year-long retreat, and I was supposed to stay in the house and look after it while he was gone. Other things had to be settled and divided.

In the meantime, as he stopped caring about anything and started revealing more and more of who he really was, the roller coaster kicked into high gear. He'd swing from elated to depressed, played the victim, exaggerated physical pains, walked around furious at everything, then be totally indifferent. He lashed out at me and even turned on Anastazja, suddenly mocking her for being religious and going to church. At one point, he said, "Why are you even worried? If it's not her, I've got a few others in line."

That's textbook narcissism. They always need backup fuel. They can't exist without it. They can't sit still with themselves and their own emptiness.

The Silence Of The Lambs And The Stranger In The Mirror

One day, he declared that he'd been "called into silence"—that he'd lost his voice and couldn't speak to me anymore. He could only write emails or notes on paper. For a few days, he just scribbled things down instead of talking. A couple of times, he forgot and said something out loud by accident, lost in thought. But then he'd catch himself and fall back into "I can't speak" mode. It was both pathetic and disturbing to watch a grown man behave like that.

Something really was unraveling in him at that point. At one moment, he told me that when he looked in the mirror, he didn't recognize his own face—and that it scared him. He said he saw a stranger.

No wonder. A narcissist doesn't see themselves, not their real reflection. So when the mask starts slipping and their true inner Self begins to show, it makes sense that the mirror suddenly feels unfamiliar. They've spent their whole life looking into their own face—and never really seeing it.

The Hollow Abyss And A Deadly Prohibition

During that time, there was one moment when I looked into his eyes, and what I saw there chilled me to the bone. It was a kind of emptiness more terrifying than death itself. At least death is something. But this was absolute nothingness. It lasted only a moment, but I'll never forget it. It left an imprint.

His panic around being truly seen spilled over into everything. Even when I decided to go back to the same real estate agent to list the house for sale, he freaked out. She had sold us the place just a month earlier, and as a kind and professional woman, I felt comfortable working with her again.

He asked, "What are you going to tell her? That she sold us the house and now she's selling it again a month later?"

I said, "I'm not going to lie. I'll just tell her we're separating."

What he called me after that... let's just say it was so vile, I'd rather not write it here—my computer might crash from the profanity. He lashed out, screaming that she didn't need to know any of that and that he forbade me to tell her.

I ignored him completely. I went to her and told her exactly what was going on and why we were selling the property. She was so stunned that she offered me a drink. We ended up forming a warm, supportive connection.

An Oscar For Manipulation

It was Maciek himself who started talking about Anastazja. Just take that in for a second—the absurdity of it: telling your current partner about the new woman you're trying to win over. No thought whatsoever about how I might feel, what it was doing to me, the fact that I'm a human being going through this, that we'd been together for over ten years, and it wasn't even entirely over yet. Nothing. He didn't see me as a person. Never did. Just as fuel. A resource.

However, I did discover some interesting things. He talked about the vacation he was planning with her (in Kraków!), how she's emotionally needy, how her pain draws him in (!), how he's there for her. He even asked me for the address of the same apartment in Kraków we always used to book! At the same time, he offered that if we were no longer a couple, he'd like us to stay friends. Of course—friends with benefits, naturally.

This really showed that relationships, for him, were nothing more than narcissistic fuel. Not believing what I was hearing and trying to grasp the absurdity of it, I said that in such a situation, he would have to inform Anastasia that he was choosing this kind of relationship with me. Otherwise, he was putting me in the position of hiding behind her back, just like he had hidden her behind mine. I had no desire to be part of any manipulation.

He said he couldn't tell her—because it would devastate her. So, let's get this straight: he had apparently spun her a story about how things were definitively over between us, and now she was "the one." To me, he was saying she was just a harmless friend he was helping out. Hmm. Interesting, then—why the need to hide my existence from her if she was just a friend?

Nothing in a narcissist's world makes sense. It's all ruled by chaos and instant gratification. Nothing else matters. And facts—meaning the truth—are the ultimate threat.

You won't believe this either—but Maciek actually made *me* responsible for Anastazja showing up in his life. He said to me, and I quote: "You called it in." When my eyes widened in disbelief and I asked him how that could possibly be, he explained that a few years earlier, during one of our many conversations about his life, I had supposedly planted that vision in his head.

It happened during one of his frequent rants—those moments when he'd complain that life was meaningless and empty, that he wanted to escape the world, disappear, cut off all ties, and that he hated his country and wanted to leave—preferably somewhere in Eastern Europe. (Just as a side note: what a wonderful thing to tell your partner—basically making it clear how little a part she is of your future.)

At that point, already done buying into his dramatic monologues and refusing to take the bait emotionally, I had said something like: "Maybe you should. Maybe you should go buy yourself a little apartment in the middle of nowhere, hire some girl to cook and clean, and maybe that will make you happy."

Now—get this—he actually threw it back at me. He told me that because I said those words back then, that's exactly what he went and did. According to him, I had energetically called this woman into his life and his space. In other words, he basically suggested that his decision to start and pursue an online affair was my fault, and he was just the poor victim of it all.

It's honestly mind-blowing how a narcissist can twist facts and reality to fit whatever narrative serves them—and to avoid taking responsibility for anything. They'll spin anything. They'll remember a comment from years ago if it benefits them, and conveniently forget everything from yesterday that might actually matter or help resolve something.

The most baffling part? He truly couldn't see the sheer absurdity of what he was saying.

At this point, the narcissistic manipulation was so out in the open that it was almost unbelievable. As hard as it was to be in the thick of it, it was also incredibly liberating, because it left me with absolutely no doubt about who I was dealing with.

"Surrender To It"

I recall a particular moment—it was during our first week in the new house. The place was a bit run-down; it'd belonged to an elderly couple who had lived there for over twenty years. In the last two, the wife had been sick and moved into a care home, where the husband pretty much lived with her. The house was full of dust and layers of neglect. The kitchen was the worst. The stove was caked with years of grease—inside and out—and appeared to be in need of replacement. But I was determined. Armed with a toothbrush and some heavy-duty cleaners, I spent the entire day scrubbing it until it looked nearly new.

I remember kneeling in front of the stove, still scrubbing, listening to something on my iPad. Maciek was out somewhere. All of a sudden, this word echoed through my mind: "Surrender. Surrender. Surrender."

Something cracked open inside me—a vast space that felt like it had no bottom. Everything I had thought was important—about the relationship, about life, the world, my beliefs, my intentions—started dissolving. It felt like it was all dying. But not tragically or painfully—it was just… shrinking. Fading. As it did, I was filled with this growing sense that it was okay to die on the inside.

There was a deep, quiet trust in that moment. Like I could strip myself bare, down to nothing, and still be safe. That the devil himself could tear me apart, and I would still be okay. That if I let go of even the tiniest grain of resistance, no fear, no defensiveness, no need for control—I could pass through some kind of eye of the needle and come out in a completely different dimension.

It really was one of those moments: "Thy will be done."

I can't even begin to describe the energies that moved through me. At some point, I became so physically weak that, still on my knees, scrubbing kitchen corners with a toothbrush, I let my forehead rest on the floor. Yet, inside, there was a power so immense that I have nothing to compare it to. The more I surrendered—letting go of every single instinct to protect myself—the stronger that inner force became. And then, something shifted. A new kind of freedom opened up inside me.

From that day forward, the outside world started showing me the most incredible synchronicities—things lining up in such perfectly helpful ways that, to this day, it still feels like a fairytale. Suddenly, my work life began to bloom. Opportunities and new paths began to appear out of nowhere.

That new freedom didn't magically erase the emotional storms Maciek was still stirring up—those had to be cleared, layer by layer. But there was something new now, a space inside that had cracked open, quietly pointing toward a different path.

It was like when you begin to feel spring in the air—subtle signs of life stirring—but winter still throws in the occasional icy wind or snowstorm just to remind you it's not done yet.

The Predator In Full Color

That moment summed up everything about who he truly was. While I was working through the waves of emotions, reactions, and beliefs that kept emerging during this emotional Armageddon, a day finally arrived when something dropped into my emotional system: it was over. Different parts of us experience the same reality in different ways. The mind examines the facts and makes a logical decision—this is unsustainable; something has to change. The spiritual Self opens to a new path and can already feel a pull toward something else. But the emotional body—that's where the deepest attachments live. That's usually the hardest part to let go of. When the moment of final release does come, it's not a graceful one. It hits like a wave of grief, helplessness, the feeling of having lost something valuable, wasted time, wasted life. Even the body can ache. These sensations might not reflect the deeper truth of the situation, but that's what it feels like when you're releasing something that held deep emotional ties.

The day came for me, too. I remember it vividly—even the sweater I was wearing at the time. At one point, I sat down at the desk chair and was flooded with those exact emotions: the sense of massive loss, of something irretrievably gone, forever. The tears started flowing because the body needs to release them in its own way. I think I sat in that chair for a full hour, letting it all happen. In my belly, I could feel these inner depths churning with energy, so intense it was almost physical pain. Maciek was in the other room.

When it had all passed through, I was physically drained. I lay down on the bed feeling completely hollowed out on the inside. Thankfully, I knew—at least intellectually—that it was a process, that there was nothing to fear, and that the more openly I allowed it, the sooner it would pass. About half an hour later, Maciek came into the room. Let me tell you, I don't think any other moment or image of him from our over ten-year relationship is as etched into my memory as this one.

He walked in very slowly, upright, with his chest puffed out slightly forward. He had this mysterious little smile on his face, his head tilted upward. I couldn't shake the sense that he was in some kind of bliss, in a deep calm. He approached me almost theatrically, knelt beside the bed, placed one hand over my chest where my heart is, and wrapped his other arm around me. He stayed like that for a good fifteen minutes. I was so emotionally exhausted, I didn't even have the strength to say a word.

Imagine this—after those fifteen minutes, he suggested we have sex. Luckily, nothing happened, but that moment exposed absolutely everything about who this man truly was. I don't think I could have had a more textbook narcissist in front of me.

He waited until I was at my lowest, when I was completely drained, and then slid in, wearing his white gloves of dominance, assuming the posture of "I'll save you" or "You need me, you won't survive without me."

This is how a narcissist forges an emotional bond, so they can later use it to siphon your essence, to feed off your energy as narcissistic supply. Like a spider waiting for the fly caught in its web to grow weak, so it can creep in, cold-bloodedly and hungrily, suck the life out of it. I will never forget the pride and satisfaction on his face as he walked into that room.

In healthy relationships, when someone is at their lowest, the natural instinct is to support or protect, not exploit. What he revealed in that moment was the textbook narcissist—a textbook parasite.

At the beginning of the relationship, he once said to me, "I am a shapeshifter." Ultimately, he revealed himself to be the Predator. In between, he just juggled various masks.

No matter what kind of mask a narcissist wears, there will come a moment when they reveal themselves fully. Stay alert, and you'll see it. Even when you're at your lowest, don't fall for the "rescuer" performance—set a boundary.

> *Notice the moments when you're feeling low—
> and they suddenly light up.*

A Hideout For Two

That moment—no matter how revolting—taught me a lot, not just about him, but about myself, too. Through that experience, I saw the traumatic bond a narcissist forms with you. Buried deep down, almost out of sight, was this feeling that he was the only person in my entire world. That realization really surprised me, because in my personal life, I'm a very independent person. I do my own thing, make my own decisions, work for myself, don't follow anyone, don't care what people think, and even create my own frameworks for understanding the world. However, in this relationship, it was different somehow.

I had a vision—like everyone else had disappeared, and only Maciek remained. When I felt that, I realized this was the pattern: the narcissist pulls you so deeply into his internal world that, over time, he becomes the only thing you see. He emotionally latches onto you, like a child clinging to a parent, and the parent ends up seeing only the child, who would even give their life for them.

For individuals with low self-worth, this is particularly dangerous because they lose faith in themselves, their independence, and their ability to take action. They start to believe they can't exist without the narcissist. That without them, they're nothing. Their entire sense of Self becomes dependent on him.

With my level of independence, self-worth, and healthy boundaries, I wasn't really in danger of falling into that trap—alongside the relationship,

I had been constantly growing and building my own life. Still, I saw the mechanism hiding at the very bottom. In my vision, it seemed as though I was trapped in a capsule with him, and there was no one else present. To make it worse, the capsule was floating in a dark and empty space—there was no world beyond it, and no one else existed.

When I saw this with full awareness, the absurdity of it all hit me, and I actually said to myself, in second person: "Are you out of your f…ing mind?" The moment I said that, the walls of the capsule melted away, and the world opened up, bursting with color and filled with millions of people. With that came the realization: "I'm in a relationship with all of humanity, not with one disturbed person."

Never let yourself be cut off from your family, your friends, and most of all—from yourself. He is *not* your whole world.

I Thought I'd Finally Catch A Break

The day finally came—Maciek was leaving for his year-long retreat. Before he left, he completed several major projects around the house to prepare it for sale. I won't even go into detail about the nightmare that was—how he cursed to the heavens, threw things around, and poured hatred out of every pore. Of course, it was all my fault. I was the one who wanted to move, I was the one who picked this house, and so on. I didn't react anymore—I'd gotten used to the standard dynamic over the years: if something was good, it was thanks to him; if something wasn't, it was my fault.

Eventually, he packed up and left. The relief was enormous. It was March, and in Palmara the summer weather had already arrived. I could finally lie out in the sun behind the house, rest, and tan. The house became quiet, calm, and spacious.

A few days later, Maciek called to say he had arrived at the retreat house where he was supposed to stay for the year, but it was such a neglected dump that the conditions were basically unlivable. He told me he was coming back because he didn't know what else to do. Apparently, he also had some kind of argument with the owner of the place because, as it turned out, she had just wanted to use him. Well, let's just say, the thought "karma's a bitch" definitely crossed my mind.

He came back a few days later and said he couldn't stay in the same house as me—that it was too brutal, too unbearable. No surprise there. The shame over everything he'd done was burning him alive, and inside, he was completely falling apart. We tossed around several ideas about what to do next. Eventually, we decided to put the house on the market immediately, rather than waiting a year. He'd go back to his hometown, all the way across the country, and I'd stay here until the house sold—then figure things out from there. He rented a place back in Pacifica, and a week later, he was gone.

That final week before he left was an interesting time. Maciek helped with a few of the heavier tasks around the house, and we took care of some last logistics. In the process, I found out quite a bit about Anastazja—because he was talking about her (!) Apparently, she'd had a husband and hadn't mentioned it to Maciek before declaring her love for him. When her husband found out about the affair, he threatened to beat Maciek up if he ever caught him with Anastazja on vacation in Krakow. So yeah—soap opera on steroids.

I just watched it all from a distance, feeling how our worlds were separating more and more, like oil and water. Nothing was holding them together anymore. He was still spinning in a state of chaos, drama, and tension. I was finding more and more peace. I didn't care much anymore about anything, really. I set boundaries when I needed to, regardless of how he felt about it. I focused on what was mine, and the only thing I was interested in was resolving this mess in the simplest, most harmonious way possible.

You won't believe what he said at the end—seeing how calmly and firmly I stood my ground, he looked at me and said, "Well, you've gotten a lot stronger compared to when I first met you. I really trained you well over the years." Wouldn't you just fall off your chair at the absurdity of that? Without skipping a beat, I replied, "That strength is thanks solely to me and my own inner work. Not to you." Though, to be fair, he wasn't completely wrong—if he hadn't presented me with that particular challenge, which pushed me deep into myself, I might not have discovered so many things. But that's not what he meant, of course.

At that point, I actually started to feel grateful to Anastazja for stepping onto the stage and taking him off my hands. I even joked with my therapist friend that I should send her flowers as a thank you.

What A Narcissist Really Bonds With

The day finally came when he left for good. He packed up his pickup truck and trailer. He got up early that morning, made coffee, started the engine to let it warm up, and came back inside for a moment. He stood in the hallway, and it was clear to both of us that this was the last time we'd ever see each other.

Suddenly, he broke down crying so hard it turned into sobbing and spasms. It was even more dramatic than the first time. You know how a small child cries—not just with their face, but with their whole body. He stood there in the hallway, sobbing like a child lost in a vast space, and even his posture looked like that of a little boy. I had flashes—literal visual flickers—of him turning into a six-year-old child, then back to himself, then back to the child again. The grief pouring out of him was so raw it clenched my chest. This was his second *narcissistic collapse*—his second contact with the original trauma he refuses to process.

If I were to compare the depth of that despair to something, imagine a family: mother, father, a little boy, and a little girl, happy together. One day, their home is attacked by intruders. Everyone is killed except the boy, who manages to hide and survive. Afterward, he stands in the middle of the house, surrounded by absence, crying into the void, hoping someone will find him—utterly helpless, abandoned, heartbroken, and shut off from life, the world, and other people. That's exactly what surfaced in Maciek at that moment.

The narcissist's original trauma carries this level of intensity. It may come from childhood or generational trauma. But the biggest problem is that the narcissist doesn't want to heal it. From my metaphorical perspective, it appears as follows: in that moment of extreme helplessness, abandonment, and disconnection from the world, life, and people, they surrender their soul to some kind of parasite, which gives them a sense of power. As if, in an act of desperation, they sold their soul to the devil in order to survive.

The parasite seems to be the only one "interested" in them at that moment. The bond is for life. They serve the parasite loyally, which is why they behave like parasites and defend it at all costs. Later in relationships, they replay the same scenario: they push the other person into helplessness, strip them of their identity, strength, and self-worth, until—just like they once did—the person breaks and hands themselves over. Not out of love, but out of desperation. Just like they once surrendered to the parasite that felt like their only savior.

The bond they develop with that parasite is so strong that they'll destroy everything just to not let it go, because in their mind, there is no alternative. Even if the alternative is right in front of them, they'll choose not to see it. This is their real relationship. Instead of having an inner connection with their authentic Self, they have a relationship with the parasite. That's why they have no true identity—because identity can only exist in connection with one's Self. So they will never be authentic in a relationship with anyone.

They'll keep searching for something and never find it. They'll continue to feed the parasite with the energy and attention of others. They'll keep controlling you and treating you the same way they themselves are being controlled and treated by the parasite. Because they gave their soul away, they are not truly present with you in the relationship. However, they will be euphoric when feeding on your essence. Don't mistake that for love.

If you're an empath and your heart is breaking, don't let yourself get pulled in. Your empathy not only won't help without their own will to change—it'll be consumed as a resource, and later you'll be blamed for it. Narcissistic disorder is a truly serious condition; normal behaviors don't work here. What's needed more than anything is your wisdom.

I stayed calm while he went through his meltdown—I just held a quiet space. Eventually, he pulled himself together and left. He called me from the road. He called when he arrived. Then he kept calling every few days—until I set a boundary with that, too.

> *You can't heal narcissistic disorder with love.*
> *Only with a decision—and it won't be yours.*

Alone, But Still In Touch

When He Leaves, You Clean Up

There I was, alone in a house that still needed a lot of prep work before it could go on the market. You might remember—it had been neglected for years by the elderly couple who lived there before. Every day after work, I scrubbed, cleaned, scraped, tossed out junk, bought replacements, and fixed things. I even painted part of the exterior, because there were ugly rain stains and rusty gutters. I repainted the doors, the bathroom cabinets—there was plenty to do. I had to call in a handyman for a few things. The yard also needed care—weeding, planting flowers, and clearing out the woods behind the house. I got through it. The real estate agent was very happy with the results.

I didn't know a single person in Palmara; I had never lived in the state before. The only person I met early on was that same real estate agent. It's funny how, once again, I ended up being the one left behind to clean up. He left me in a strange place with the significant task of prepping and selling the house while he headed off to his hometown, where he was immediately surrounded by old friends eager to help him. Someone found him a place to stay, and someone else invited him to group meditations. He was rekindling old friendships, meeting new people, and getting involved in local activities.

"I'll Do Anything—As Long As It's Against You"

I knew all this because he would call me to tell me about it. You see how incredibly one-sided things are with a narcissist? He created total devastation out of our life, left me standing in the ashes to do the cleanup, and then called to share how supported and welcomed he was feeling. The tact, the empathy—truly breathtaking. Not a shred of consideration for how I might feel. Meanwhile, he was still charming Anastazja.

He told me proudly how he was starting to feel better, how he had started therapy, meditation, support groups, and how he had finally quit smoking that certain substance. He started using it when we were still living in the woods in Westmont. He knew I hated it, but insisted it was good for him, that it helped him. I didn't fight it—there was no point. He smoked it for all those years, right up until he left Palmara.

All the things I thought were important for the sake of our relationship—like getting help, finding a meditation practice, a tool to soothe the chaos inside, giving his body a break, detoxing—he always refused. He'd say nothing worked for him, and to stop trying to control him. But the moment we broke up? Not only did he start doing all of it, but he also made sure to let me know.

It felt like emotional cruelty, even abuse. Or like a child finally doing what his mother asked and then expecting praise. Either way, this had nothing to do with the partnership. Honestly, I don't even know if any of it was true or just another manipulation, another lie. But one thing is clear: the narcissist's primary goal is the destruction of the relationship and the other person. It's a mirror of his own inner wreckage. He proved that to me in a phone call.

"Leave Him There, That's His Place"

He called me and, in a grave, flat voice, started telling me how devastated and lost he was—how he couldn't find his way, how his life was over. He said he already had a plan, had taken care of his affairs, and sorted everything out. He was taking his backpack and going off into the void, disappearing so that no one would ever find him. He said it with such cold determination as if he were completely detached from life.

Maybe the thought crosses your mind that he was telling me he planned to end his life. But let me tell you—after years of hearing the same kinds of stories and pulling him out of emotional holes, it doesn't shake me anymore. At first, it would hit me hard, and my soul would leap to help. But eventually, once it became a pattern, I realized it was just another way to extract narcissistic supply. As soon as he got his emotional fix, the "need to die" disappeared.

This time, after everything he had done, and now that I understood it was just another manipulation trying to suck me into his emotional black hole, I simply said, "Okay, do what you need to do." Later, he told me that during that breakdown in the hallway, when he was leaving Palmara, he had seen that heartbroken and abandoned six-year-old inside himself again.

I'll admit, I felt a flicker of hope in that moment. Because if a narcissist tells you he's seen his core trauma—seen his true Self totally rejected and cut off—there's a chance for healing, for integration. I even told him that now that he had touched something so deep and real, he'd reached the ultimate destination of his search, something many never manage to find. You won't believe what he said next. That moment was a life lesson for me—my final release from the belief that everyone is striving for happiness and that we're all here to support one another on that path. Maciek said, "I don't want to get him back. I want him to stay right where he is. I built a fortress with thick walls around him so he'd be safe, and that's where he's staying."

I said, "But he's miserable there—alone, lost, desperate, crying, looking for 'Mom and Dad,' helpless, just waiting for someone to reach in and help. Those walls aren't protecting him; they're hurting him. They're keeping him cut off from life. All it would take right now is to take him by the hand, and everything could change."

Maciek replied, "I'm not interested. He's staying there as he is."

If his goal was to shock me, he succeeded.

The Place No One Can Enter

It hit me that within the vast architecture of the universe, life, and the human being, many things can intertwine, mix, support each other, complement, even imitate one another—but at the very center, there's a space where no one else exists. There is only you. Everything that happens in that space is just between you and your Creator. In that place, the only thing you truly have is your will. Nothing else. No one enters there, no one saves you, no one helps you, no one decides for you. Not even the Creator steps in—that space is yours alone. It's the place where you choose what kind of relationship you want to have with life, and the Creator delivers it. Your will is sacred there. Whether you choose to use it constructively or destructively, the Creator will honor it completely. That is both the greatest gift and the greatest privilege of being human and self-aware, and at the same time, the most dangerous tool.

There's a saying in America: "You can lead a horse to water, but you can't make it drink." That's exactly how it felt—I was walking alongside Maciek on that path, but only he could decide what to do with his deepest Self. He could either bounce back or sink deeper. No one has control over that—not even the universe itself, the one that brings everything into existence. That's the phenomenon of the created form: it has been granted independence and entrusted with the power to create. Everything a person has and everything they experience is their own creation—born from that innermost place.

Sacred Will

That moment was also a liberation for me. I could see clearly that he was fully responsible for his fate and his life. Now that he had reached the core of himself—where there was no more running, no more hiding in illusion or ignorance—what he chose from that point on was conscious. When you choose consciously, it's one hundred percent yours. He could no longer shift the blame onto anyone else or escape responsibility. Maybe that's the whole point of this earthly journey and the evolution of self-awareness—to realize that you are the creator, and what you create is secondary?

It also became crystal clear to me that in my desire to help others, I am only responsible for how I show up, for the quality of who I am and what I offer. What someone does with that, whether they accept it or reject it, is not my business. I'm not responsible for it, and I don't need them to use it the way I believe they should.

In his twisted way, Maciek gave me everything I needed to claim my independence and freedom. Of course, it was up to me—and my deepest will—what I would do with those lessons. Would I sink into them and blame Maciek, or would I see it as an opportunity for profound transformation and expanded self-awareness? Maciek made his choice too, and it finally hit me: I fully respect his will. I don't need to influence it or even have an opinion about it. It's his and his alone.

The next day, after that long phone call and his solemn promises that everything was in place for his "disappearance," he sent me a casual text message about something unrelated. I asked how he was doing after what he'd shared the night before. He said he felt fantastic—that it was just a moment of weakness, and now it had passed. I didn't believe a single word. Things like that don't just disappear overnight. He had simply run from himself again, temporarily filling the void with something external and riding a wave of euphoria. Maybe Anastazja had told him he was the most amazing man on earth.

Yet, some part of me stays open to the possibility that that moment of contact—when Maciek came face-to-face with his deeper Self—did happen. That it's recorded in time and space. It cannot be erased, because it has already occurred. And maybe, one day, it will become the point from which he begins a new path—this time with himself, holding that six-year-old boy by the hand. If he doesn't? That's his will. I remain open to all possibilities independently.

The next swing of the emotional pendulum didn't take long to arrive. One day, I got an email from him with a poem. He would occasionally write poetry—sometimes about me—and send it to me. This time the poem was about his suffering, about the end of our relationship, about how he missed me, how he sat by the phone waiting for me to call, how devastated he was, how I once came after him and found him (during the first exodus), and so on. I was absolutely speechless. I thought, "Man, you blew up the relationship, you couldn't even be in the same space with me, you left and started a new life, treated me like an object, and now you're crying on my shoulder? What the hell else do you want from me?"

This was a classic example of *hoovering*—the narcissist's way of sucking you back in for more emotional fuel, even after the relationship is over. I had no idea what else I could possibly say to get through to him. So I came up with the idea to write my own poem about how I felt in this relationship. Since poetry was his language, maybe it would finally cut through. Going completely no-contact wasn't an option yet—we still had a house to sell and unresolved practical matters, so we had to stay in touch.

Never Enough

I woke up from a dream
of a bottomless pit
of never enough

They say that unconditional love is enough
they say it heals everything
it does not

I will love more…
it's not enough
the abyss is empty again

I will forgive one more time…
it's not enough
I'm the enemy again

I will understand harder…
it's not enough
my understanding is wrong again

I will be more caring…
it's not enough
it's just another annoyance again

I will say what I think…
it's not enough
my opinion is an attack again

I won't say anything…
it's not enough
I just don't listen again

I will give him some space…
it's not enough
I'm just ignoring him again

I will enter his space…
it's not enough
I'm just another intruder again

I will focus on myself…
it's not enough
I'm a cold-hearted bitch again

I will focus on him…
it's not enough
I'm the evil controller again

In the bottomless pit
everything has to be rejected
nothing can be received

Colorful and shiny masks
flying in the abyss
posing as truth

Luring the innocence
consuming the essence
leaving nothing behind

Moving to the next shiny mask
good only for the time being
until the shine wears off again

Illusion of strength but no true ground
only transient attention of others
to stand on in the abyss

Illusion of love but no true flow
just moving masks
creating fantasy movement

Illusion of direction but no true light
only shiny masks
deceiving into another trap

There is boundless space in the abyss
but no room for anyone
only for a carnival of shiny masks

I woke up from a dream
of a bottomless pit
of never enough

The next day, he wrote back saying how difficult it was for him to read that I had felt that way in the relationship, but that he hadn't seen it like that at all. Of course, he hadn't. If he had seen it that way, he would have had to take responsibility for himself, and a narcissist won't do that, because it would mean facing yet another narcissistic collapse.

This was already the tail end of the Armageddon. Some final scraps of energy were still being released, but our worlds—mine and his—were clearly separating and drifting farther apart. Inspired by writing that first poem, I ended up writing two more. One was a goodbye. The other came more from a place of shamanic abstraction—a reflection on the narcissistic reality I now felt I knew inside and out. I posted all three poems on my blog. I didn't send them to him, but he found them anyway, as he later mentioned them in an email.

Time To Say Goodbye

Time to say goodbye
all roads have reached the end
all ended up in the void
of nothingness

Time to say goodbye
the distance shows the truth
all illusions unmasked
leaving nothing to look at

Time to say goodbye
I'm watching false ancient gods laughing
as they move to the next believer
to charm and consume

Time to say goodbye
and save myself
from the web of deception
that trapped me in the mirage

Time to say goodbye
to fantasy words that had no meaning
to the angry voice that branded my skin
to the heartless wall that bruised my bones

Time to say goodbye
hope betrayed me again
it's cold and ruthless
dressed in a gown of comfort

Time to say goodbye
some things can't change
same play, different actors
same theatre, different masks

Time to say goodbye
and leave the whole play
the show must go on
hypnotizing those who stayed

Time to say goodbye
sharp edges of truth
cutting into wisdom
that's the only road for me

Time to say goodbye
the time of offerings ended
'be your own rock'
new world ahead without rocks

Time to say goodbye
I'm closing all gates to this space
not looking back
never opening it again

Time to say goodbye
old blossoms of love purged
no trace of it left
I can finally breathe freedom

Time to say welcome
to the new space and time
the past is dead
I am alive

The Diamond

I found the Diamond
in the deepest chamber of the I
it dwells in plain sight
but in a blind spot

Looking in its direction
and nothing there
the blind spot created by comfort
that makes your soul blind

Desperate to find it
the cornerstone of your existence
lost without it in a vast space
no foundation, no direction

And here it is — I see it
a shiny object on the horizon
appeared mysteriously as a savior
'It must be my Diamond, I'm home'

I feel like I've known it forever
the lure of familiar is so powerful
I lose my discernment and will
my soul sold to comfort

The ancient passenger in my soul
wakes up alive, posing as God
energy rising up hot and powerful
it feels so real, I can't resist

it takes over my senses
it takes over my heart and thoughts
it gives me power
by consuming my own essence

In the moment, I feel like God
the false diamond feels like God sent
not interested in consequences
the power in the moment is all it wants

Deceptive comfort of the ancient past
going in circles, back to the same
the familiar is not freedom
it's the soul's forever yoke

I finally beat the game
of ancient false gods
who possessed people's souls
confusing familiar with freedom

Old gods didn't work
but they don't want you to know it
so you worship them again
and nothing changes

They deal false diamonds
creating comfort that is your blind spot
so you can't see the true Diamond
in the deepest chamber of your I

I left the comfort and the familiar
false power and false love
the discomfort almost killed me
right in the center of my soul

I didn't move, I didn't run away
I stayed and surrendered
I chose death and collapse
didn't buy into any savior to pull me out

Pressure of pain got stronger
compressing my soul more and more
then the discomfort washed my eyes
and the blind spot disappeared

I saw it — the Diamond
transmuted in my soul by fire
and by the pressure of unknown
pain was only an illusion

It's the false gods that felt hurt
scared of being unneeded anymore
turning truth into pain
so you run back to their trap of familiar

I finally beat the game
saw the sham diamonds of comfort
and claimed my own true Diamond
through the sober truth and unshaken will

The enslaving power of hot desire
run by a desperate need to feel alive
replaced by the power of refreshing peace
all is here, nothing else needed

You can leave now, phony gods
take your gifts of fake diamonds
and your fantasy stories used as a ruse
I choose freedom from you

I left the game of ancient gods
game of self-consumption through 'the other'
they exhausted their right to be here
free world opened beyond the familiar

End Credits Of The Movie

The real ending came on its own. He called me, gave a quick update about what was going on in Pacifica, and then started pouring on the flattery so thick it made me recoil. It felt completely unnatural, forced—even fake. That over-the-top style wasn't him at all. He went on about how amazing I was, how much I had accomplished, how much he admired me, how deeply I understood life and reality, how much he had learned from me, and how he was still just beginning to grasp it all. I didn't buy a single word. I realized he was saying all this right after reading my poem "Time to Say Goodbye", which he'd responded to with just a single line in an email the day before. I could feel the love bombing.

Then, in the same conversation, he said that we had covered all the logistics about selling the house, but that we still needed to discuss our relationship, what was going to happen with us. I said that we could occasionally check in and have a casual phone call, just to say hi, that that was all I was open to. And then he said, "What about the other part—meeting in person sometimes?" (we both knew exactly what he meant). I said no, that this was where I was drawing the line for myself.

His voice instantly shifted from syrupy and praising to cold and detached. He said, "I can't do that. I need either both options or none at all." I said, "Then you've made your choice." He hung up. That was the last time I ever heard his voice. After that, any remaining communication—about the house or anything else—was strictly written.

He couldn't have made it clearer what the relationship was really about for him all along. Everything else had just been a necessary evil.

> *If you ever realize that it was never **you** he cared about–*
> *only what he could get from you–you're free.*

The Movie Script–"Explained"

The very next day, I got a message from someone from the past, asking me what was going on. They had just received a message from Maciek in which he wrote that he had been in a relationship with a narcissist (!) for over ten years—that I had emotionally abused him the entire time, that I used him physically because all I ever wanted from him was to fix houses for me, that people like me prey on people like him—those with a difficult past, easy targets. He said he had been blind and never saw what I was doing to him, that all the signs were there and perfectly matched the textbook definition of narcissistic abuse, that I accused him of having a mental illness, but really, I was the one who was sick. And a few other gems like that. Of course, not a single word about the fact that I ended things after he started professing his love to someone else.

Let me tell you, I was so stunned I nearly fell out of my shoes. Both my therapist friend and I were completely speechless.

This is a textbook narcissistic response to rejection, especially final rejection. It's called a *smear campaign*. I turned down his "friends with benefits" offer, and that hit him right in the core of his original wound. He had to discharge the pain somehow—by projecting it outward, denying all responsibility for the breakup, and, of course, blaming me for everything. Then he went around spreading this twisted version of events to anyone who would listen, even people from the past he hadn't spoken to in years. Anything—just to dodge responsibility for the wreckage he left behind.

> *When you walk away from a narcissist–*
> *get ready for the smear campaign.*
> *They'll accuse you of everything they did to you.*

You're Not His Echo–You're Your Own Voice

Being treated this way by a narcissist takes a real toll on your self-worth. If you enter a relationship like this with already low self-esteem, it's like leaving the door wide open for him to lower it even more. Over time, you start to believe you're nothing, that you have no power, and that he's the only one who gives your life any meaning. You stop believing in yourself, in your individuality, and your ability to make things happen.

If this is how you begin to feel in a relationship with a narcissist, it's a sign that somewhere earlier in your life — most likely in childhood — someone already treated you like this. Someone criticized you, rejected you, put you down, constantly compared you to others, didn't believe in you, clipped your wings, and kept telling you that you wouldn't amount to anything because you're not good enough. More often than not, it's someone from your closest family — someone whose love and approval you deeply needed. In many cases, it's a parent who's a narcissist themselves, locked in a constant need to compete with their own child, always needing to be better, and needing the child to stay inferior.

I once knew a man who had a grown son. His son suffered from severe anxiety, isolated himself from the world, and was dealing with serious health issues. The father tried to "help" him by telling him what to do with his life, pushing him to get it together, and laying out the steps he needed to take. But the son, gripped by his own fears, was terrified of all that. He couldn't make decisions, constantly imagining worst-case scenarios, and so he never followed the advice. Eventually, the father said the son had no respect for him and told him flat out, "You're dead to me." Then he deleted his phone number and email.

You read this and can't believe a parent would do that to their own child. But yes, a narcissistic parent absolutely can. The only thing that matters to them is control and obedience — and if you don't comply, they will destroy you. A parent like this doesn't see their child as a separate human being with their own personality and soul, but as an extension of themselves. And if that extension isn't "worthy" of praise, they'll cut it off and crush it without remorse.

So if you come from a home where you weren't truly seen or respected as a person, where your boundaries were crossed over and over, being in a relationship with a narcissist will feel like hell. Because the part of you that still hopes for the love you never received back then will receive exactly what you received back then. And it will hurt you, again and again, until you build your own boundaries — especially those internal ones that protect your sense of wholeness and Self.

That's why, even if you're still in a relationship like this and feel like you're breaking down, don't lose hope. There is a way forward. Turn inward.

Begin building a real relationship with yourself. This is the ONLY path to freedom. You don't need to make drastic changes overnight — unless your safety requires it — but you can begin reconnecting with yourself today.

I'm living proof that having a healthy relationship with yourself — knowing your worth and who you truly are — becomes your emotional immune system. It knows how to detect and neutralize any "virus" that tries to invade and take over. Even though I had no prior experience with narcissists and hadn't studied the topic in depth, I did have a strong sense of inner integrity and self-worth. That's what allowed me to stand tall in the middle of the chaos and hold onto my center, even as the tornado raged around me.

For years, I wondered why I ever got involved with this man. It never made any sense. I read all the books, studied everything I could find on the subject, but I still couldn't find the answer that fit me. The answer finally came — but it didn't come from the books. It came from within, once Maciek was gone and I was alone in the house—more on that in Part Two.

Completely On My Own

A Whole New Level Of Freedom

So there I was — completely alone after that final phone call. My main task now was getting the house ready for sale. At the time, I had no idea how I was going to handle it all, as I also had to dispose of all the furniture and belongings before selling. I'd accumulated heavy exercise equipment, a bike, hundreds of books, and many other things over the years, even though I'd already donated a lot when moving from Deserta. What was I supposed to do with all this? Palmara was completely new to me; I had just arrived, didn't know a single person, and had no idea how things worked there.

I had no plan and no destination where I could take any of it. So I decided to let go of everything. Absolutely everything. I would keep only a few personal suitcases and boxes that could fit in my car. The moment

I made that decision, I felt an incredible sense of freedom. I wasn't just leaving behind a toxic relationship or the emotional wreckage it caused — I was letting go of every physical item tied to my past. And not just the past with Maciek, but my entire past, going all the way back to childhood. I had saved a few sentimental items — things that might be considered keepsakes or personally meaningful — and I let them all go.

I decided to keep only what was practical and useful in my life right now. Everything else could go out into the world or into the ether. And the moment I made that choice, the synchronicities that began to unfold were nothing short of magical.

Symphony Of Reality

After Maciek left for Pacifica, I reached out to Autumn, an old acquaintance of his who happened to live near the house in Palmara. She turned out to be an incredibly kind person—we're still in touch to this day. Autumn is a real go-getter with a vast network of local contacts, and sometimes all it took was one phone call from her to get things moving. She found people who needed exactly the kind of furniture I was trying to get rid of. She found someone who had been dreaming of buying a treadmill because she wanted to lose weight, but summer was approaching, and in Palmara, that meant heat so intense that outdoor exercise was discouraged. A treadmill allowed her to walk in the comfort of her air-conditioned home. She didn't have the money for it, so I gladly gave mine away. She came with her husband; they loaded it into their car, and off they went.

I managed to sell another piece of expensive, heavy workout equipment through a marketplace section on one of the social media platforms. A guy showed up, paid for it, loaded it into his truck, and left.

One day, a handyman came by to make a few repairs before the house went on the market. We started chatting, and it turned out he'd been in a very similar relationship with his ex-wife. Now he was in a new one, building a much happier life. He had this big dream of creating a library in his home—just books and comfy chairs, a space for reading and relaxing. I asked him if he'd be interested in a few hundred books on spirituality and psychology. His eyes lit up. He ended up taking a big load of book boxes off my hands.

That same handyman came over again a few days later, and once more, we ended up talking. He told me about bike trips he takes with his son. I asked if he wanted a mountain bike from me—practically brand new—for his new partner. You won't believe it: every time he'd been at my place before, he came in a work van. But this time, he happened to stop by on his own, and he came in his personal car. Guess what—it had a bike rack on the back. He strapped the bike on, beaming with happiness.

Everything was unfolding in harmony and with ease, and everyone involved was genuinely pleased. Even the new buyers of the house fit perfectly into this flow. The house was listed for sale in early April. Still, I had some professional commitments at the time and couldn't afford to move yet—I needed stable conditions and a reliable internet connection. The earliest I could relocate was June 3rd. That meant the new owners could move in no sooner than two months after the sale. The couple who fell in love with the house and the little forest the very first time they saw it? They couldn't move in before June 4th (!). She was a teacher and had to wait until the end of the school year before she could start the move.

Conjured Violins

There were dozens of synchronicities. But the most touching one happened when I was letting go of my violin. I had sold my guitar, but I wanted to give the violin to someone. At one point, Autumn suggested I join her on a Sunday for a gathering hosted by a group focused on personal and spiritual development. Every Sunday had a different theme and a different kind of meeting. If a variety of people came there, maybe there would be a child who wanted to learn to play the violin. So I tossed the violin into the trunk of my car.

Before the meeting started, people were sitting at tables, chatting or walking around, striking up conversations. I was sitting at a table with Autumn and another woman, telling them a bit about myself—that I'd be moving out of Palmara soon and getting rid of things. I mentioned I had a violin in the car and asked if anyone might want it. The woman at the table went silent and then said, "You have no idea what just happened." She pointed to a young woman sitting two tables away with her twelve-year-old daughter. She told me that just half an hour earlier, she'd spoken with this woman, who was only at her second meeting with the group. She had recently lost her home and was currently bouncing between motels with her child, trying to get back on her feet. Just today, she had shared how much she missed playing the violin—how she used to play seriously, even in an orchestra, and how badly she wanted to start playing again because it relaxed her. But in her current situation, affording a violin was out of the question. This time, I was the one left speechless. I went out to the car and brought her the violin.

A few weeks later, at another gathering, she approached me again to thank me, telling me she had started playing again and how wonderful it felt. Those few months in Palmara felt like true alchemy. In the deepest depths, old energies and structures were breaking down and clearing out, while in the world of light, small miracles were unfolding, offering a sense that everything really is okay. You just have to let go and allow.

Life Is Good

The entire process of preparing the house for sale went so effortlessly that it couldn't have been easier. Everything seemed to fall into place. I met wonderful, kind-hearted people—some offering practical help, others just a kind word. I even struck up a little rapport with an older man at the local dump, where I went once a week to drop off trash. He worked the recycling stations—a warm, lovely immigrant from Croatia who always had something kind to say. Whenever I pulled up, he'd call out, "Hey, Polska!"

On moving day, I lined up everything I'd kept after giving away the rest. It all fit into my car. To mark that liberating moment, I snapped a photo as a keepsake.

I didn't even get a simple thank-you text from Maciek for taking care of everything. He left the entire burden on my shoulders, conveniently collected his share of the money from the house sale, and that was that. On one hand, it was exactly what I should've expected. On the other hand, it just added another piece to the bigger picture of who he really was. What mattered most, though, was that I could look at myself in the mirror with a steady gaze and know I had a completely clear conscience. There's nothing more valuable than that.

I stayed in Palmara for another month, renting a room in a part of the state I'd always wanted to visit. I turned it into a little vacation. I bonded with the lovely older woman who owned the house where I was staying—she ended up inviting me to come back anytime.

I also spent time with Autumn, met her family, explored a few local spots, went on long walks and swims, and listened to audiobooks. It was a deeply relaxing time.

I'll admit that I look back on that whole time in Palmara—from the disaster of Anastazja's message to my final vacation there—as something

truly magical. The most important thing was not to resist anything, to trust that the Universe was on my side and guiding every step, to know there was a bigger purpose working for my good, and to wait patiently for the next sign to appear.

Destination: Africa

In the meantime, while transformation was happening at the speed of light, the question arose: "So where is my place now?" Suddenly, the whole world opened up. I didn't have to be anywhere, I had no obligations, no attachments, no debts, and I could do my work from anywhere on the planet—so what do you do with that kind of freedom?

I started discussing with my therapist friend and her husband the possibility of going to Thailand or somewhere in that part of the world.

And then, completely "by accident," the opportunity appeared to buy a beautiful apartment in a newly built resort on a tropical island in Africa, right on the beach by the Indian Ocean. It took me about thirty seconds to make a decision. Over the following year, everything fell into place, and I became the owner of that apartment on a paradise island.

Until then, after my Palmara vacation, I spent some time in Poland, where I met amazing people and new career paths opened up for me. Later, I returned to the States, where I stayed with a friend who offered me a place to live (for free) while I waited for my apartment in Africa to be ready. Work opportunities began to open up for me there, too, and I leaned into them. I also started meeting wonderful people. Life was simply overflowing with goodness and abundance.

I also wrapped up all the loose ends that had been left dangling from that relationship—things like undoing the paperwork I had already started to arrange for Maciek's Polish residency, and other details. At last, there were no strings left connecting us.

Only now did I truly feel how much weight Maciek's presence had placed on my inner space. And even though the relationship didn't stop me from growing—both personally and professionally— it was still a burden.

It seems that the burden mainly manifested in my body, as I was generally my usual self emotionally and mentally: positive and full of energy. I suspect it had more to do with ancestral trauma—something rooted much deeper in the body, not tied directly to events that happened after I was born. And as it turned out later, that's exactly what it was.

When The Mind Is In Disbelief, The Body Tells The Truth

During the time I was in a relationship with Maciek, I started experiencing joint pain and headaches, which eventually turned into migraines. I had never dealt with either before. The joint pain started back when we were still in the forest house in Westmont. It must have been some kind of inflammation, because sometimes the pain in a single joint would last two months and be so intense I couldn't even lift a kettle of water. Then the pain would subside and reappear in a different joint. It just moved all around my body.

At first, I thought it was the damp climate in Westmont affecting my joints. But after we moved to the bone-dry Deserta, the pain didn't go away. Same with the headaches. In the Deserta, they became so intense that they turned into full-blown migraines with vomiting that lasted for three days. I even went in for testing to make sure I wasn't developing a brain tumor. But everything came back clear.

Another physical issue I'd never struggled with before was sleep. I had always slept soundly. But from the moment we moved to the forest house in Westmont, I started waking up about ten times a night. I would only wake up for a second and fall right back asleep, so technically I was getting enough hours, but the sleep was fragmented. In the Deserta, it got worse. Sometimes I'd wake up and stay awake for an hour or two—or even the whole night. It didn't matter whether Maciek was home or away; my sleep was still disturbed.

The answer came after the breakup. As soon as Maciek disappeared from my space, all my joint pain vanished. I really had thought arthritis was coming for me "in old age." The migraines lingered for a bit longer, but after a few months, they, too, were gone. I don't get headaches anymore, just as I did before the relationship. As for sleep, after more than ten years, I finally started sleeping through the night again. That deep, uninterrupted sleep returned after the house was sold, and I took a month-long vacation in another part of Palmara. To this day, I sleep well.

When I dove into professional literature on toxic relationships with someone who has NPD, I learned that unexplained physical symptoms are standard. No wonder—the amount of toxicity such a person dumps on you daily could knock down an ox. They can't process it themselves, so they "vomit" it onto you.

> *A toxic relationship can manifest in the body as physical symptoms.*

Portal To The Next Part

I'm now in Kraków, slowly making my way toward the end of this story. I walk the same streets and paths I once walked with Maciek. The lightness I feel inside and in my body is the best proof that everything is truly okay. So many burdens—even ones I wasn't consciously aware of—have been released from deep within my subconscious.

The state of my awareness now, thanks to all the inner work I did throughout this relationship, fills me with immense gratitude. Without it, I wouldn't have recovered so many pieces of myself—pieces I've now reconnected with through these life experiences. And that reconnection, that contact with the lost parts of myself, is the most blissful experience there is. Everything else is just an extension of that.

In the second part of this book, I'd like to invite you to look not just more deeply at the difficult relationship with a narcissist, but also at the broader path of human experience. That larger context gives all our experiences a different perspective—and therefore a different meaning. Through it, we can see that nothing is random, nothing is divine punishment, or the universe being cruel.

If someone asked me today whether, knowing all that'd happen, I'd still choose to go through this relationship, I'd say "yes". Not because I'm a masochist, but because the inner place I reached through these challenges is worth everything. If, on this path called "Kasia Dodd," this was the experience I subconsciously chose to meet myself truly, then so be it.

The challenge itself is not what brings awakening, growth, or a return to your true Self. It's *what you do* with that challenge that determines whether it becomes your liberation and freedom, or your prison and suffering.

So I invite you, in the next part, to explore the wider perspective—and that place within.

PART 2

THE ALCHEMY OF LIGHT

CHAPTER 10

A WIDER PERSPECTIVE

In the second part of this book, I'd like to expand the mainstream perspective on relationships with people who have NPD. Typically, we focus on the causes, symptoms, and effects of narcissism—on the emotional devastation and relational damage it leaves behind. And that's completely valid. Naming these wounds is a necessary part of disentangling yourself from the confusion and beginning the journey back to your own Self.

But once you've returned to yourself, gained some distance, caught your breath, and begun to see things through a new lens, it's possible to stretch that understanding beyond the usual boundaries.

If, while reading this book, you're still in a relationship with a narcissist—or you've left, but find yourself stuck in unresolved emotions—this section may feel a bit premature. You can only truly expand your view once the pain has loosened its grip on your perception. Otherwise, what I share here might seem outrageous, unfair, or just plain absurd. That's not a flaw—it simply means your system is still tending to something more urgent.

So check in with yourself and decide whether Part Two is for you right now, or whether it might make more sense sometime down the road.

Is A Healthy Childhood Everything?

When I finally found myself alone—still living in Palmara—and began digging into the topic of covert narcissism, my eyes flew open. As I read articles, books, and listened to various lectures, I had the overwhelming sense that everyone was talking about Maciek. There was just one thing I couldn't quite reconcile. Almost every source claimed that people subconsciously choose narcissistic partners because they themselves carry unresolved childhood trauma, often coming from a dysfunctional home, a narcissistic parent, or emotional abuse.

This really gave me pause. My home wasn't dysfunctional, and there was no abuse. My parents were ordinary people who lived honestly and took care of our family. They loved each other until the day my mom passed away. I always felt safe and well taken care of. I honestly can't remember a single time when anyone in our house raised their voice. Any conflicts I had with my parents were the usual teenage pushbacks—me wanting to stop being treated like a child. Neither my mom nor my dad was a narcissist. My mom was energetic, capable, and generally upbeat; my dad was quieter and more reserved, often staying in the background of their relationship. Mom was excellent at managing money, so even though both of them worked regular jobs, we never lacked anything. No one ever went hungry; we always had enough for vacations, and sometimes even for a little extra.

My parents had a close, affectionate relationship. I observed how they supported and took care of one another. They were loyal and faithful. They didn't fight—if there was ever tension between them, no one raised their voice. There'd be a brief exchange, and then each would retreat to their own "corner of the field." After a short while, once things had settled, everything would go back to normal. Life just felt generally balanced.

I grew up with a healthy sense of self-worth and confidence. I had friends—both girls and boys—and I did well in school, regardless of which one I attended. I never got pulled into addictions. I briefly experimented with cigarettes, but I didn't like them at all and never went back. I wasn't in any trouble at home or school. I had various interests—I played instruments, took extracurricular classes, and liked doing things my own way and thinking for myself.

When I look back on my childhood, I see it as ordinary and safe, with a healthy balance of discipline and freedom. Any friction was normal—nothing dramatic or traumatic.

A Kind Of Normalcy That Didn't Protect Me–But Actually Did...

Looking back now, my parents placed a great deal of trust in me, and that trust became my most effective form of discipline. I had a lot of freedom within that trust, but I always felt the boundary of it was their trust itself—I didn't want to break it. So I made sure to use my freedom, but never abused it. That's how I learned both external and internal responsibility.

One thing was particularly interesting: in our small two-bedroom apartment, I had my own room. And it was truly MY room. No one ever went in there. When I think about it now, it feels almost unbelievable—but that's how it was. I didn't demand it, and I wasn't even fully aware of it at the time. It was just an unspoken rule in our home—my room was my space, and I was responsible for it. If I cleaned it up, it looked nice. If I didn't and invited friends over, that was on me. No one ever monitored me—it was up to me to stay on top of it.

My mom kept some fabric in a storage cabinet in my room—she used to sew clothes occasionally. On the rare occasion she needed to grab something, she would knock and step in just for a second, always letting me know she was only coming in to get her materials. It was almost as if she was apologizing for stepping onto my turf. When I think about it now, that level of respect for a child's boundaries—combined with gently teaching responsibility—was truly remarkable.

I remember when I was eighteen, my ENT doctor sent me to a health resort to strengthen my throat. I spent three weeks in the mountains.

Later, at a holiday dinner, my uncle asked me about the resort and then turned to my dad, asking if he hadn't been worried about letting me go there alone. You know, the usual "resort stories"—one woman, one man, and… well, you can imagine the rest. And my dad replied, "What should I be afraid of? I trust her, so why wouldn't I let her go?"

I still remember the heat that rushed through my body when I heard that. It was such a simple, straightforward answer—but it went so deep.

Even today, my dad sometimes tells me how impressed he is with the way I live and lead my life. My mom has passed away. She and I had very different personalities and tastes, so we had our share of friction, but not once in my life did I ever feel unsupported by her. She handled my rebellion and tendency to push limits with a lot of grace.

Overall, I can say I had a normal childhood—no trauma, no dysfunction—just the usual challenges of life. The most limiting part of it all was the kinds of beliefs that often get passed down from generation to generation as life rules or social norms. But that's something you can work through on your own as part of your personal growth.

So there I was, pulling my hair out, trying to make any sense of my relationship with Maciek. Nothing fit what I had learned about the nature of these kinds of relationships. I truly wanted to understand. I thought about it, analyzed it, meditated, did exercises, and set clear intentions for the answer to come to me. And it did—in a dream.

The Answer Came In A Dream

It was about a month after Maciek had left Palmara and returned to Pacifica. That month had been an extremely intense time for me on every level. I was undergoing deep internal shifts, emotional processing, and preparing for significant life changes. I was preparing the house for sale, letting go of belongings, and clearing physical space.

One night, I had a dream. In it, I was with Maciek in Kraków, in my grandmother's apartment on my mother's side. In real life, my grandmother passed away more than thirty years ago. I inherited that apartment after her death and even lived there for a year or two before selling it just before I moved to the U.S.

So in my dream, I'm in that apartment with Maciek. I can't quite wrap my head around why I'm even there. At the same time, I'm aware that his new "girlfriend" is in the neighboring building. He thinks I don't know. Suddenly, he says he needs to go for a walk, just for half an hour. Of course, I know he's going to meet her. But I pretend not to. He leaves. Comes back an hour later, visibly disgruntled. I don't say a word. I'm completely calm and relaxed throughout the entire dream.

Then I suddenly woke up in the middle of the night, and in that half-sleep state, I saw my grandmother's face. A memory surfaced—something my mother once told me. Oddly enough, my mom rarely spoke about her childhood or her past. I only know bits and pieces.

What came back to me was something she told me long ago: When I was born, my mother brought me over in a baby blanket to introduce me to my grandmother. And my grandmother growled, "Take her away." She didn't even want to look at me.

The story with my brother was the complete opposite. He's much older than I am. When he was born and my mom brought him over, my grandmother was thrilled. He was her little prince, the apple of her eye.

The Unconscious Is Inherited Too

It turns out there were some deep generational traumas and dysfunctional collective beliefs running through my mother's side of the family—patterns where boys and men were seen as more valuable, while girls and women were treated as second-class. That's why my brother was so warmly welcomed, and my grandmother instantly rejected me.

Of course, I don't remember any of this myself—I only learned about it when I was already a teenager. But I never liked my grandmother. My mom used to push me to visit her now and then—"because that's what you do, she's family"—but for me, it was torture. My grandmother was always negative, always upset or angry about something. To be fair, she treated me normally when I was older—I never experienced anything from her like what happened when I was a newborn. Maybe by then, things had shifted. But still, I avoided her apartment whenever I could.

I also knew from my mom that when she was a child, living with her younger brother in their mother's home, the story was the same. Her brother was adored and treated like a little prince, and my mom was the "Cinderella"—pushed aside and always made to do some kind of chore.

Looking at it now from this perspective, my grandmother was a textbook narcissist—the kind that casts one child as the "golden child" and the other as the "scapegoat." That's a classic dynamic in families with a narcissistic parent. No wonder I disliked her so much.

Interestingly, my mother's brother—the so-called "golden boy"—turned out later to be an extreme egotist (possibly even a narcissist...?), and he ended up emotionally wrecking his own sons. My mom, on the other hand, managed to break that generational cycle of trauma to a significant extent. She was "normal" enough that if I hadn't heard those family stories, I probably wouldn't have guessed there had ever been a problem at all.

Still, I suspect that while my mom managed to break free emotionally and consciously, there may have been unresolved material lingering on the biological level—unprocessed or pushed down. When she was pregnant with me, halfway through the pregnancy, she developed a severe allergic reaction to the fetus, to me. Her body was physically trying to reject mine. There was a real risk she'd miscarry. She did everything in her power to protect the pregnancy and carry me safely to term—she went through a lot and spent several months in the hospital. Emotionally, she accepted me completely and genuinely cared about my well-being. But something must have remained, embedded in the unconscious layers of the body—unspoken, unhealed.

Dad Didn't Let It Break Him Either

Not long ago—actually, while I was already writing this book—my dad told me something surprising. For the first time in my life, I heard him speak about his childhood in a way that wasn't just nostalgic memories of a beautiful garden and a big yellow dog. He said that his father really didn't like him. He belittled him, called him names, humiliated him, and forced him to do hard labor. He never once heard a kind word or any encouragement from him.

His two older sisters, on the other hand, were adored by their father. They were cherished, praised, and spared from work and responsibilities. Dad said that, overall, his childhood was hard, and that for many years he had a severe stutter—he could barely get a word out. But then one day, he said, something in him snapped. He decided he'd had enough of being mocked by other kids, and he made up his mind to stop stuttering. He did—just like that. From one day to the next, it was gone.

On the other hand, he had a beautiful relationship with his mom. My grandmother was truly like a walking angel—calm and gentle—such a stark contrast to my other grandmother, who seemed to embody pure resentment.

What's most remarkable is that if my dad hadn't told me all this, I would've never known. I've always known him as a calm, easygoing man, always ready with a joke, with a healthy sense of humor and distance from life's chaos.

Both of my parents, it turns out, had pretty difficult childhoods. Additionally, when they were just three years old, World War II broke out. Their families lived in constant fear for their lives. My dad, especially—he grew up in Warsaw and still remembers the sound of bombs whistling past the windows, the explosions nearby.

He once told me that he actually saved his mom's life during a bombing raid. She had been standing by the window when, suddenly, he started crying in a full-blown panic attack from the other side of the room. She rushed to him, and in that very second, a bomb fell and exploded right where she had been standing. The window shattered into pieces. I can't even imagine that kind of childhood—growing up in such constant fear and tension.

Yet, both of my parents not only survived—they didn't let that trauma destroy them. They managed to build a healthy, stable life, grounded in normalcy.

The Last Link In The Line

Going back to that dream—when I suddenly woke up in the middle of the night, half-asleep—I saw the entire ancestral chain stretched out in front of me. My narcissistic grandmother, my mother, was cast in the scapegoat role—but only about a third caught in it, the rest of her somehow free, reaching beyond—and then me, at the very end of the chain. In that moment, it all made sense. It looked like the task of healing the wound of disconnection in our family had landed squarely on my shoulders. I was the one who had to close the loop.

The most fascinating part is that several years earlier, while I was still in a relationship with Maciek, I'd gone through a few sessions of body-based energy healing. At the time, I had unexplained liver pain, and—seemingly out of nowhere—I crossed paths with a woman who specialized in this work. After her first reading of my body's energy field, she told me something surprising: it looked like I had come into this life to finish a lineage.

She did some clearing—on the level of both my body and ancestral trauma—and I'm certain now it was part of the greater process of cleansing I'd already begun.

What that woman said actually lined up with something that happened when I was ten years old. I remember it clearly—it was November 1st, All Saints' Day in Poland. My mom, my uncle, my cousin, and I had gone to visit our relatives and the graves of our ancestors on my mother's side. After the cemetery, we went to a relative's house for lunch. There were other extended family members there—people I didn't know—including a young woman with a baby who couldn't have been more than a year old.

My cousin, who was a year younger than me, started playing with the little one. They were laughing and chasing each other around the room. The baby was still crawling, but managing to keep up surprisingly well. I sat nearby, just watching them play.

Then suddenly, this thought and feeling came over me so clearly: I would never want children, and I would never have them. That wasn't what I came here for. I have no idea where such a knowing came from in a ten-year-old, but it felt completely obvious. And it hasn't changed to this day.

I've always felt that my path here on Earth is about something else. What truly drives me is the desire to understand the deeper structure of life—to crack the code of self-awareness that frees us from being entangled in unconscious patterns and inherited programming. My task is to grow the Inner Parent within myself, the one that makes this freedom possible, and to expand the space of the Inner Adult—the state of inner wholeness.

My one true passion is to share this understanding—to contribute to the collective Inner Parent and Inner Child. So far, I like doing this job a lot. I've been having deep, seemingly out-of-nowhere insights for as long as I can remember—since I was seven, in fact.

Through The Looking Glass: The Meaning Of The Relationship

In this light, my relationship with Maciek became an integral part of my path. Inner integration—which includes embracing both the personal and collective shadows—requires us to come into contact with that shadow and truly understand it. I didn't experience much of it in my childhood, so I couldn't rely on my own past to explore that territory.

It seems that my innate passion for "the engineering of life and reality," the inherited ancestral material from my family line, and the intensely challenging relationship with Maciek—these were exactly the ingredients needed to fulfill my life path. A relationship with a covert narcissist in adulthood, at a time when my boundaries were already strong and I had a well-established connection with my sense of Self, gave me a unique opportunity to experience the shadow and gain insight into it, without being traumatized by it.

If I'd had narcissistic parents or other forms of dysfunction in childhood—anything that prevented me from developing healthy boundaries—then a relationship with a narcissist in adulthood would have been devastating. But it seems my higher Self cleverly bypassed that key stage of life—childhood—and placed me in a family where, on the surface, things were fairly normal and moderately healthy. That gave me the chance to build those boundaries. Meanwhile, in the "underground waters," the unhealed wounds of past generations flowed quietly through the unconscious.

Adulthood brought the time to confront that "underground current finally." Maciek played a crucial role in bringing the shadow into my life, along with all the distortions of Self that hide within it. With my healthy boundaries and a passion for inner inquiry, the conditions were perfect for deep self-awareness and discovery.

That's why the more dysfunction Maciek brought into the relationship, the deeper my consciousness dove, uncovering more and more of the "dark side of the moon." Looking back now, with a clearer understanding of how reality works, it truly makes sense.

CHAPTER 11

HOW CONSCIOUSNESS COMES TO KNOW ITSELF

When I talk about human consciousness here, I'm using the term in a very loose and intuitive way. Consciousness can be explored through many lenses—philosophical, metaphysical, psychological, biological, and now even quantum.

In our context, when I speak about human consciousness, I'm referring to a kind of inner awareness: the ability for self-reflection, the movement of thought, the activity of the creative mind, our capacity to grasp abstract concepts, and the innate drive to understand ourselves.

By nature, consciousness is light and fast—it vibrates at a high frequency, which makes it elusive and quick. Thoughts move at the speed of light.

Matter—our physical, earthly reality—is much heavier in energy. It moves slowly and has a low frequency. But "low" and "heavy" don't mean "bad" or "negative." That's just the frightened projection of a consciousness that hasn't yet come to understand the foundational principles of reality.

A Dance Between The Poles: Consciousness And Physicality

Self-awareness is the capacity of a human being's consciousness to grasp the underlying principles of existence—principles that are embedded in the way the physical world functions, including the body and the natural world. In other words, when consciousness seeks to know itself, it uses the human and physical worlds as its mirror and trainer.

This training in self-awareness opens up an entirely new dimension of reality. A reality where the human being experiences a pull between two poles: the lightness of consciousness and the density of physicality. In the space between them, there's a constant dance—a calibration, a tuning in, a rhythm of highs and lows, success and failure, fullness and emptiness, light and darkness.

It's a training ground where consciousness comes to know itself through physical experience, where it learns the art of creation by engaging with matter. It's the realm of will and choice.

The poles of light consciousness and condensed physicality are so vastly different in their nature that they can't communicate directly. This is the root of the constant conflict between body and mind.

The bridge that allows for connection and understanding between consciousness and the physical world is the realm of emotion—a unique network of information and energy flow. It's through these emotional channels that the principles embedded in matter are translated into the language of the mind.

The body speaks in sensations, but the mind doesn't understand the language of feeling. The mind speaks in ideas, but the body doesn't think—it reacts through impulses. Emotions serve as the energetic bridge, carrying the body's charge and the mind's meaning.

This is why so many people either drown in emotional turmoil or feel completely numb inside, because the mind still doesn't know how to use the emotional system. And when it can't, it becomes disconnected from reality and from the true Self, which lives deep within.

Our deepest Self—our essence—holds the clearest connection to reality. That's what the mind should be aiming to connect with. Only through that inner connection can it truly understand itself and the laws of life.

> *The body doesn't think, and the mind doesn't feel.*
> *Emotions are the language they share.*
> *Only through emotional presence can the mind*
> *hear the body–and only then can the body*
> *respond to the light of the mind.*

Why Do We Still Need Pain?

In a reality designed the way ours is, certain mechanisms exist to help consciousness and the mind discover the deeper truths of creation.

Imagine that consciousness and the mind are as light as a feather. They float high, effortlessly gliding through space. Physicality and matter, on the other hand, are dense, slow-moving, more like molten lava—heavy, thick, inching its way through the depths.

Now, how is that feather supposed to understand the laws of creation embedded in the lava? First, it's too light—gravity can't pull it down. Second, it's terrified of the lava's intensity, convinced that if it touches it even once, it'll be scorched to ash. So the feather drifts around aimlessly in the clouds, high above everything, wanting to steer life because it sees so much from up there—but it can't. To truly learn the art of creating and navigating life, one would have to descend underground and study it from below.

So, how did the system of self-awareness ensure its own growth? It introduced pain, both physical and emotional.

Notice what happens when a person is in pain: they're instantly pulled into a lower vibration and begin to recognize what really matters. Suddenly, all the superficial things lose their appeal. Priorities shift. People start questioning their beliefs and lifestyle choices. They begin to look at what hurts, in order to heal it. While doing so, they start learning the rules of life. They develop humility and perspective.

Pain forces consciousness to engage its intelligence—to discern, to choose what's real and what truly matters.

If you don't use your free will to consciously grow and discover the wisdom encoded in the physical world, pain will push you there. You can't bypass this system—not if you want to truly live. Of course, you can numb yourself with alcohol, drugs, screens, or any other escape. But that's not the path of self-awareness. That's the path of self-destruction. And that's not what we're talking about here.

The Original Choice-The Source Of All Other Choices

If you want to avoid pain and suffering, you absolutely can—by turning inward, toward the space where the emotional world lives. This is the realm that connects the physical with the spiritual. It's the most important choice that consciousness can make.

When the mind engages willpower and learns to work with this emotional system more effectively, it begins to experience greater harmony and inner peace. That peace leads to integration, wholeness, and an expanded awareness of life. You begin to manage yourself and your life more consciously—you're no longer a lost child in the fog searching for a mom or dad. You become your own parent. When you can truly be a wise Inner Parent to your Inner Child, you step into the role of your Inner Adult.

Now you have independence, freedom, and a healthy distance from life's drama. You get to play with creation instead of trying to survive it.

The ability to control is now used for just one thing: managing your inner world and its state. Not the outer world.

When your inner reality is harmonious, quiet, open, and flowing, your outer reality starts to mirror that. Inner integrity is akin to releasing control and learning to trust the infallible laws that govern the structure of reality. In this place, the inner Self yields to the higher Self—the part of you that has access to the whole of creation, not just the tiny sliver that is your physical body.

This kind of system enters a new stage in the evolution of self-awareness: the Inner Adult becomes the Child of the Higher Self, and the Higher Self becomes the Cosmic Great Parent. At that point, emotions are so well understood and integrated that you no longer need to think about them or process them using willpower or conscious effort. The inner worlds communicate effortlessly and automatically.

It's like moving to a foreign country. At first, it's exhausting trying to learn the local language. However, after a few years, you come to understand it so naturally that you become an integral part of the community. Now imagine never bothering to learn the language at all—you'd always feel like an outsider. That's what happens to the mind when it refuses to learn the language of emotions. It will forever be cut off from the native world of the body and from the laws of creation that existed long before the mind ever "moved in."

I truly believe that the evolution of self-awareness is heading in this direction. And with each generation, we're getting better. For now, we're still in training—learning how to use the will and learning how to direct it in the right way.

Trauma Bond

Another mechanism that consciousness uses in its path toward self-understanding is *bonding through trauma*. Some parts of us exist on such a deep level that even our will can't reach them. Consciousness has no access, unless it enters through experience. Because, as a species, we're still evolving in terms of self-awareness, it's natural that we all carry pieces of ourselves that lie beyond the current reach of consciousness.

On these deeper layers live generational traumas—imprints of unresolved and unprocessed stress, usually tied to life-threatening situations. These experiences gave rise to survival mechanisms that worked in those specific times of danger. But now, when the danger is long gone, those same mechanisms become dysfunctions. And yet they remain—buried deep, passed down through generations like inherited survival blueprints. Until, eventually, in one generation, consciousness awakens just enough to start questioning them.

It works something like this. Imagine you've broken your leg. The surgeon sets the bone and puts it in a cast. You wear the cast for six weeks—not only does it help the bone heal, but it also lets you move around, even if with limitations. After six weeks, the bone has healed, and the cast can come off. But… no one takes it off.

A year goes by. Two. Fifteen. You're still walking around with the cast on, even though you no longer need it. Your life is restricted by it—you can't run, can't ride a bike, hike, swim, or wear a normal pair of shoes. Not to mention how that cast looks when you try wearing a mini skirt ;-) Your leg is screaming at you that it's healed and wants to live, but you ignore it. When someone points it out or reminds you that you could get rid of that burden, you either want to lash out at them or you panic, terrified that without the crutch your whole life will fall apart and you won't know how to walk anymore. Absurd, right? Yet, this is exactly the kind of absurdity we all subconsciously train ourselves into—until we finally wake up.

The function and meaning of something—like a cast on your leg—depend entirely on its relationship to reality, not on what that thing is in and of itself. In the case of a broken leg, the cast is helpful and necessary for functioning. But once the leg is healed, it becomes an obstacle.

It's the same with the defense mechanisms we develop—our own kind of "cast" to stabilize a fractured sense of inner integrity. These mechanisms help us survive when things feel dangerous or destabilizing. But once the threat is gone, they don't just get in the way—they start creating new problems. And eventually, they need to come off.

The tricky part is that these mechanisms are buried so deep that we can't even access them consciously, let alone do anything about them directly. The only way to make contact with those parts is through our interactions with something—or someone—outside of us. Most often, it's other people. They act like mirrors, reflecting those deeply hidden aspects of ourselves back to us. And suddenly, we can see them out there in the world.

When it comes to learning about yourself, one of the most important things to understand is that your awareness of what draws you to someone—or irritates you about them—is never really about the other person. It's a part of you. But you're seeing it in a mirror, not feeling it directly.

It's like trying to find out what color your eyes are. You can't see them directly. The only way to know is by looking in a mirror. You catch a glimpse of that rich brown or striking blue and think, "Wow, beautiful eyes!" But you're not actually seeing your eyes—you're seeing their reflection. You know they're yours, but you're aware you're only seeing them indirectly. To truly experience them, you'd have to go inward and train your mind to perceive through feeling. That's the only way to know them from the inside truly. Otherwise, you're forever dependent on mirrors.

When your awareness becomes sharp and present enough, you start to recognize that any emotional reaction—whether it's admiration or aversion—reveals a piece of yourself reflected back at you from the outside world. That's when the real adventure of self-discovery begins.

The House That Lives In Shadow

At the current level of self-awareness on this planet, all close relationships are a blend of light and shadow dynamics. The parts of us that dwell in shadow also enter into relationships with each other. And those connections often feel even more intense.

Why? Because the parts of us that live in the shadow are still unknown. They can't connect to another person directly, so they reach out through emotional dependency. And emotional dependency is rooted in survival instincts—in fear of death, or of the kind of lack that feels like death.

What's more, the shadow is where generational traumas and inherited life patterns live, still unprocessed and unreleased. When these patterns get activated, they feel deeply personal, like something that's uniquely and undeniably ours. The more personal something feels, the more intense and important it becomes in our experience. And the deeper it lies, the older and more "familiar" it tends to feel, like an ancient part of home.

So when two people fall in love and immediately feel like they've known each other forever, like they can't live without one another, like they're each other's missing half—when it feels like being "home," and that feeling is so intense it's almost physical—what's actually happening is that two shadows have met. Two sets of unconscious patterns, unhealed wounds, or dysfunctional coping mechanisms are resonating with each other. The intensity of the connection is mistaken for love—a mutually expanding and nourishing flow of affection. Yes, there is a strong current of energy—but in the shadow, there is no conscious Inner Parent. So the energy that flows isn't conscious, and it doesn't flow outward through giving. It flows inward through taking, fueled by a sense of lack. That's why there will be friction, drama, disappointment, blame, tension, insecurity—so that something deeper can emerge: self-awareness.

Notice that these two people don't actually know each other at all, and yet they're under the illusion that they've known each other forever. This is the psyche's way of trying to access parts of itself it can't yet reach directly, so it latches on emotionally to something outside that feels strangely familiar. When the spell of the "familiar and perfect" begins to wear off, that's when the real journey begins. Either there will be disillusionment and blame, or a deeper meeting with the self. Whatever has been left unresolved in your relationship with your own inner self—whether it comes from ancestral trauma or childhood wounds—will rise to the surface in this dynamic.

In classical psychology, trauma bond is often described as an emotional dependency that forms through cycles of emotional abuse interwoven with moments of relief and closeness. This mechanism is typically associated with relationships in which a person with past trauma—especially childhood trauma—repeats familiar dysfunctional patterns, often attracting partners with narcissistic or abusive traits. It's generally understood that this bond forms in an atmosphere of threat and relief, creating a strong, chemically anchored attachment that's extremely hard to break.

However, this perspective doesn't always take into account the deeper roots of such attachment—roots tied to inherited patterns, unconscious survival mechanisms, or deeper shadow structures that may not stem from personal biographical trauma at all, but instead have ancestral or even archetypal origins.

The Trauma Bond As A Mechanism Of Consciousness

So, regardless of how painful or dramatic a trauma bond may be, in itself it is not "wrong." It's a mechanism of evolution—an impulse of consciousness attempting to lead us toward the growth of individual self-awareness, and by extension, collective awareness. To see it that way, though, we have to be able to step far enough outside of it. The real question becomes: what do we actually do with this experience? Do we use it as an opportunity to grow and take responsibility for ourselves, or do we keep spiraling into it, deepening the trauma?

One thing is certain: the more self-aware a person becomes, the less they need to enter into trauma-based relationships in order to learn who they are.

CHAPTER 12

THE LESSON OF DARKNESS

Looking back now, with all I've learned about life and myself, I can say that my relationship with Maciek was a lesson in darkness. But I don't mean that in a terrifying, horror-movie kind of way. It was about coming to understand what darkness really is.

From early childhood, we're taught to fear the dark. We're scared of it, warned about it, and told that "dark" characters lurk within it. That's what we perceive and feel on the surface level of darkness. Usually, that's enough to make us want to run the other way, treating darkness as something bad, threatening, and unsafe.

However, as my relationship with Maciek drew me deeper and deeper into the darker aspects of myself, I began to uncover something profoundly different. It was only then that I understood: there is no true integration of the Self without understanding and embracing darkness.

The light wants to reject the dark—but in truth, it can't exist without it. That's where the inner conflict comes from. It's why we often feel incomplete and keep searching for wholeness outside of ourselves. Inside, we idealize the light and demonize the dark. In doing so, we separate ourselves from ourselves.

Rejecting the darkness within ourselves—essentially, cutting off half of who we are—leads us to search for our "other half" outside of us. That's exactly where we end up meeting our own darkness: in another person. It manifests as conflict, emotional drama, disappointment, jealousy, fear of loss or abandonment, unmet expectations, demands, control, and a subtle or overt emotional dependence on the other person for our sense of well-being. No matter how hard we try to run from our shadow or deny our darkness, it will always find a way to show up. You can't outsmart this system.

Pure Darkness, Without Contamination

I've been fascinated with emotions and the inner world for as long as I can remember, and over the years, I managed to uncover many hidden layers within myself, at least as much as I was able to access. I was never afraid of what lived inside me. Later, in adulthood, when I discovered EFT, the process of uncovering and releasing went even deeper.

But as life would have it, there were still central, deeply buried places I couldn't reach on my own, just like you can't see your own eyes—unless you look in a mirror. And my relationship with Maciek was that mirror.

As I mentioned earlier, month by month, year by year, through all the challenges he brought into my life, I kept going inward, clearing everything I met along the way.

And then, finally, in December, when the house in the Desert was under contract and we were packing to move out, my consciousness entered a state of pure darkness. When I say pure darkness, I mean just that—PURE darkness. Not the kind where dark or evil energies hide out, but the kind where there's absolutely nothing left—because everything has been cleared. It's just space. And it was the most beautiful thing I've ever experienced.

It all unfolded more or less like this: without fear of the various things hidden in the darkness—whether they were my own life experiences or imprints from collective or ancestral programs—I continued to move inward, releasing everything that came up along the way. Every obstacle eventually dissolved, making space for the next step inward. And then the next. And deeper still.

It was like hacking through a jungle with a machete. One by one, the fallen and decaying trees disappeared, the tangled vines loosened their grip, the snakes and other lurking creatures, the condemned and shadowy beings, the guardians of the dark—all of them faded away.

Until finally, the jungle ended. And what opened up before me was a vast expanse. The space of PURE darkness.

Darkness That Gently Envelops With A Matte Softness

Pure darkness, the kind where nothing obstructs anymore, has such an extraordinary quality that when my awareness entered it, I could've stayed there forever. Its essence is so unearthly soft and enveloping, so nurturing and kind, that nothing else is needed. There's a stillness, a safety so complete that there's no more striving. You could stay in that softness for eternity, simply because you know—everything is just fine.

There are no dilemmas here, no inner friction or conflict, no need to choose. Nothing is missing, because everything is already present. It's pure being, in wholeness.

There's not only an absence of light, but also of sound. Have you ever been in a recording studio or a soundproof room lined with acoustic panels, the kind that absorb every echo? That muffled stillness creates the smooth, velvety voice you hear on high-quality radio—so pleasant, so rich.

In the pure darkness, there's the same sound-dampening effect. No wave travels through it. You're not transmitting or receiving anything—you just are.

It's as if that matte darkness itself is the dampening panel, absorbing everything, where your energy, instead of rippling outward, sinks into a soft, unmoving presence. You simply exist. You remain forever. There's nothing more to do.

This quality of life is the complete opposite of what comes from light. It's radically different. Most importantly—for integration, for the feeling of wholeness, of being yourself, for freedom and independence—both qualities are essential.

Unraveling Before Rebirth

Maciek led me perfectly through the path of darkness. With every manipulative move, every twisted behavior, he pointed straight to the demons still hiding along the way. What I learned from that journey is that the greatest mystery of life lives in the dark. And you know what? It's actually a brilliant setup. Everything shaped by light is just there, out in the open, visible, available, ready to be taken.

But the path that runs through the dark? That's the territory we're meant to discover ourselves. It's the space where we must allow ourselves to see, to know, and to own. It's the place where true will lives—not that grasping kind of desire that light tends to chase after.

This is the school of independence. The school of courage. The school of becoming who you are, and stepping into your rightful place. It's where you learn to trust—because you can't see anything, you can only feel. You begin to see the world through different eyes.

It's where you prove to yourself that you're ready to walk among the conscious creators. That no demons, no obstacles, no old programs, not even death will stop you, because it's all worth it if it means becoming fully, truly YOU.

The realm of soft darkness is the space where disintegration takes place. But it's a beautiful process—not dramatic or violent, the way it's usually portrayed. That's where the real distortion lies: demonizing darkness, associating it with all things evil, enveloping it in tragedy, and scaring us into running from it—creating even more negativity that ends up being projected into the dark.

But life can't exist without darkness. It's essential to the life cycle. It's where we release what's no longer needed.

When we can't let go of what has run its course—whether it's material things, old relationships, outdated ideas, memories, or inner structures of the Self—our inner space becomes cluttered and overloaded. The system gets drained, confused, and overwhelmed. We end up stumbling around blind, unable to see.

Letting go happens in the dark—in the depths. Yet we're taught to fear it. But it's in that darkness where everything breaks down into its most basic elements and returns to the field of pure creative potential.

It all depends on your awakened awareness—whether you claim your innate capacity to be a conscious creator of life. No one can hand it to you. You gain it through your own will, your determination, your clarity that this is what you want, and your trust that you can let go of absolutely everything, until there's nothing left but bare darkness. And there, at the end of it all, you'll find the source of life.

> *Light is the creator of life.*
> *Darkness is the source of life.*
> *Together, they generate infinite forms of existence.*

The flow of life—what we often call love—can only happen because there's a pulse at the heart of it all. Each pulse of life is a cycle of creation and dissolution... creation and dissolution... creation and dissolution. Whatever has broken down returns to the field of pure potential. It becomes the raw material for something new.

Darkness is what dissolves. It's the resource, the reservoir where everything exists. If something has run its course and it's time to let it go—to hand it over to the dark so it can break down—and you try to cling to it out of fear, you're actually going against the flow of life. You're stepping out of love, out of that state where energy moves freely. And when energy gets stuck, when emotions get blocked, that's where trauma begins.

When Light Acknowledges Darkness

Our task on the path of growing self-awareness and becoming whole is to break free from the deeply ingrained distortion of rejecting half of ourselves—half of life, half of creation—namely, the realm of darkness.

It's about releasing the habit of projecting our mind's rejected creations—negative beliefs, destructive patterns—into that space.

Anything created by the mind and then pushed away into darkness doesn't simply dissolve; it lingers there as a negative presence, kept alive by the emotional umbilical cord of rejection. Darkness itself is not bad. What circulates through it are the unwanted or "failed" mental creations that we've refused to take responsibility for and consciously let go of. That refusal to own our own projections turns what could be a beautiful, fertile realm of darkness into a toxic dumping ground. No wonder we have to wade through all that mess before reaching the purity at its core.

Consider how this dynamic unfolds in our physical world. Many cultures and traditions associate masculine energy with light, the creator, and consciousness. God is often referred to as the Father. The sun, which radiates light, is linked with masculine energy. Feminine energy, on the other hand, is connected to the moon, the night, rhythms, and feeling. It's the mysterious subconscious. It's Mother Earth.

Look at what's happening to human civilization. When darkness is rejected on the level of deep consciousness, the feminine aspect of humanity becomes secondary in the physical world. It's expected to serve, to submit, to endure everything without complaint. It's denied the same rights as "the light." It's told it can't learn, can't vote, can't have its own opinion, can't control its own means of survival. I'm referring to historical times here to provide some perspective. And how is the Earth treated? As property. Something to be used, exploited. She exists to serve—period.

The price of this imbalance is high. Constant creation with no space for release leads to control, possessiveness, war, competition, perfectionism, the race to be "better," the generation of massive waste, and the disregard for nature. Internally, it leads to emptiness, form overshadowing substance, disconnection from the deeper Self, emotional immaturity, and the suppression of what is true, valuable, and unique. All of this manifests as a lack of authenticity—life lived behind a glossy façade. And that, in turn, is the recipe for depression, anxiety, and a sense of meaninglessness. Which, sadly, we have in abundance—everywhere you look.

Now that the feminine side of humanity has started pushing back—tired of being treated as second-class—we're beginning to see some pretty interesting collective shifts. Of course, I'm not talking about the "weaponized" version of feminism that wants to bite through every man's aorta. That's just another mask.

The real shift is this: as more and more women begin to reclaim their place in the design of life—not as lesser, but as equal—a deep hunger for authenticity is rising in the collective consciousness.

Have you noticed it? It's everywhere—not just in books, workshops, and courses, but even in movies and TV shows. The message is getting louder: there's nothing more important than being real. People are starving for it. They crave it like parched land waiting for rain. They want to just be—without shame, without fear of rejection, without guilt, and without the belief that there's something wrong with them.

There's a growing exhaustion from this disconnect, from living inside a polished illusion, trying to impress others while feeling empty and echoing inside. People want to be real—and to feel good in that truth.

When a person brings both halves—light and darkness—into balance within themselves, when both are clear and in harmonious cooperation, when they complement each other and form a whole, the inner friction begins to fade. Conflicts disappear. Even wars lose their fuel.

The light must mature enough to recognize darkness as an equal and free partner, not as a subordinate servant stripped of identity. This must happen first within each individual, long before it manifests in the physical world.

Dear woman, it's your responsibility to claim your independent identity. It's time to shine your own light.

Dear man, learn to see what exists beyond your own light, because blinding yourself with it creates illusions of lack and loneliness. It's time to let go of control and trust that there is an entire universe outside of you, rooted in the dark. Just look at the cosmos...

When my consciousness was resting in that velvety, muted darkness, wrapped in otherworldly peace and stillness, I had no idea it was the beginning of a process that would soon unfold in the physical world. As you know, after I arrived in Palmara in January, it only took two months for the entire structure of that relationship—carefully built over more than ten years—to start cracking. One more month, and it all collapsed completely. And just a few months after that, there was nothing left. Not even rubble.

Everything was broken down, dissolved, and cleared. Returned to circulation. And from that, a new reality begins to take shape.

Behind The Curtains Of Earth's Theater

As human consciousness expands and begins to see beyond the boundaries of its own survival story on this planet, it starts to realize that each individual life is just one small puzzle piece in the vast complexity of reality. Things don't happen solely as the result of personal processes—every living being is immersed in a greater field of life, being nudged, pushed, and positioned by it.

When consciousness detaches even further from the physical experience, another space begins to open—not outward, but inward. This is what we refer to as the spiritual realm. From this wider lens, everything—even something like a relationship with a narcissist—takes on a completely different meaning. However, this perspective won't emerge and won't become accessible until a person has released the trauma that narrows their field of perception. As long as consciousness is still trapped in the vibration of wounding, that's where the focus must stay first. It's a bit like this—if I were to put it in a metaphor…

Earth is like a giant Hollywood, endlessly producing films of every genre—series, short films, blockbusters, documentaries, and fiction. It's a forge of stories. Now imagine looking at Hollywood from afar and saying, "That looks like a cool place—I'd love to play a role in one of those films. But which one? Maybe a romantic part? Maybe a tragic one? Or maybe I'll play a psychopath—now that would be quite the experience!"

From the spiritual perspective, every role is fascinating because, in that dimension, we don't identify with the role. The Self remains the same, and the role is something we step into temporarily to explore certain experiences.

From the wide-angle view of the soul, there are no mistakes, no real injustices or wrongdoings. From up there, all of humanity is simply in the process of learning consciousness, awakening it to self-awareness. And like any learning process, that journey is filled with effort, errors, breakthroughs, and uncertainty.

When this broader view first opened up to me, I realized that before we even enter the physical body, in the spirit realm, we see—and choose—our role. We pick our path and our life theme. And to walk that path, we need others who will help us carry out the lessons and experiences we've signed up for.

I saw that we only agree to go through difficult experiences on Earth with souls with whom we share a deep spiritual connection with. It's not easy to play a role like that for someone on their earthly path.

I remember that throughout my relationship with Maciek, I would occasionally get these piercing glimpses "from the other side." And in those moments, it was crystal clear—everything was unfolding exactly as it was meant to. That there was a soul-level agreement between us. I had this strange and powerful sense that, in that other realm, Maciek had already reached such an advanced stage of growth that he was able to choose this difficult role—and hold it. A weaker spirit wouldn't have been able to withstand it. And that this wasn't about some childlike fantasy of life being all cuddles and holding hands. This path was about something entirely different.

At times, I even felt like he was guiding me from some other dimension—and that my role was to learn, to go deeper. That nothing would be handed to me. It was my responsibility to discover it all for myself and own it. He agreed to play the hard part for me—and to stay in that role without breaking character, not even once. And I agreed to receive the teaching, in exactly that form.

The Power Of Learning Through Shadow

Native American teachings speak of two kinds of learning—positive and negative. Positive learning is when a teacher offers you clear, direct knowledge, and you simply receive it. Negative learning, on the other hand, happens when you cross paths with someone who plays the role of a dark figure or antagonist. Their purpose is to affect you in such a way that your soul is pushed to awaken the opposite energy within itself—the truth and the light. This kind of knowledge isn't handed to you from the outside. It rises up from deep within you. And that makes it the most valuable kind of knowing—because it's yours. It's real. It can't be faked. You feel it in the depths of your soul. And you know.

As your awareness expands, you start to see that life unfolds across many layers. There's an entire spectrum—from the deepest dimension of spirit and light, all the way to the physical body and material world. Life is happening on all these levels at once. The more you understand that, the more skillfully you can navigate your experience.

Becoming What You Carry

A long time ago, I had a dream—one of those rare dreams you never forget. And now, all these years later, it finally makes sense.

In the dream, I was a soul, but a very young one. It felt like I was still a child, just beginning my journey. I was flying through dimensions and vast open spaces at the speed of light. It was pure fun, like cosmic play. At some point, I drifted into a dimension where a line of people—though really they were souls—stood waiting. They all seemed older than me, more mature, like grown-up souls.

Curious, I paused to watch. What were they waiting for? I floated up to the front of the line, where a gateway, a portal, lay ahead. On the other side of it was a descent—an entryway to Earth. Standing at the threshold was someone, another soul, clearly playing a specific role in that space.

I watched as the first soul in line stepped forward, holding out their hands. The figure by the gate handed them a bundle—something carefully wrapped. The soul took the bundle, passed through the portal, and descended toward Earth.

As I focused on this curious moment—when the soul would receive the bundle—I noticed something fascinating. Just before stepping through the gate, while still holding the bundle in their hands, each soul had this thought, this feeling: "I am, and I carry this burden." But the moment they crossed the threshold, something shifted. That inner statement changed to: "I am this burden."

When I woke up, the meaning was instantly clear.

Before we incarnate into the physical world, we're fully aware of our true spiritual identity. We see the role we're about to take on as exactly that—a role. Just like an actor in a movie who knows he's playing a part, but still remembers who he truly is: his name, his life, his family waiting at home. He acts out the role, but never loses himself in it.

But something strange, almost magical, happens as we cross that threshold into physical existence. Our spiritual identity merges with the "bundle"—with the role, the burden, the task. And suddenly, we forget who we are. The role becomes the identity. The burden becomes me. And the truth of who we really are fades into the background.

Someone might ask—what's the point of all this? To me, the answer is this: that very merging and forgetting allows us to take our path and our role extremely seriously, because we don't see any other option. We fight to survive, we push through the hardships, because we can't just step out of the play. There's no "offstage" we remember.

But here's the thing—the forgetting is also part of the design. It's the school of self-awareness. The lesson is about gradually peeling away from the role, waking up to the memory of our true identity. To return with an understanding of what it truly is, with gratitude that it even exists at all, and with the ability to take responsibility for it.

Three Layers Of Vision

Let's return to the topic of my relationship with Maciek. When my awareness shifts to the physical level, there's a clear boundary and firm stance: in the physical world, Maciek and I have nothing to do with each other anymore. The path has ended. I don't want to see him again. My door is permanently closed.

At the same time, that doesn't stop me from expanding and shifting my awareness to a less dense level—the emotional one—where I can see the human lessons, the path through pain and suffering. Here, I feel compassion for the fact that, on the human level, someone has to struggle so much and carry out the role of a fragmented Self. This is the dangerous zone for empaths who haven't yet learned how to keep their distance, because the impulse to help kicks in right away. I'll come back to that in a moment. And then there's the wider, spiritual perspective. From here, Maciek is simply a fellow traveler on the journey.

The Dream That Closed The Circle

I remember it clearly—it was near the end of my time in Palmara, after I had let go of most of what was left from that relationship. I had this dream twice. In the dream, I was alone again, free. Suddenly, Maciek walked into the room where I was. He came up to me calmly, said nothing, kissed me on the forehead, looked at me for a moment, and walked out.

That dream told me everything I needed to know. Everything is exactly as it should be. All we need to do is wake up and truly see the system we're living in. That it spans the full spectrum—from spirit to matter—a mix of all kinds of energies and layers. And our task is not only to recognize and distinguish them, but also to know how to move through each one in the right way.

In a sense, it's about giving to Caesar what is Caesar's, and to God what is God's—every dimension has its own rules. When we stop mixing up the laws of different realms, we live in harmony, and no one suffers. In the realm of spirit, everything is accepted and supported because there's no division. But in the physical world, we must make choices—accept or reject—because here, things take form, and it's through form that we learn discernment, self-awareness, and resonance.

You can't just decide to expand your awareness or gain perspective. It doesn't work like that. It only comes naturally when you go deep inside and release every uncomfortable thing along the way. Only then can your awareness encompass both the physical space, where there's no room for contact, and the spiritual space, where a shared journey unfolds.

If you try to force your way into the spiritual space without first freeing yourself from the trap of feeling wronged, you'll only end up creating more harm. And if you try to hold your boundaries while still carrying that hurt, it will either lead to guilt or to disconnecting from a part of yourself.

CHAPTER 13

COMPASSION AND DISTANCE – THE MOST IMPORTANT CHAPTER FOR YOU

I want to talk about what might be the most important thing, especially if you're in—or have been in—a relationship with a narcissist and truly want to be free. If you're an empath and feel compassion when you think about how deeply wounded the narcissist is, you need to install a giant red STOP button.

Between Empathy And Self-Erasure

The desire to help is beautiful, but without being armed with wisdom, meaning clear boundaries, it will lead you straight into destruction and feed the parasite known as guilt.

If you see the narcissist suffering—lost, disconnected from themselves, drowning in inner despair—know this: nothing you do for them will ever make a difference. And you'll ruin your own life in the process.

At the core of narcissistic personality disorder is an escape from the Self—a disowning of responsibility, and the misuse of will to manipulate others. The will must be used to help oneself, turned inward. But for the narcissist, it's reversed: they use their will to get you to help them. And it won't lead anywhere. Your energy will just get swallowed by a bottomless black hole.

Because there is no will in them to find themselves, anything you give won't be used for healing—it'll be consumed like free food. They won't draw from themselves—they refuse. So they'll draw from you. But this is completely against the natural order, against the design of creation itself—and that's why it causes such devastation.

If your heart feels compassion for his suffering, that's okay. Wish him well. Pray for him, if that's something you practice. Send him light, good energy, do whatever feels right to you in that dimension. But stop there. Don't extend that into the physical world. That's where you need to draw the line. Shut the doors and windows. As long as he doesn't use his own will to care for his inner world, to do the work, and to integrate his fractured Self, you'll remain nothing more than a source to be used.

Love Will Not Heal A Narcissist

Your task is to heal yourself from the illusion that your love can save him. Not in the case of NPD. That's not how this works. Your love—even your self-sacrifice to the point of losing yourself—doesn't stand a chance against a narcissist's reversed and unyielding will. Sure, it might create a moment of euphoria in him, but it will quickly shift into a desperate hunger, one that you will be held responsible for. And suddenly, it becomes your job to feed him again. Don't fall back into codependency. Not anymore.

Here's another important reminder—if your heart feels compassion, but your mind holds you back from helping, and then guilt shows up, pause right there. That feeling of guilt means there's a part of you that's still disconnected from your whole Self, and it's trying to regain that connection by controlling the narcissist and "fixing" his suffering. But that will never work—because that's not the path to reconnecting with yourself.

Where The Mind And Heart Fall Short

Not long ago, I came across a quote rooted in the wisdom of the North American Indigenous people. It stayed with me:

> *"Don't listen to the heart—the heart can be blinded by longing. Don't trust the mind—the mind is easily deceived by illusion. Listen to the spirit—the spirit always knows the truth."*

This idea stands in stark contrast to what we often hear in Western culture—the constant encouragement to "follow your heart" or "listen to your heart." That advice has always made me pause and reflect, especially when I look at real life. If that were truly the whole truth, then why do so many people who follow their heart end up in emotional turmoil, heartbreak, or even tragedy? And why do just as many people who follow their minds end up lost, drained, or stuck in equally painful experiences?

That quote above gives such a clear answer. The spirit is something that reaches beyond both the heart and the mind. It sees farther, wider. It has access to both feeling and intelligence. The real art lies in learning to listen to both the heart and the mind. We've been given both for a reason. It's their cooperation that creates inner peace, harmony, and the ability to make aligned, wise decisions.

The heart is drawn to what feels familiar—what's yours, what's known. It fears the unknown. That's why it needs to be supported by the courage that comes from the mind's vision and dreams. The question is: what truly belongs to you because it flows from your divine potential? And what feels like yours only because it comes from past or inherited trauma?

The heart doesn't know the difference. It just follows what it recognizes. So sometimes it will lead you toward your wholeness—and other times, straight into your emptiness. Be prepared: when you follow only your heart, without engaging your mind, you might find yourself swept around by all sorts of inner currents.

The mind, on the other hand, is pulled toward the new and the unknown. It gets bored with the familiar. That's why it needs to be rooted in the heart, which knows your Self. The real question becomes: which paths are truly yours—just not yet discovered—and which ones are not yours at all and will lead you astray? Be prepared: if you follow only your mind, without the heart that knows what belongs to you, you'll likely go on many journeys into emptiness.

Both the heart and the mind are meant to guide us. And we only gain real access to both when we expand our awareness and drop into spirit.

> Life unfolds in the space between the heart and the mind—
> it's the relationship between them that shapes our experience.
> The heart and the mind exist thanks to the body, and the body
> itself is rooted in spirit.

When The Heart Understands That Love Means Boundaries

If you want to free yourself from a narcissist—both on the outside and within—and you're an empath, you need to get to know yourself well enough to sort out these different inner spaces.

1. On the **physical level**, you must cut off contact. If you absolutely have to interact due to children or shared responsibilities, that's fine—but keep it diplomatic—no emotional openings, no personal disclosures. Otherwise, you'll spill over again—and you'll pay the price.
2. On the **heart level**, if you're an empath and feel compassion, or you're drawn to give where something's missing, use your mind. Know this: you can offer something, but not in the physical world. That's where you'll be taken advantage of. In a relationship with a narcissist, that natural instinct won't work the way it should. So turn your heart toward the spirit. Set the intention for goodness and healing—for them and

for you—but release it into the hands of spirit. Let spirit arrange it all in the way that's truly best for both of you.
3. On the **spiritual level**, when you widen your awareness and can see the bigger picture, remember: all is well. Your experience is part of something larger. And your role in it matters.

This way, you're taking care of everything: your body and physical health, which need boundaries, and your heart, which longs to connect. Now your heart is equipped with reason, guiding how and when to connect in ways that actually fit the situation—no more blind giving. You're no longer going against your body or against your heart. You're simply being wise.

Not Every Intensity Is Love

Once this inner order settles in, you'll begin to notice the difference between love and emotional dependency. The latter is a craving to possess and is often confused with love. From that place, you'll be able to recognize those strong emotional pulls that are actually rooted in emptiness—and avoid acting on them. Let's examine the core differences between love that stems from wholeness and love that arises from a state of lack, between genuine love and the desire to possess.

True love doesn't resemble the kind we often see in romantic movies. It doesn't start with "I love you" and end in declarations. It's not built on promises but on presence. It doesn't need proof—because it is the proof.

Love doesn't say, "Make me happy." It says, "Your happiness matters to me." Love doesn't ask, "What do I get out of this?" It asks, "How can I support you, even if it's harder for me right now?"

Real love isn't blind—it sees clearly. It sees the shadows and the contradictions, yet still chooses to stay. Not because it ignores them, but because it recognizes something in the other person that's worth caring for—even if it's not perfect.

Desire, unlike love, wants to possess. Love wants to understand. Desire is nothing more than addiction. It doesn't want to know you truly—it wants to own you. It's not interested in your freedom. It wants your predictability, your attention, your constant "supply." It wants to be right. It plays the game of who gives more and who takes more. It treats you like a source of pleasure or validation. It hurts you, and then it says, "I did it because I love you."

But that's not how love works. Love doesn't need winners—because there's no battle to be won. There are only souls who want to dance with life. Real love is freedom. Love doesn't control—it trusts. It doesn't keep you in a cage—it opens space. It doesn't condition—it accepts. It doesn't demand—it invites. It doesn't reward or punish—it's not training. It's not "perfect"—it's real. It doesn't reject you when you grow or change.

Love doesn't just happen—it's not some feeling that drops out of the sky. It's a choice you make every day. A decision to stay fully present, even when it's uncomfortable.

Love doesn't require sacrifice. It requires truth. And the truth in a relationship with a narcissist is this: your love will disappear into a bottomless well. And in that case, the most loving thing you can do is draw a firm boundary.

From The Passion Of Pain To The Passion Of Presence

It's worth touching on something we often hear about: passion. Live with passion, follow your passion, find a passion, love with passion… or that something is "so passionate." But did you know that the word "passion" comes from the Latin *passio*, meaning "suffering"? So does passionate love mean… painful love?

Yes—and no. It all depends on the state of a person's self-awareness—how much their mind and heart have become integrated. Or, in the language of the Inner Parent theory, how developed that Inner Parent is, and how well they know their Inner Child.

"Passionate" means emotionally alive, emotionally charged. And when do emotions lead to suffering? When they're disowned or rejected.

The Self lives deep in the center of our inner system, at the heart of our consciousness structure. Everyone, consciously or unconsciously, longs to reconnect with that inner Self. That connection, deep within, will either be filled with suffering or filled with bliss. Both are passionate because they are emotionally intense and full of life.

So what did the ancients mean when they said passion equals suffering? They were referring to the condition where the mind is disconnected from the deep Self, desperately longing for it, yet only pulled into that depth through pain. As we talked about earlier, if the mind doesn't choose to reconnect with the Self, pain will do the pulling instead.

In pain, in passion, the most breathtaking creations, breakthroughs, and ideas are born. But is suffering truly necessary for this kind of passion? No, it isn't.

When the mind is no longer drifting in the clouds—detached from reality, stuck in its controlling programs and "being right"—but instead slows down, softens, and connects with the deep Self through mindful awareness, then passion transforms. It stops being rooted in pain and becomes filled with bliss and a quiet kind of upliftment. From this place, works of equal beauty are born. And love—real love—becomes spacious, generous, and free. Not a desperate, dramatic attachment. Not a suffocating knot of control and unmet expectations.

We're entering a time when the need for authenticity and inner freedom is becoming increasingly clear and urgent. So let's get to know a new kind of passion—one that's free from suffering. Let conscious will—not pain—be the doorway to our inner depths. Let's rewrite the meaning of passion.

Disconnected At The Root

I remember a conversation I had with Maciek early in the relationship, back when we'd just moved to the woods in Westmont. That was when the first wave of complaints began—he said I was too independent, that there was nothing he could do for me, that he felt useless because I seemed content with myself. I told him, honestly, that yes, I did feel good about my life. I didn't need rescuing, nor did I need anyone trying to buy my affection. I had everything I needed, both inside and out. The only thing I didn't have—because it wasn't mine to give—was the presence of another person. His presence. That's all I wanted. For him to just be there, present. That was enough for me. He didn't have to do anything for me, prove anything, provide anything, earn anything.

And that was the great paradox of the relationship. The only thing I lacked—the one thing that wasn't mine to supply—was his presence. And ironically, it was the one thing he couldn't give. A narcissist, having rejected their own Self, can never truly be present inside. All they have to offer you is emptiness.

He sought a relationship characterized by a lack of independence and dependency. I wanted one rooted in presence and freedom. For him, the point of being together was pleasure. For me, it was happiness.

Pleasure is driven by dopamine. Happiness—by serotonin. Dopamine gives a quick hit of satisfaction. Serotonin brings lasting peace. The most ironic part? Excess dopamine actually lowers serotonin production. So the more we chase pleasure and tie our well-being to it, the more miserable we ultimately feel.

Just look around—depression and anxiety are becoming the new norm in cultures where instant dopamine gratification has become a lifestyle.

The Absence That Awakened Presence Within

This was the final lesson in independence for me—the release from the collective programming that says happiness and a sense of safety require someone else's deep personal presence. Maciek did everything in his power NOT to give me that, and in doing so, stripped me of all illusions. It led me to a deeper awakening, where I finally met just myself, and it turned out everything was perfectly okay.

Where did all those beliefs go? The ones about being incomplete, about needing someone else to "complete" me? That quiet insistence that something must be wrong if you're not in a deep emotional partnership? What a brutal illusion—so deeply embedded in human consciousness.

What comes to mind is this line from T.S. Eliot[4]:

---

4 T.S. Eliot, Four Quartets: Little Gidding, 1942.

> *We shall not cease from exploration,*
> *and the end of all our exploring*
> *will be to arrive where we started*
> *and know the place for the first time.*

When I finally arrived there, something clicked into place. The light merged with the pure darkness, and something began to circulate inside me. A sense of wholeness settled in, along with a deep, otherworldly feeling of fulfillment. And I can say with complete honesty—I have never felt this good in my life. And it's not just a sense of inner wisdom or peace; it's showing up in my everyday reality.

Sometimes we carry wisdom inside us, but when it comes to making real-life choices based on that wisdom, there's a gap—a kind of inner split. But now, there's no disconnect between what I feel and how I live. My awareness has found its home and fully settled into it. And that's enough.

That's what I want to encourage you to do. Not to follow my life path—because yours is your own. But to walk the path that leads inward, toward yourself. That direction is the same for all of us. What unfolds in your external life as a result of that inner connection—that doesn't matter right now. Because it will naturally mirror whatever is happening inside.

And when it does, it will show up in harmony. In peace. In truth and authenticity. And with that comes a sense of wholeness and fulfillment—the kind that can only be found within you.

I would like to reiterate and remind you of something important. The connection to your true essence looks the same for everyone: it's about turning your awareness inward, embracing your deeper Self, and reaching a sense of inner wholeness. But the life path—that's unique for each person. Everyone comes to this Earth with their own set of experiences to live and their own potential to express.

Reaching inner wholeness doesn't mean there's a single, universal outcome, such as suddenly dropping everything and becoming someone else. Whoever you are, whatever your soul's assignment is on this planet, that inner fullness will fuel it, not erase it. It will help you not only discover yourself and live up to your unique potential, but also do so with a sense of deep fulfillment.

If your purpose is to be a mother, you'll do it with joy, wholeness, and fulfillment—because you're rooted in your essence. If your deepest calling is to be in a relationship, you'll be able to show up in that connection from a place of truth and alignment with your Self. If your path is about letting go of attachments and living as a hermit, that too will be rich and complete, because it's coming from deep within.

It's not about what you do. It's about whether you're doing it in alignment with your inner potential. The goal isn't to chase a specific role—it's to discover yourself through the role you've chosen. So if you feel unfulfilled or unhappy on your path, it likely means one of two things: either you're playing a role someone else handed you, or you're living your role without being connected to who you truly are inside.

All roads lead inward. That's where the mystery of life lives—and everything you need to feel authentic, safe, grounded, and fulfilled. Everything else that plays out in the physical world is simply an extension of that. Life happens in the space between your inner essence and the outer world.

CLOSING WORDS

At the very end, I want to share a passage that found its way to me just as I was finishing this book—a beautiful bit of synchronicity. I received it from Autumn in Palmara. It was a YouTube video, and the message struck me so deeply that I transcribed it. Honestly, I couldn't imagine a more perfect summary of this whole life adventure.

This quote speaks about a woman, so that's how I'll present it here. However, individuation is a human process—it applies to all of us, regardless of gender. So wherever you see the word "woman," you can just as easily say "man." The meaning stays the same.

The Truth About Women Who LIVE ALONE Without A Man | Carl Jung[5]
https://www.youtube.com/@SoulSync-04

Have you ever wondered why some women live alone? Without a boyfriend, without a partner—and they don't even seem like they're looking for one. The

---

[5] Carl Gustav Jung (1875–1961) – Swiss psychiatrist, psychologist, and thinker, best known as the founder of analytical psychology. His work laid the foundation for our modern understanding of the unconscious, archetypes, and the process of individuation. He believed that true psychological healing happens through confronting the shadow and integrating the many aspects of the Self.

answer isn't loneliness, lack of options, or a broken heart. The real reason runs deeper—something more uncomfortable, more unsettling, something that shakes up everything we were taught about a woman's role. Because when a woman chooses to be alone, it doesn't mean she's lost—it means she's finally finding herself.

And that process of finding herself doesn't come with applause, likes, or company. It comes in silence, in strength, and in a kind of freedom most people still don't understand. No, she's not lonely—she has the freedom to choose. She's not withdrawn—she's just tired of burning herself out for people who never asked for her fire in the first place.

A woman who lives alone, without a partner, is not lost—she's operating on a different level. A level where nothing needs to be begged for—everything is consciously chosen. Where she doesn't chase approval, her presence alone is enough. And maybe that's exactly why she gets so much criticism, judgment, so many attempts to label or explain her. But what many still fail to see is that behind her seeming absence is a presence that fills space, breaks boundaries, and challenges the emotional status quo. She is whole. She is complete.

You may not fully understand it at this time. You might think it's an exaggeration, or pride, or masked hurt. But somewhere deep inside you, quietly pulsing, is a question you're trying not to hear: What if this quiet path is the only one that leads to the most important love of all—the one that starts with you?

The silence surrounding a woman who lives alone isn't emptiness—it's a sanctuary. And those who don't understand the value of that space call her distant, cold, maybe even arrogant. But what most don't see is that she didn't build that space to shut the world out. She built it to have herself.

Carl Jung once said that everything we don't face within ourselves, we begin to project onto others. Maybe that's why so many women still confuse solitude with absence, when in truth, it can be fertile ground for discovering who you really are. While most people try to fill themselves up through external relationships, this woman turned inward. And there, in the vastness of her own unconscious, she faced her ghosts.

She didn't stop believing in love—she just stopped accepting what others called love when it only diminished her. This woman knows chaos, but at some point, she woke up. And that awakening wasn't sudden—it was a series of disappointments that stopped hurting and started teaching.

What you see today isn't withdrawal—it's emotional maturity. And maturity can be intimidating, because it requires presence, depth, and truth. She's no longer drawn to promises, but to real presence. Maybe that's why so many perceive her as unavailable—because she doesn't want to be rescued. She wants to be seen. And that takes more than charm or sweet words—it takes courage to dive into depths that few dare to enter. And that's where many give up—not because she's difficult, but because she's whole.

When a woman becomes whole, she awakens two extremes in the world: admiration and fear. Admiration for those who are also searching for that fullness. Fear in those still living in halves, waiting for someone else to make them whole. She isn't here to complete anyone.

Carl Jung once said that where convention rules, there's little room for authenticity. And this woman doesn't live by convention—she lives by her essence. She hears things like, "You're too picky, you should be more open, no one's perfect." And she just smiles softly. Because she knows that what others call being picky is simply her absolute minimum—the kind of minimum it took her decades to understand.

The discomfort she evokes doesn't come from what she says, but from what she represents. She's living proof that you can be happy without needing anyone. And that strips away masks. Men who feed on a woman's insecurity feel threatened. Women still trapped in the need for approval feel judged. But she didn't come to confront anyone—she simply is. And the authenticity of someone who's broken free is, in itself, a brutal mirror for those still living in chains.

This woman is in no rush. She doesn't speed up to please anyone. She honors her own pace. And that alone stirs a quiet resentment in a world addicted to instant gratification. She longs for depth while the world chases distraction. She seeks presence, and the world offers only surface-level availability. And when she says no, it's not a game—it's the truth. When she walks away, it's not a drama—it's a boundary. When she chooses to stay home rather than meet with someone empty, it's not arrogance—it's clarity. And that clarity, forged through pain and surrender, is her greatest revolution. Because she doesn't live to please—she lives to be. And that simple act—being—makes her dangerous to the system. Maybe what unsettles people most about this woman isn't her solitude—but the peace she's found within it.

Carl Jung once said that those who look outside, dream—but those who look inside, awaken. And that's exactly the journey she took—an inward path. It wasn't easy. It was an exhausting process of peeling off masks, facing the ghosts of emotional dependency, and rebuilding herself piece by piece. She no longer defines herself through the eyes of others. She sees herself with her own eyes. And that changes everything.

Her path isn't a straight line. There are days of doubt, moments of longing, nights steeped in deep silence. But there is also a strength that grows with every choice made in awareness. This woman is the embodiment of the individuation process Jung described. She broke down, confronted her shadow, descended into her subconscious, and returned more whole than ever before. And now that she truly sees herself, she refuses to ever again be someone's "other half." She doesn't want someone to complete her. That can be intimidating because it demands emotional responsibility.

She no longer needs to prove anything to anyone. And that kind of certainty—born from the deepest part of her soul—shifts everything around her because a woman who has reclaimed herself becomes dangerous, not because of her armor, but because of her clarity.

Carl Jung once said that the tree that reaches to heaven must also have roots that reach down to hell. And that's exactly what she lived through. She descended into the hell of her own history, faced generational fears, inherited pain, and traumas that didn't belong to her alone but to all the women who came before her. She broke the cycles. She said no to relationships that kept repeating the same toxic script. She learned that it wasn't her role to heal, save, or settle for crumbs just to please someone else. And when she stopped accepting less, the world tried to convince her she was wrong. But she didn't back down—first with uncertainty, then with awareness, and finally with unshakable strength because someone who's walked through their own abyss no longer fears emptiness.

She learned how to be nourished by silence, how to be warmed by her own presence. She's not unattainable—she just no longer allows herself to be violated. There's a huge difference between opening your heart and letting *someone tear it apart. Yes, she opens—but only to those who show up in truth, not with rehearsed lines or hollow promises. She's seen enough now to know the difference between presence and a performance.*

Her intuition has become razor-sharp. Her energy acts as a filter. She can sense a lack of depth from a distance and walks away from it without hesitation. Her transformation isn't superficial—it's archetypal. As if she reached into some ancient wisdom, an old memory that says a woman was not created to serve, but to express; not to be molded, but to flow. And when she tapped into that memory, something inside her awakened. And no matter how hard the world tries to label her, nothing sticks. Because she no longer lives to fit in, she lives to expand her consciousness.

She no longer fights for attention—she radiates presence. She doesn't wait to be chosen—she chooses. And that shift in logic unsettles those who are still trying to control womanhood. But she's no longer there. She's crossed the threshold. On the other hand, she discovered that a true relationship begins only when you love yourself enough to no longer need anyone.

There is something sacred about the way she moves through the world. She doesn't need applause or public approval. Her confidence is quiet. And it's in that quiet where her true power lives.

Carl Jung said that what we wrestle with within ourselves eventually becomes our destiny. And maybe that's exactly why this woman, choosing herself again and again, became the author of a destiny few can understand—but many quietly long for.

She no longer fills voids with promises, nor tries to convince anyone that she's worthy. She doesn't ask for a place in someone's life, because she's learned that presence should never have to be begged for—it should be invited. And when that invitation doesn't come from truth, she simply declines. Not with anger or bitterness—she walks away with the dignity of someone who's gotten lost too many times to let it happen again.

This isn't pride or rebellion—it's wisdom. The kind of wisdom that can only be born in silence. The same wisdom Jung called individuation—the process of becoming wholly yourself, with no masks and no compromises. And when that happens, nothing outside of you holds more power than the truth that pulses in your own chest.

That truth doesn't need to be shouted. It reveals itself in the quiet way she closes doors without resentment, in how she retreats when the space no longer resonates, in the soft smile she wears even when no one is standing beside her. Because she's discovered that being with herself isn't a punishment—it's a vow of loyalty to her own soul. And the soul of a woman who has awakened doesn't chase, doesn't shrink, doesn't plead—it simply is. And that… is enough.

The world will keep telling her she's missing something. It will keep tossing distractions her way—plastic princes and love made for display. But she's already peeked behind the curtain. She already knows: it's not about finding someone—it's about never losing herself again. And when that awareness begins to take root, everything changes. Desire turns into discernment. Emptiness becomes choice. Waiting becomes the path. And what once hurt, now teaches. What once bound her—now sets her free.

You feel it somewhere deep inside—an echo, a spark. Maybe it's a memory, an old wound, a longing that never made sense. Maybe it's the image of a woman you once knew—or the woman you've become. In every version, something inside you is asking to be seen more clearly. Something that no longer fits into old shapes. Something that—if you allow it—might completely transform your relationship with love, with others, and most of all—with yourself.

This woman isn't just someone who doesn't fit the mold. She's a living symbol of emotional freedom—a reminder that you can rebuild without rushing, without fear, and without proving anything to anyone. She doesn't walk ahead of anyone, but she doesn't trail behind either. She carves her own path—unique, untouchable. And along the way, she lights small fires for others who are just beginning to awaken.

If something stirred inside you while reading this story, maybe it's because, deep down, you're ready for a new kind of love. The kind that begins with reconciliation—with yourself. A love that's nourished by silence, presence, and truth. A love that can't be negotiated, begged for, or faked. And if that love hasn't arrived yet, maybe it's because you first had to become the kind of woman who no longer settles for less than she truly deserves.

And if these words reached you at just the right moment—or awakened a part of you that you had long forgotten—don't keep them to yourself.

Share this message with other women who also need to remember their strength.

I hope this book has been an inspiration for you on many levels. No matter what has happened in your life—or what is happening now—there is one thing you can always do, because only you have access to it: your connection to your Self. No one can forbid it, take it away, or destroy it. And yet, it is the very foundation of your existence, your happiness, your fulfillment. It is both the beginning and the end—and then, once again, the beginning.

Just think of the power in that: having a source within you that belongs only to you, and is here for you. And what you choose to do with it, once you truly claim it—that, too, is your will.

And may that will be done.

Author's Note

Thank you for walking through these pages with openness, courage, and honesty toward yourself.

If this book has touched something meaningful in you — even if it was painful, confronting, or liberating — it would mean a lot to me if you could **share a short reflection on Amazon,** or on the platform where you found this book (Apple Books, Kobo, Google Play, or others).

Your words may become a lifeline for someone who is still searching for clarity, validation, or a way out.

Continue Your Healing Journey

If you feel the need for gentle, structured support after reading — I created a therapeutic EFT app with a guided recovery program specifically for those healing from emotionally harmful or narcissistic relationships.

You can explore it at the link below, or by scanning the QR code if that feels easier.

Your healing is yours.
Your timing is sacred.
This is simply a place designed to hold you.

— Katarzyna Dodd

Website / App access: www.peakpowereft.com
or simply scan the QR code below:

About the Author

Katarzyna Dodd is a European-licensed psychologist, therapist, and author with decades of experience in emotional healing and personal transformation. She is the creator of the *Inner Parent Theory*—a groundbreaking framework that introduces the missing piece in the widely known Inner Child narrative. Her approach reframes healing as the development of the Inner Parent: a conscious, guiding structure that supports clarity, emotional safety, and deep integration.

Katarzyna also developed the Inherence® Process, a transformative method born from years of work in expanded states of awareness. It helps individuals reconnect with their deep Self and embody greater resilience, presence, and coherence. In 2006, she introduced Emotional Freedom Techniques (EFT) to Poland, significantly influencing its integration into therapeutic practice.

Born and raised in Kraków, Poland, Katarzyna lived in the United States for over two decades before relocating to the Indian Ocean coast of Africa, where she continues to write, teach, and explore the inner architecture of human transformation.

Her first book, *You Are the Dream of the Universe*, guides readers through the emotional dynamics between the Inner Parent and Inner Child.

Her second book, *The Chameleon's Game*, explores the hidden architecture of relationships with covert narcissists, exposing the emotional cycles that undermine self-trust and create confusion. It's both a revelation and a roadmap to reclaiming personal power.

For More Ways to Work With Katarzyna Dodd Check Out The Link Below:
www.katarzynadodd.com

Made in the USA
Studio City, CA
November, 2025

www.ingramcontent.com/pod-product-compliance
Lightning Source LLC
Chambersburg PA
CBHW070614030426
42337CB00020B/3791